MEDIA DEBATES

MEDIA DEBATES
ISSUES IN MASS COMMUNICATION

Second Edition

Everette E. Dennis
*The Freedom Forum Media Studies Center
Columbia University*

John C. Merrill
University of Missouri

**Media Debates:
Issues in Mass Communication,
Second Edition**

Copyright © 1996, 1991 by Longman Publishers USA.
All rights reserved.
No part of this publication may be reproduced,
stored in a retrieval system, or transmitted
in any form or by any means, electronic, mechanical,
photocopying, recording, or otherwise,
without the prior permission of the publisher.

Longman, 10 Bank Street, White Plains, N.Y. 10606

Associated companies:
Longman Group Ltd., London
Longman Cheshire Pty., Melbourne
Longman Paul Pty., Auckland
Copp Clark Longman Ltd., Toronto

Acquisitions editor: George T. Hoffman
Associate editor: Hillary B. Henderson
Production editors: Dee Josephson, Ann P. Kearns
Editorial assistant: Jennifer A. McCaffery
Cover design: David Levy
Production supervisor: Winston Sukhnanand
Compositor: Atlis Graphics and Design, Inc.

Library of Congress Cataloging-in-Publication Data

Dennis, Everette E.
　　Media debates: issues in mass communications/by Everette E.
　Dennis and John C. Merrill.—2nd ed.
　　　　p.　　cm.
　　Includes bibliographical references (p.) and index.
　　ISBN 0-8013-1470-4
　　　1. Mass media—United States.　2. Journalism—United States.
　I. Merrill, John Calhoun, Date-　　. II. Title.
　P92.U5D445　　1996　　　　　　　　　　　　95-18677
　302.23′0973—dc20　　　　　　　　　　　　　　CIP

1 2 3 4 5 6 7 8 9 10-MA-9998979695

CONTENTS

Preface		xi
Introduction		1

1 Freedom of the Press — 5

Dennis:	The American press is not free.	6
	Argument summation	11
Merrill:	The American press is free.	11
	Argument summation	15
Topics for Discussion		16
Topics for Research		16
Further Reading		17

2 Media–Government Relationship — 19

Merrill:	The media and government should not be adversaries.	20
	Argument summation	24
Dennis:	The media and government should be adversaries.	25
	Argument summation	29
Topics for Discussion		29
Topics for Research		30
Further Reading		31

3 Media and the Public Trust — 32

Merrill: The media chiefly desire to make profits. — 33
Argument summation — 37
Dennis: The media mainly serve the public interest. — 37
Argument summation — 40
Topics for Discussion — 41
Topics for Research — 41
Further Reading — 42

4 People's Right to Know — 44

Dennis: There is no right to know. — 45
Argument summation — 49
Merrill: There is a right to know. — 49
Argument summation — 52
Topics for Discussion — 52
Topics for Research — 53
Further Reading — 53

5 Public Access to the Media — 55

Merrill: The public has no right of access. — 56
Argument summation — 61
Dennis: The public has a right of access. — 61
Argument summation — 66
Topics for Discussion — 67
Topics for Research — 67
Further Reading — 68

6 Media Bias and Political Leanings — 69

Dennis: The news media are not biased. — 70
Argument summation — 73
Merrill: The news media are biased. — 73
Argument summation — 75
Topics for Discussion — 75
Topics for Research — 76
Further Reading — 76

7 Power of the Media — 78

Dennis:	The media are quite powerful.	79
	Argument summation	84
Merrill:	The media are not so powerful.	85
	Argument summation	88
Topics for Discussion		88
Topics for Research		88
Further Reading		89

8 Quality of Media Content — 92

Dennis:	Media content is generally of poor quality and getting worse.	92
	Argument summation	98
Merrill:	Media content is generally of good quality and getting better.	98
	Argument summation	103
Topics for Discussion		103
Topics for Research		103
Further Reading		104

9 Journalistic Objectivity — 106

Merrill:	Journalistic objectivity is not possible.	107
	Argument summation	112
Dennis:	Journalistic objectivity is possible.	113
	Argument summation	118
Topics for Discussion		118
Topics for Research		119
Further Reading		119

10 Deciding What Is News — 121

Dennis:	Market forces, not editors' judgments, should decide what is news.	122
	Argument summation	126
Merrill:	Editors' judgments, not market forces, should decide what is news.	127
	Argument summation	130

	Topics for Discussion	130
	Topics for Research	131
	Further Reading	131

11 News-Gathering Tactics   133

Merrill: News-gathering tactics should be situational and relative. — 134
    Argument summation — 138
Dennis: News-gathering tactics should be consistent and universal. — 138
    Argument summation — 143
Topics for Discussion — 144
Topics for Research — 144
Further Reading — 145

12 Journalistic Ethics   146

Merrill: Journalists are essentially unethical. — 147
    Argument summation — 150
Dennis: Journalists are essentially ethical. — 150
    Argument summation — 153
Topics for Discussion — 153
Topics for Research — 154
Further Reading — 154

13 The New Communitarianism and Public Journalism   156

Merrill: Communitarianism in journalism is a healthy trend. — 158
    Argument summation — 160
Dennis: Communitarianism in journalism is an unhealthy trend. — 160
    Argument summation — 163
Topics for Discussion — 163
Topics for Research — 164
Further Reading — 164

14 Propaganda and the Media — 166

- *Dennis:* Media are defenses against propaganda. — 167
  - Argument summation — 169
- *Merrill:* Media are instruments of propaganda. — 170
  - Argument summation — 173
- Topics for Discussion — 174
- Topics for Research — 174
- Further Reading — 175

15 Race and Ethnicity — 176

- *Dennis:* Diversity needs rethinking and reassessment. — 178
  - Argument summation — 181
- *Merrill:* Diversity is still one of the media's greatest failures and needs constant attention. — 181
  - Argument summation — 184
- Topics for Discussion — 184
- Topics for Research — 185
- Further Reading — 185

16 Advertising — 187

- *Merrill:* Advertising is a negative social force. — 188
  - Argument summation — 191
- *Dennis:* Advertising is a positive social force. — 192
  - Argument summation — 195
- Topics for Discussion — 195
- Topics for Research — 196
- Further Reading — 196

17 Public Relations — 198

- *Dennis:* Public relations manipulates the news. — 199
  - Argument summation — 201

Merrill:	Public relations provides an essential news service.	201
	Argument summation	204
Topics for Discussion		205
Topics for Research		205
Further Reading		206

18 Journalism as a Profession 207

Merrill:	Journalism is not a profession.	207
	Argument summation	211
Dennis:	Journalism is a profession.	212
	Argument summation	215
Topics for Discussion		216
Topics for Research		216
Further Reading		217

19 Globalism and the Media 218

Dennis:	Globalism greatly benefits people, the media, and freedom of expression.	220
	Argument summation	223
Merrill:	Globalism harms national and local media and can only impair freedom of expression and individual liberty.	223
	Argument summation	226
Topics for Discussion		227
Topics for Research		227
Further Reading		228

Index 229

PREFACE

When earlier editions of *Media Debates* appeared, reviewers kindly described it as "one of a kind," a distinctive approach to presenting otherwise complex material about media and modern society in a format that "engages students and forces them to make choices." In the field of mass communication, where many issues, problems, and controversies endure, sometimes for decades, finding a new voice pertinent to the contemporary scene is often difficult. But that is what we have tried to do in this book, which represents a fusion of ideas, intelligence, and engagements.

In comparing himself with his father, Yogi Berra's son Dale once said, "Our similarities are different." And so it is with this book. While the authors are scholars with experience in the media, universities, and foundations, both have deep respect for the world of professional practice on the one hand and the world of systematic research on the other. They believe that experience and scholarship can inform each other and that feedback between practice and theory is a healthy interchange. They also believe that the dogmatic pronouncements of many professors in the academy and all-knowing commentators in the media are often wrong.

One can walk through the halls of any school of journalism or communication and hear lectures about the motivations of media owners given, unfortunately, by people who have never ventured inside a corporate boardroom and have never had a conversation with the people they so facilely understand and so often denounce. By the same token, it is not hard to find media professionals, such as editors and broadcasters, who immediately dismiss research conducted by university professors, asserting that "they don't know what they are talking about." The authors of this book have met and known the leaders of media industries, the famous and the lesser known in communication, as well as leading scholars, researchers, and other commentators. They have traveled widely both in the United States and in nearly every other part of the globe and have studied similarities and differences between U.S. media systems and those elsewhere.

The result of this experience is humility about what we really know and understand. The field of communication and media studies is not as easy as some might imagine but rather is multifaceted and multidimensional. Different people with different life experiences, perspectives, political outlooks, and, indeed, vested interests will come to different conclusions. There are, in fact, different ways of "knowing" the same subject. Nowhere is this more the case than in media, where entry-level reporters will differ sharply with the owners of their enterprise, and news managers see things differently than do people in advertising and public relations. Similarly in the university, historians of the press will have one view, social science researchers another, and critical theorists still another. These differences are often in play, swirling around in the midst of debates between and among people with different interests and motivations. Thus it is left to the students to absorb varied perspectives, sift through a range of evidence, and come to their own conclusion.

In the field of media studies there are few fixed points on the compass, few imperatives that are always, under every circumstance, true or false. Communication issues and communication policy, whether expressed at the individual, group, organizational, or societal level, are matters of human decision making. A "fact" or trend that one person or organizational leader thinks terribly important may seem irrelevant to another. Where one person sees radical change, another sees an exceptional lurch not likely to be repeated. Yet however one resolves a media debate, many of the abiding issues and principles do endure. Whatever conclusions one reaches, they are benefited by a clear assessment of the issue at hand in the context of institutional memory, history, scholarly assessment, and personal experience.

As we have said before, this book was the outgrowth of a conversation between media scholars and analysts who admired each other's work but often disagreed with the other's conclusions or the way that evidence about a given topic was weighted. When one of our team suggested a coauthored book, that seemed highly unlikely until the idea of a debate was proposed. Since that time, two editions of a book of media debates have been prepared and have been well received by reviewers, teachers, students, and media professionals. The book has been widely used in American universities and abroad as an indicator of what U.S. media professionals and scholars are debating and within what context.

In this approach one author takes a position and then builds a case and assembles evidence, as a lawyer would, to support a strong conclusion. The other author follows and tries to demolish the first's argument, evidence, and conclusion. Then there are opportunities for rebuttal. In the end, students are offered divergent models of discourse and are given both study and research questions that ought to help them reach their own conclusions. There is a danger in this approach, however, because the authors are not simply dishing out their own positions and prejudices but rather are playing the role of advocates for positions (which may not be their personal views at all) in order to put forth a strong and compelling case for the proposition at hand. In some instances we have drawn straws for the position, while in others we have picked that side of the case we know best, whether or not it is a personal conviction. We invite students to consider our other published work, widely available, if they are truly interested in our own views as opposed to those we champion for the cause of lively discourse here.

The format of the book is straightforward: A neutral description that reflects prevailing sentiment on what the issue under discussion means is followed by a challenge and then a response. In the challenge and response the authors have attempted to assemble the best evidence from both scholarly and professional sources to support their positions. While we've mined a good deal of material that covers several recent decades and also harks back to historical references, we have at the same time developed a detailed bibliography of pertinent source material for later consideration.

We have added several new chapters to this edition, including "Media Bias and Political Leanings," " The New Communitarianism and Public Journalism," "Race and Ethnicity," and "Globalism and the Media."

This book was developed for courses in mass communication, journalism, media studies, and related fields, especially those just beyond the introductory level. Earlier editions of this book have been used by sophomores, juniors, seniors, graduate students, and media professionals. It has been used most often as a text in "Mass Communication and Society" classes and in others called, variously, "Contemporary Problems (or Issues) in Journalism and Mass Communication," "Media Ethics," "Communication Ethics and Law," "Introduction to Media Studies," and several others.

As always, we are grateful to the busy people who served as critics for this and earlier editions of this book, namely: Carol Reuss, University of North Carolina; Gary Pettey, Cleveland State University; Dominic LaSorsa, University of Texas, Austin; Vince P. Norris, Pennsylvania State University; and Dwight Teeter, University of Tennessee, Knoxville. To our original editor at Longman, the late Gordon Anderson, and to our present editor, George Hoffman, we are indebted for their support, guidance, and many kindnesses.

This book also owes a considerable debt to several generations of students whose lively inquiries and blunt assessments shaped what we have written here, as well as to many faculty and other professional colleagues who joined vigorously in the debates developed, recreated, and extended here.

MEDIA DEBATES

INTRODUCTION

Public communication provokes arguments. When the various elements of our system of communication in the United States are functioning, they are almost always bumping into controversy. Because by definition their work is displayed in full public view, they are vulnerable to criticism of all kinds. People who make up the media audience like to talk about the various messages directed toward them. Sometimes they do so with considerable knowledge and apparent insight. In any event they have a right to express their views, to put forth their impressions and concerns. This book presents some of the many arguments that arise in regard to the process of mass communication—whether in the media generally, in media institutions such as newspapers and television, in individual communicators such as reporters, producers, photographers, public relations personnel, and advertising executives, or in the content of communication, both written and visual.

Although many media issues may seem trendy and ephemeral because they themselves are part of the news, they are really part of a larger mosaic of enduring debates that stretch back decades, even centuries in some cases. A county prosecutor tries to stop a reporter from covering a trial. A grieving parent wants the press to leave the scene of a tragedy. A government blocks publication of a book. A television producer intrudes on the privacy of an individual. A terrorist organization holds an editor hostage. An advertiser cancels sponsorship of a popular television show. A critic decries a media corporation. Minority persons say they are portrayed unfairly in television news. Residents in a developing country complain that their economy is hampered by their image in the western hemisphere. These and hundreds of other "media issues" arise and are discussed daily. At first they seem quite short-lived, and many are, but all of them are linked to similar controversies that have arisen in the past and that will recur in the future. A text about media does not serve the reader well if, in striving for clarity, it suggests agreement or consensus. Issues are not that settled in this field. We are instead aiming to stir up further debate and reader reaction, in the belief that controversy creates interest.

Public communication issues are important because they can affect people's lives both directly and indirectly. The content of communication—for example, the image of African-Americans or Latinos in the media or the coverage of health issues, the economy, or the environment—almost always arouses criticism. So does the way reporters and other media people perform their jobs, whether or not they are ethical. There is concern too about the way a given medium such as a radio station, magazine, or newspaper behaves in its community. Since folklore (as well as reality) says that those who "pay the piper call the tune," the ownership and control of communication are always on the agenda of those who care about the media system. Beyond these considerations, the social consequences of communication also attract attention and comment. The system of freedom of expression and its relationship with government and other institutions of society are always worthy of hard thought and public scrutiny.

This book examines some of the persistent arguments that perplex editors, broadcasters, critics, educators, and others concerned about the purposes and practices of the mass media in America. We have selected nineteen of the most common recurring themes in debates about journalism, the media, and the press. We hope that this book will stimulate the thinking of students and media professionals alike as they confront these issues that have continued to plague, perplex, and excite over the years. The subjects are organized to encourage the reader to explore the nature, purpose, and operations of mass communication in America. Some of the issues raised have large social implications while others border on internal "shop talk." Taken together they help us understand the relationship of the communications media to society, as well as the relationship of social forces to the press and mass communication.

In selecting the issues presented here, we perused scores of books, articles, bibliographies, and other scholarly inventories to assure ourselves that we were choosing both the most prevalent and the most important arguments for analysis. The nineteen issues singled out are developed with more than a hundred subsidiary issues.

Whenever possible, we point up the links between the various professional and scholarly controversies considered here, explaining how and why they are interrelated. We begin with freedom of the press, the most fundamental of all issues in any media system, and move to the closely connected issue of the relationship between media and government. We follow with considerations of the media and the public trust, an essential link between communicators and their audiences. Several connected concepts considered next are the people's right to know and public access to the media, as well as media bias and political leanings. While these early chapters are philosophical underpinnings for any media system, their importance is then determined by ascertaining the power of the media. Two succeeding chapters look at content issues: the quality of media content and journalistic objectivity. Behavioral considerations—including factors involved in deciding what is news, the nature of news-gathering tactics, and journalistic ethics—continue to define and sharpen our inquiry. One of several new chapters examines the rise of communitarianism and public journalism. Matters of persuasion and public opinion—propaganda and the media, advertising, and public relations—are addressed in three different chapters. We also take up the perplexing problem of how the media handle race and ethnicity. There is then a sharp focus on journalism as a profession, again a vocational application of earlier and more theoretical discussions. Finally, we take issues to the world stage by looking at global communication dominance.

In most instances a lively contemporary controversy can be examined in the context of a conventional tenet or "article of faith" about the media in America. It is not uncommon for antagonisms to flare over whether the prevailing thought about the issue is adequate or needs to be reconsidered. We have tried to recreate that spirit in this book.

As noted earlier, this book is a departure from standard journalism texts in several respects. Each of the nineteen issues is succinctly defined and explained. The prevailing sentiment on each is identified. Then one author challenges the contemporary view and the other offers a response. Though each of us argues a particular position, we are not necessarily presenting our personal viewpoints. We are acting as advocates for the position, trying to marshal the best evidence possible. Indeed, since the last edition we have traded a few of the positions. It is important to identify the central questions at the core of the debate and to demonstrate how and why people legitimately reduce a number of complex subjects to stark pro and con arguments. We do this primarily as a catalyst for discussion. We use this procedure because it is the way two people naturally discuss any debatable subject, trivial or significant. But we also indicate that many complexities ought to be considered before anyone comes to a reasoned conclusion, especially in the area of media. Even though issues are resolved through compromise, such decisions require choices that relate evidence, values, and practical solutions to problems.

After the first edition we received many calls from students and professors in various universities who wanted to argue with us about the views expressed in the book. We explained again and again that the positions we argued were not necessarily our own views. Just as lawyers argue the very best case for their clients, we argued as strongly as we could, on the basis of evidence, for the side of the argument we each agreed to take. And just as the lawyer knows that the client is not always an angel, we know that all issues have many sides and that few of them are resolved in such stark fashion. Most of us, however, when confronted with a media issue, eventually do take sides. We decide whether a given story was of high quality or not; whether a reporter was ethical or unethical; whether public relations is generally good; and so on.

One gratifying response to the first edition of this book was the many letters that reached us from other countries. We were repeatedly told that the book helped readers "make sense" out of the steady flow of media issues coming out of the United States and other countries. One reader wrote, "Now I understand better why Americans get so agitated about government intrusion in press matters." Said another, "At last issues like professionalism and objectivity came into sharper focus for me." Still another said, "After reading your book, I decided that both of you were wrong and I decided to make up my own mind, drawing on some of your arguments while rejecting others." This, of course, is exactly what we had hoped to accomplish.

Media issues belong to people, not to institutions, governments, scholars, or critics. They are matters that affect all of us as members of the many audiences to which media messages are directed. Because we are all targeted by advertisers, editorial pages, television entertainment programs, radio news, and much more, it is vital that we become better consumers of the media by being more critical about the processes that create public communication, as well as the consequences of this communication. Each of us needs to engage in the debate, to argue about communication that affects us, to try to influence it, and to talk back.

We can start by building awareness of the great media debates. In the end we ought to marshal evidence and confront the arguments in our own way for our own purposes. In doing so, we can all reach our own conclusions, recognizing that on the issues set forth here there are no right or wrong positions.

Chapter 1

FREEDOM OF THE PRESS

On one campus a faculty-run board of publications tells editors of a student newspaper they cannot run an abortion rights (pro-choice) ad, while at another, students are under fire for printing an allegedly racist column. Passions run high in both scenarios, with profound disagreements on both sides. Words like *censorship* and *freedom* fly back and forth, yet all who are involved in these controversies would probably say they are staunch advocates of freedom of speech and press, an idea that surfaces daily in communities and nations the world over.

Freedom of the press is usually defined as the right to communicate ideas, opinions, and information through the printed word without government restraint. A deeply held value in America, press freedom is also legally guaranteed in the free press clause of the First Amendment to the Constitution of the United States:

> Congress shall make no law respecting an establishment of religion, or prohibiting the free exercise thereof; or abridging the freedom of speech, or of the press; or the right of the people peaceably to assemble, and to petition the government for redress of grievances.

A central purpose of freedom of the press is to promote an educated and informed electorate that can make decisions about public affairs. For some early commentators freedom of the press meant simply the absence of government licensing of printing and publishing. Later it came to mean "no prior restraint" of publication. This is the idea that prepublication censorship is out of bounds.

Freedom of the press is said to ensure satisfaction of society's need for a maximum flow of information and opinion and the individual's right to self-fulfillment. Freedom of the press is also a promoter and protector of other rights: In America a free press is regarded as central to the functioning of democratic government and a free citizenry. Of course freedom of the press also means protection from arbitrary and despotic control.

There is continuing debate about the essential nature of this concept of freedom: what it actually means, to whom it extends, whether it is an individual or institutional right—that is, does freedom of the press belong to every citizen or only to those organizations that constitute "the press," such as newspapers and television stations? In large part the contemporary interpretation of freedom of the press depends on legally sanctioned definitions of such terms as *Congress, no law,* and *press. Press* once meant only the print media, but in an age of broadcast and computer technology the concept of "the press" has been greatly expanded.

CHALLENGE

Dennis: The American press is not free.

Freedom of the press is one of those noble expressions that slide easily off our tongues, though it is not always fully understood or documented. There is a persistent, romantic notion that freedom of the press flourishes in America and that it is an essential linchpin of our democratic system of government. Many of us want to believe that, but such a belief eludes the truth. The American press is simply not free in any accurate sense of the word. The press fights for freedom and from time to time achieves fragments of freedom, but press freedom is far from full-scale attainment.

I make this argument knowing that the press in America is better off and under fewer restraints than media enterprises in many other countries and cultures. I would still argue that bona fide freedom of the press is a distant dream that will probably never be achieved. Why do I say this? Because when all of the romantic rhetoric of press freedom is pushed aside, the most basic formulation of freedom of the press is what the great constitutional scholar Thomas Cooley called "the right to publish whatever one may please and to be protected against any responsibility for so doing." Cooley wrote those words in the nineteenth century in one of the earliest treatises on our constitutional law, but he added this important qualification:

> except so far as such publications, from their blasphemy, obscenity, or scandalous character, may be a public offense, or by their falsehood and malice they may injuriously affect the standing, reputation, the pecuniary interests or individuals. (Cooley, 1888, 885–86)

While Judge Cooley's 1888 statement effectively summarizes the battlefield on which many of the fights for press freedom have been waged, it also is a chilling inventory of exceptions that make freedom quite conditional. And all of Cooley's conditions, except blasphemy, are still alive and well in the trial courts, clearly constraining freedom.

In part, confusion over the idea of press freedom stems from the word *freedom* itself. *Freedom* can mean the total absence of restraint. The term *liberty* comes closer to Cooley's meaning, because *liberty* is commonly defined as freedom from all restraints except those justly imposed by law. Liberty of the press assumes a system of rights and duties, while freedom of the press does not. The framers of the U.S. Constitution were not simply stating philosophical maxims but were trying to devise a workable system of government. Thus freedom under our system had a narrower focus than did liberty.

The originators of our legal basis for freedom of the press, the framers of the Constitution, were influenced by the Enlightenment philosophers who wrote about the "rights of man" in broad-based, idealized fashion. When the framers inserted the words *freedom of speech or of the press* in the First Amendment, they were doing more than stating a philosophy. They were trying to find practical means of letting the press have considerable latitude but not unrestrained freedom. Those simple words unleashed a lively, continuing debate. Two factors have fueled this controversy:

1. The general lack of agreement about what is meant by freedom of the press.
2. The recognition that freedom of the press does not exist in a vacuum but must coexist with other rights accorded to individuals under the Constitution.

Only the most naive dreamers could look on the history of the American media and think that they have ever been completely free from restraint. From the earliest times, laws were enacted, mainly at the state level, to protect citizens from the press, just as the Bill of Rights protects citizens from the government and its police. As Cooley suggested, those restrictions included libel (in police terms, false arrest), invasion of privacy (in police terms, unreasonable search and seizure), and many others. It was generally accepted by society that the press should *not* be free to destroy reputations; undermine the confidence of the community; promote violence, murder, and mayhem; or incite other activities deemed to be harmful. The debate over the extensions (or limits) of press freedom has often centered on whether that freedom is absolute or conditional.

The idea of literal or absolute freedom of the press has found few champions more fierce and steadfast than Hugo Lafayette Black, who served on the U.S. Supreme Court from 1937 to 1971. To Justice Black, the First Amendment was a literal command. It says that "Congress shall make no law . . . abridging freedom of speech, or of the press," and to Black *no law* meant *no law.* "I am," he wrote, "for the First Amendment from the first word to the last. I believe it means what it says" (Cahn, 1962, 53). Justice Black (and sometimes his colleague Justice William O. Douglas) was often adamant about the absolute nature of the First Amendment. His brand of First Amendment absolutism is not limited to the lofty chambers of the Supreme Court. I recall encountering a vehement expression of this idea by an editor at the *Milwaukee Journal* as I was speaking to the staff. I was speculating about some of the tradeoffs that citizens expect from the press as a result of the First Amendment franchise. The editor exploded, telling me that there was nothing about that in the Constitution. "*No law,* that's what it says," he told me. "Sounds familiar," I replied.

There are many laws made by Congress and by state legislatures that constrain and complicate freedom of the press. They range from libel and privacy statutes to laws governing copyright and the publication of government secrets. Even the resolute Justice Black would sometimes admit that at certain times, under certain circumstances, and in certain places there could be limits on freedom of expression. So much for the foundations of First Amendment absolutism. It should also be noted that Black's position on this issue, even when unyielding, was never the view of a majority of the Supreme Court.

The philosopher Sidney Hook argued that freedom of the press is not absolute and must yield on occasion to national security needs or to the rights of individuals—for example, the right to a fair trial as guaranteed in the Sixth Amendment or the right of privacy.

There are many complex positions on facts, values, and policies as the intricacies of press freedom are explored, and almost all observers agree that press freedom is fragile and volatile, lacking real stability. Critics point out the negative nature of the First Amendment, which figuratively slaps the hand of Congress in advance while saying little about what the powerful executive and judicial branches of the federal government may do. The so-called strong presidency and the "imperial judiciary" could not have been foreseen by the framers. Some critics argue that the First Amendment really refers to "all government" instead of Congress per se. Even though the Fourteenth Amendment has been interpreted to extend the provisions of the Bill of Rights (including press freedom) to the states, it was not until 1925 that the Supreme Court, in *Gitlow v. New York,* told the states not to impair these rights with laws of their own. But even this court ruling and many subsequent decisions that have defined the conditions and contours of so-called press freedom have failed to wipe out a complex series of state and federal laws and court rulings that place severe limits on freedom of the press.

Most people who have studied freedom of the press agree that one of its fundamental conditions in America is the doctrine of "no prior restraint" of publication. This doctrine holds that the press must be free to publish what it wishes without interference from the government, while remaining subject to various types of legal scrutiny after the fact. This is, of course, a kind of muted freedom, but even here the record is by no means unsullied.

In *Near* v. *Minnesota* (1931) the Supreme Court struck down a gag law in that state and established the principle of no prior restraint of the press firmly in American constitutional law. On a number of occasions since, however, there have been government attempts to block publication of controversial material. In 1971, for example, the *New York Times* and *Washington Post* published some material about the Vietnam War from classified government documents two weeks before the Supreme Court conceded their right to do so; in the meantime the two newspapers were enjoined from further publication. A similar issue arose in 1979 concerning *The Progressive* magazine when that publication was prevented for several months from publishing a story about the hydrogen bomb.

While there may have good reason for the government's actions in both instances, they hardly contributed to a sense of freedom from prior restraint. There are scores of examples of courts' placing restraining orders and other gag rules on reporters attempting to cover the judicial system. These restraints may be fully justifiable, but their presence is *not* press freedom. Of course such actions are perfectly permissible under our legal system in spite of the First Amendment.

I believe that constraints on press freedom in the public sector by the judiciary, the executive, and the legislative branches of government are only part of the barrier to freedom of the press in the United States. There are also many restrictions in the private sector. These include aspects of contract and property law that severely restrict the press in carrying out its fullest exercise of freedom. In addition, the law of literary property (copyright) sometimes inhibits republication of particular material.

The noble purposes of press freedom, as envisioned by the Enlightenment philosophers and others since, would clearly elevate society, but in most instances these are still distant goals, not the reality of the situation today or perhaps even. Some commentators say "the structure is the message" in any consideration of media organizations and their behavior. The structure of the newspaper or broadcast organization dictates rules under which reporters and editors operate. There are conventions against certain kinds of behavior. Some stories get covered; some don't. The written or unwritten rules or newsroom policies, so fully documented in studies of media gatekeepers, are also constraints on freedom. Professionalism itself restrains free will and limits individual choice. Many of us would agree that such private restraints (also called *responsibility* and *ethics*) actually limit press freedom, but for the right reasons. There are many forces that have an impact on the performance of the media. They condition and control. They slow and mute freedom.

While there are theorists who believe that freedom of the press has a preferred place in our scheme of individual liberty and freedom, both because of its symbolic primacy* in the Bill of Rights and because of its importance to the functioning of democratic government, the fact remains that freedom of the press, if it exists at all, is engaged in continuous bargaining with other rights and interests, both individual and social. This has been called a process of reconciliation, wherein rights exercised by one person or group can be reconciled with equal opportunity for others to enjoy them. Thus we have a complex, interrelated system in which rights, principles, practices, and institutions interact. A local newspaper may severely limit my right of privacy today in the name of press freedom, but I might be able to restrain that freedom tomorrow by arguing that pretrial publicity is impairing my right to a fair trial.

The American press lives with rules and regulations, conventions and constraints, but by worldwide standards it is relatively free, even with all of the limitations on its freedom. It has a mechanism which, under most circumstances, allows for the adjudication of disputes that constrain freedom. Freedom of the press presupposes the free flow of information and the free dissemination of a wide spectrum of opinions. In most instances we have a rather muted version of this enlightened view of a free press. Even the most perfunctory surface view of the condition of the press in America tells us that it is not really free. A more penetrating look at the social and psychological factors that can have a chilling effect on freedom—such as the subtle influences of one's peers, bosses, or community—yields a haunting indictment of any claim of press freedom. Finally, as we examine the legal sphere, there is a subtle message that ought to be understood: Through the years spokespersons for the press have fought vigorously for greater and greater press freedom. If it is necessary to do this, the press is hardly free.

Some of my journalist friends tell me that "nowhere does the Constitution say anything about responsibility; the press has no responsibility to do anything." Perhaps, but the same people are fond of enumerating the rights of the press and the rights of reporters. All rights, as anyone who has studied law knows, usually have corresponding *duties.* And any system of free expression that presupposes that there are rights also assumes that there are duties. Whether these duties are also responsibilities is partly a semantic quibble. However, what appears to be a victory for the press one day, such as the *New York Times* decision rendering it difficult for public officials to sue for libel, later can emerge as a constraint. In a late 1970s Supreme Court case, *Herbert* v. *Lando,* the *New York Times* standard for defining malice ("reckless disregard or knowing falsehood") was used to force a producer of television's "60 Minutes" to account for his private thoughts in planning a story. What had been a new

---

* Historians note that the number one placement of the First Amendment was really an accident, not the result of calibrated planning by the framers.

right came back to haunt—and also to restrain—the media. Sometimes the action of the legislature or court to define and extend freedom can become the loophole by which it comes back to check the media.

One thoughtful champion of press freedom, Alexander Bickel of Yale Law School, observed that the more we have to define freedom, the less freedom we have. This statement is not inconsistent with Justice Black's view that we should not have tampered with the command of the framers in the First Amendment. But the fact remains that we have taken considerable license in interpreting its meaning and reach. What remains is hardly a pristine vessel. The charter of press freedom is now somewhat the worse for wear. It is less than whole. It exists mainly in our minds as a social goal, not as a realistic description of the American press today.

Argument summation: The American press is not free.

Freedom of the press is a noble social goal, but in reality America does not have the unfettered rights implied by "freedom" of the press. While not as restricted as in some countries, American press freedoms are conditioned on numerous exceptions. The exceptions are necessary because press rights often must yield to other interests, such as libel, defamation, privacy, and national security. In addition to legal limits on the press, there are numerous private restrictions, including civil laws such as copyright and contract, concentration of media ownership, public relations manipulation of news, and press policies in editing and publishing news. It should be noted that, although the First Amendment says Congress shall make no law restricting freedom of the press, several restrictive laws do exist. The courts have said that only an absolute freedom from prior restraint exists, yet newspapers have been enjoined from printing certain items. These official and private limitations on the press mean that there are active American media, but they are far from a "free" press.

RESPONSE

Merrill: The American press is free.

When we say that America has a free press, of course we do not mean that the press is completely, totally, absolutely free of any and all restraints. Anyone who thinks even minimally about press freedom—or any kind of freedom, for that matter—knows full well that freedoms require some kind and degree of restriction and responsibility.

It may well be that press freedom is a romantic notion and that it really doesn't flourish in the United States. But that is true of all objectives of a society, and freedom, like "truth," "law and order," "friendship," and "loyalty," is relative, incomplete, and hedged with inadequacies. And nobody has maintained that press freedom flourishes in the United States. Dennis, I feel, exaggerates when he says that the American press is simply not free in any real sense of the word.

The press is indeed free in the commonly understood sense of the word: In a nonabsolutist, pragmatic, reasonable sense it is free and can be referred to as free. This is so, of course, with the implicit understanding that it is not absolutely free of all the extrapress and self-imposed restrictions that can easily be brought up by critics.

Even Justice Black and others who have taken basically an absolutist view of First Amendment freedoms have recognized some limitations to press freedom. Obviously nobody—most of all the Founding Fathers—has ever considered the press completely free, nor would any responsible and moderate person want the press to be. I am not talking about an anarchistic or nihilistic press; I am referring to a free press—free in the sense of having minimal government restraints placed upon it. I am talking about a press in the real world of social and political frictions and problems; I am not considering some theoretical level of freedom for press that might exist in the minds of absolutists and sophists. Just as I might say that the United States is a democratic country (knowing full well that it is not really or totally so), I can say with assurance and pragmatic validity that America has a "free press."

Of course Sidney Hook has been quoted asserting that press freedom must yield on occasion to national security. But note that the term *press freedom* is used; it is this press freedom that "must yield." Such freedom must obviously be assumed by Hook in order to be yielded. What American would really want an unyielding concept of press freedom? Reasonable persons, and certainly the framers of the Constitution were reasonable, would not want an unyielding freedom in a nation based on law and social cooperation.

A number of factors limit freedom of the press. Some are external to the press, such as considerations of national security, court rulings, libel actions, pressures from advertisers and other groups, and subscriber desires. Some are internal, such as professional codes of ethics, the editorial power structure itself, press councils, and the like.

I maintain that the core of press freedom in the United States is editorial autonomy and that this country's press system can be considered "free" in the sense that it has editorial autonomy—even in the broadcasting aspects of "the press" (those concerning news and commentary, at least). The American press can make its own editorial decisions and, as a result, can legitimately be considered free. And certainly in the context of the press systems of other countries—even those in the United Kingdom and Sweden—it is free. Relatively free, of course, but free in a meaningful and realistic sense.

Essentially in the United States there is no prior restraint on the press by government. This means that the media are free to publish or broadcast what they want to without government interference or prepublication censorship. The press can criticize the government without fear of being shut down. This is a key factor. Although, as Dennis has pointed out in his "Challenge," there have been a few instances where the courts have instituted some prior restraint on publication, these must be considered exceptions and aberrations; they should not be cited to negate press freedom in America. General statements that are valid are not to be invalidated by pointing to occasional exceptions.

As to the argument that newsroom policies restrict freedom of the press, nobody would deny that internal journalistic decision making and management control by the news media's own executives have a restrictive and directive role in journalism. But is this a restriction *on* the press? No. It is, if it is anything, a restriction *by* the press. And it is an inevitable result of freedom *of* the press. Managers of the press must have the freedom to make their own decisions vis-à-vis editorial content; so they make these decisions and, in so doing, are not restricting press freedom but are exercising it.

Freedom does not mean simply "free from." To be free from everything—free from other people, free from laws, free from morality, free from thought, free from emotion—is to be nothing. Unrestricted freedom is impossible, in fact, and should not be demanded by reasonable people. The truth is that any freedom that is possible and desirable does and should have some limitation. Realistic freedom must have some base point or ground.

An example of this grounding of freedom can be found in Confucian ethics. Here the ground or limitation to freedom is goodness. A person should choose good, not evil. If evil prevailed, freedom would probably disappear. Hence from an ethical perspective we should permit only the freedom to select good and not the freedom to choose evil. In Confucian ethics choosing good is the only freedom.

Confucius confirmed this principle in his own life as it related to freedom of speech. He was free to speak as he pleased, and he thus recognized "freedom of speech"; he would oppose only the speaking of bad words or empty words—that is, words without corresponding "right" actions. Incipient authoritarianism? We have seen rationales for limiting freedom in the writings of Plato, Immanuel Kant, Walter Lippmann, and others who have argued that any freedom that harms others or the foundations of society must be curtailed. Certainly one might speak of a degree of authoritarianism in Confucius in the same way, and only in the same way, as one might speak of a degree of authoritarianism in Kant or even Jesus Christ. The Categorical Imperative of Kant or the Golden Rule of Christ carries authority, but this authority is self-realized and in no way externally imposed.

So we can talk about self-determined restrictions within an environment of freedom. And still we have freedom—of speech or of the press. A contemporary proponent of ethical restraint, very much Confucianist in this respect, has been Professor Walter Berns. In *Freedom, Virtue and the First Amendment* (1957) he issues an articulate call to public virtue. While disassociating himself from intolerance and censorship, he favors certain censorship from a moral perspective. Salacious and pornographic publications, he maintains, can be censored. American Communists have no claim to free expression since they are disloyal. Like Confucius, Berns contends that "bad" speakers and "bad" speeches deserve no protection. Government, he believes, should be engaged in raising the moral quality of the community and therefore must judge and limit public discussion according to the moral quality of the writer or speaker. For Berns and others there is a set of moral principles which, though hard to state with precision, are obligatory on all reasonable persons.

Walter Lippmann (*The Public Philosophy,* 1955) would restrict the concept of freedom also, or more precisely, would have it restricted voluntarily by the individual. Essentially he believes as does Berns: As long as they contribute to forming the public mind, speech and writing should be free. Lippmann believes that the criterion of loyalty is "an indubitable commitment to defend and preserve the order of political and civil rights." To Lippmann and Berns the disloyal have cut themselves out of the basic agreement that supports the process of public discussion. Lippmann maintains, for example, that there can be no right (freedom) to destroy a liberal democratic state—in this he echoes Plato—and Berns points out that we can limit disloyal speech or writing that would generate an American Lenin or Hitler.

So we can see that there have been, and are, thoughtful persons who recognize the necessity of limiting freedom or placing certain moral restrictions on certain forms of communication—whether it is falsely shouting fire in a crowded theater or advocating something that will do harm to national security, public morality, or the continued environment of responsible freedom.

There is, indeed, some danger of authoritarianism implicit in the ideas of these persons. Like the much-maligned Commission on Freedom of the Press (Hutchins Commission) of the 1940s, they are often seen to pose a threat to freedom by stressing responsibility or virtue. And perhaps they do. The debate still rages as to the relative benefits of virtue, responsibility, and social stability against the benefits of freedom.

We certainly will not get into that at this point, but the reader might like to reassess the pronouncements of John Stuart Mill and others (Locke, Milton, Burke, Jefferson, and Voltaire) who base their belief in free expression largely on utilitarian principles. There are, of course, a relativity and an incompleteness to press freedom, but I believe that such qualifications are implicit in the term itself and that, when we think of restrictions on press freedom, we are thinking largely about these restrictions placed there by U.S. journalists themselves. By and large the American press is free to be about as free as it wishes—recognizing, of course, that along with this exercise of freedom come certain responsibilities and obligations to the society that permits it to exist.

In conclusion, let me reiterate my position. In a realistic sense, there is press freedom in the United States. It is quite legitimate for such a term to be used to describe the American press, in spite of the fact that such press freedom is not absolute. The U.S. Constitution protects "freedom of the press," so there must be something to protect. Journalists think they have press freedom, and what they *think* they have, they have. Basically they are thinking of their own individual self-determinism, not of limitations and restrictions imposed on them by the press hierarchy itself.

When I say that America has a free press, I am saying that it has a relatively free press, a freer press than perhaps any other country. I am not saying that it has a *completely* free press, nor is anyone else who talks about freedom of the press in the United States. In addition, I am not saying that the media in the United States use their freedom to the degree they might. The freedom is there, but it is not always used. I agree with Philip Wylie, who said:

> The image of our media turns out . . . to be cowardly and unfree in a very great though not inclusive degree. . . . The media, in their mass-circulation or mass-viewed forms, either foster industry's synthetic image, or remain silent about the rot, mess, lies, human debasement, and the rest of the unfavorable truth hid behind the idol. They go along, too, with the support at least by silence, of pious interference with liberty. (1969, 212)

Wylie is right—not that there is no implication in his words that the American press could not do better and be *freer* if it would *will* to be. The freedom is there; the fact is that the press often chooses not to use it. Such self-imposed restriction does not negate this freedom. It simply sets it temporarily aside until a stronger will, coupled with more courage, will project the press toward a more forceful and responsible utilization of the freedom that it does, in truth, have.

Argument summation: The American press is free.

The American press is free in the ordinary sense of that term. This does not mean license or anarchism, but legally controlled, socially responsible freedom, permitted by the First Amendment to the Constitution. Naturally, journalistic freedom is not total, since there are various social pressures on media managers. But press directors can publish what they wish—without prior restraint by government, and this is what is meant by *press freedom* in the United States. The core meaning has come to approximate "journalistic autonomy." Newsroom policies and directives are not relevant to press freedom, although they do apply to the freedom of individual journalists. The First Amendment protects press freedom (the press's freedom); therefore, there must be "press freedom" in the United States to be thus protected.

TOPICS FOR DISCUSSION

1. Discuss *freedom,* giving all the possible meanings for the term relevant to the freedom of the press. Now do the same thing with the term *press*.

2. Should the media be able to publish or broadcast anything they wish? If not, what should be forbidden? Where should the press freedom line be drawn? Who should draw it?

3. What is the problem with the concept of "a responsible use of freedom"? For example: Who—or what entity—should define responsibility?

4. Why do many persons feel that press freedom is to be preferred over responsibility or virtue?

5. If there is press freedom in the United States, does it belong only to media managers and owners, or to all journalists? Many say that it belongs to "the people." How could it?

TOPICS FOR RESEARCH

1. Thomas Jefferson and other American presidents have typically made positive and negative statements about press freedom. Write an essay indicating why this is the case. Find examples of idealistic pro-press freedom statements from Jefferson or another president. Also find a negative statement. From studies of this topic or biographies of the president, see if you can find public controversies that might have made the given president "go sour" on the press.

2. Find an example of a press freedom issue either in this country or elsewhere. Put the issue in some historical context and use appropriate sources to explain why the issue is still unsettled. This might involve book or film censorship, freedom of information, or libel.

3. Do a short paper on your personal freedom of the press. Do you have

First Amendment press and speech rights? How can you exercise them? Does the present structure of American media help or hinder you in your exercise of press rights?

4. Read the biography or autobiography of someone who has helped extend and expand freedom of the press. Assess the person's contribution and indicate how it is relevant to modern media issues.

5. Using the material in this chapter, critique the arguments of the authors and their use of the sources they quote to document and defend their arguments. If you could question those sources (or the authors) about the down side of the cited material, what would you ask? Prepare your own inquiry into the authors' approach and conclusions. Pretend that you are their adversary and are trying to find coherent middle ground in fashioning a sensible argument.

FURTHER READING

Altschull, J. Herbert. *From Milton to McLuhan: The Ideas Behind American Journalism.* White Plains, NY: Longman, 1989.

Becker, Carl. *Freedom and Responsibility in the American Way of Life.* New York: Vintage Books, 1960.

Berns, Walter. *Freedom, Virtue and the First Amendment.* Baton Rouge: Louisiana State University Press, 1957.

Bodenhamer, David J., and James W. Ely, Jr., eds. *The Bill of Rights in Modern America After 200 Years.* Bloomington: Indiana University Press, 1993.

Cahn, Edmond N. "Dimensions of First Amendment 'Absolutes.'" A public interview in Dennis et al., *The Media at War,* pp. 41–53. Also see *New York University Law Review* 37, no. 4 (June 1962):549–63.

Chafee, Zechariah. *Government and Mass Communication.* Chicago: University of Chicago Press, 1947.

Chamberlin, Bill, and Charlene J. Brown. *The First Amendment Reconsidered.* White Plains, NY: Longman, 1982.

Cohen, Jeremy *Congress Shall Make No Law: Oliver Wendell Holmes, the First Amendment and Judicial Decisionmaking.* Ames: Iowa State University Press, 1989.

Commission on Freedom of the Press. *A Free and Responsible Press.* Chicago: University of Chicago Press, 1947.

Cooley, Thomas. *A Treatise on Constitutional Limitations.* Vol. 2, 2d ed. Chicago: Callaghan, 1888.

Dennis, E. E., D. M. Gillmor, and David Grey, eds. *Justice Hugo Black and the First Amendment.* Ames: Iowa State University Press, 1978.

Dennis, Everette E., et al. *The Media at War, The Press and the Persian Gulf Conflict.* New York: Gannett Center for Media Studies, 1991.

Emerson, Thomas I. *The System of Freedom of Expression.* New York: Random House, 1970.

Friendly, Fred. *Minnesota Rag.* New York: Random House, 1981.

Gillmor, Donald M. *Power, Publicity and the Abuse of Libel Law.* New York: Oxford University Press, 1992.

Haiman, Franklyn S. *Speech and Law in a Free Society.* Chicago: University of Chicago Press, 1981.

Hocking, William E. *Freedom of the Press.* Chicago: University of Chicago Press, 1947.

Lewis, Anthony. *The Sullivan Case and the First Amendment.* New York: Random House, 1991.

Lippmann, Walter. *The Public Philosophy.* Boston: Little, Brown, 1955.

MacArthur, John R. *Second Front: Censorship and Propaganda in the Gulf War.* New York: Hill and Wang, 1995.

Meiklejohn, Alexander. *Political Freedom: The Constitutional Powers of the People.* New York: Harper, 1960.

Merrill, John C. *The Dialectic in Journalism: Toward a Responsible Use of Press Freedom.* Baton Rouge: Louisiana State University Press, 1989.

———. *The Imperative of Freedom.* 2d ed. New York: Freedom House, 1990.

Soloski, John, and Randall P. Bezanson, eds. *Reforming Libel Law.* New York: Guilford Press, 1992.

Stevens, John D. *Shaping the First Amendment.* Beverly Hills, CA: Sage, 1982.

Tribe, Lawrence. *American Constitutional Law.* Mineola, NY: Foundation Press. See especially Chapter 7.

Wylie, Philip. *The Magic Animal.* New York: Pocket Books, 1969.

Chapter 2

MEDIA–GOVERNMENT RELATIONSHIP

Name any American president from George Washington to Bill Clinton, and you can find an instance of his getting mad at the press, even though he steadfastly affirmed his belief in freedom of the press. The fact is that governments and the media do not always see eye to eye. Governments and their leaders want public support for their policies, and the press is often the prickly critic and irritant.

As we saw in Chapter 1, the role of government in relation to the media is most often stated negatively. For example, government is commanded by the First Amendment not to intrude on press freedom. It is also relevant to note that the press is regarded as a fourth branch of government or as a fourth estate which serves as a check on government.

The media, especially those involved in public affairs, are said to play a watchdog role and thus keep the government under surveillance. One of the primary purposes of a free press in a democratic system, it is often said, is keeping the public informed about government activities. However, since the media often run into a resistant government that is not eager to disclose all, a natural conflict results.

When the press probes the activities of government and attacks government secrecy and possible corruption, this fosters what has been called, generally by press people, an "adversary relationship" between government and the press. The government can exercise its adversarial role by withholding information the media want. Some critics say this antagonistic relationship has a "checking value," wherein the press checks on government and makes certain that it is performing properly. This concept leads to a related question: Who checks on the press and sees that *it* is performing properly? Whether such an adversarial relationship actually exists—or should exist—is open to debate.

CHALLENGE

Merrill: The media and government should not be adversaries.

It is commonly assumed in the United States that we have an adversarial media or press system—and furthermore, that we *should* have one. The press and government existing as adversaries is usually seen, at least in the United States, as a proper and necessary relationship. The concept is embraced especially in the rhetoric of journalists.

This assumption is one that needs to be challenged. Granted, many of the hackneyed expressions of American journalism such as that the press is a "fourth branch of government" or a "check on government" or a "watchdog" suggest the validity of the notion of a press–government adversary relationship, but is it really justified? I believe not. In the argument that follows, I shall try to explain, first, why there is no adversarial relationship under American libertarian theory, and second, why the communications media would not want such a relationship to exist.

Why should the press and government be adversaries? Why not friends? Why not foes at times and friends at times? Why, then, should not the relationship be ambivalent, especially in a free and pluralistic press system? These are questions it would seem unnecessary to ask in the United States. But evidently they are necessary, for the press has taken unto itself the role of an adversary to governments, and it boasts about that role.

I maintain that theoretically the relationship is not really adversarial (the laws are on the side of the press) and should not be adversarial—any more than it should be cooperative and harmonious. It should be an ambiguous relationship, a freewheeling one, a changing one. That relationship would be consistent with the nature of independent editorial determination, with the spirit of pluralism, and with press freedom.

Beyond this theoretical problem with the adversarial relationship, I maintain that the press does not really want such a pragmatic relationship. The press wants to be an adversary by itself: It basically desires a helpless and law-bound government forced to provide the press with anything it wants, with no secrecy on the part of the government, with no attempts to influence or control any activities of the press, with no criticism of the press. What kind of adversarial relationship is this?

Does not press freedom imply, in effect, that any unit of the press system can take any stance it likes toward government? If I am the editor of newspaper A, I may want consistently to support all government policies. I am free to do so. Or I may want to oppose some weaknesses. I may want to be ambivalent toward government, sometimes pro and sometimes con.

I may indeed want to determine for my newspaper an adversarial role vis-à-vis government, to see my newspaper as a vehicle for fighting against government: to check on government, to criticize government, and to have a policy of rooting out government excesses and wrongdoing. In short, I may decide to use my newspaper as a watchdog on government or as artillery with which to bombard government.

In reality, in a libertarian society the relationship between press and government is so varied and splintered that it cannot be expressed in any monolithic way. To call it adversarial is a travesty of rhetoric and reality. It is utterly ridiculous for a press to cast itself as an adversary of government: Such a stance would imply that the government is always wrong and the press is always right; it would also imply that the press sees itself as an institution dedicated to portraying for the public their government as a flawed, negatively disposed one that must be constantly watched lest it do great harm to the people.

The government, of course, is really closer to the people than is the press, for at least portions of the government are elected by the people. Not so with the press. The press, largely a profit-making private enterprise, has simply set itself up as a representative of the people and a check on government.

Kurt Luedtke, a former executive editor of the *Detroit Free Press* and screenwriter of the film *Absence of Malice,* courageously aimed strong words at the American press in this regard:

> You [the American press] are forever inventing new rights and privileges for yourselves, the assertion of which is so insolent that you apparently feel compelled—as I certainly would—to wrap them in the robe of some imaginary public duty and claim that you are acting on my behalf. If I am indeed involved, then I would like you to do a little less for me. But of course I'm not. Your claims of privilege have nothing to do with any societal obligation, because you have no societal obligation: That is the essence of what the First Amendment is all about. (1982, p. 16)

Let me follow up this extremely relevant quotation of Luedtke with a brief statement by Paul H. Weaver, associate editor of *Fortune* and *The Public Interest:* "The romantic image of the 'adversary press,' then, is a myth: 'functional' for certain purposes, but wholly inaccurate as a model of what newsmen actually do or can hope to achieve" (1974, 95).

Traditionally, U.S. journalism has been rather close to, dependent on, and cooperative with official sources. Undoubtedly this closeness has caused problems, but it has been one of its strengths. Perhaps at times it has led to some press "cheerleading" for government policies, but it has also maximized the amount of information and disinformation available to citizens. If I, as a government official, see the press as an adversary, how will I respond to it? With caution, with distrust, with skepticism, with a minimum of openness and frankness, and with a certain hostility. In addition, I certainly will turn my caution and hostility into considerable secrecy and distortion of information that I give out. Solid and balanced information, therefore, is often the victim in this adversarial warfare, with the consumer (the public) receiving the distortions and informational shreds from the battle.

Further, it seems strange that journalists find any comfort in the concept of an adversarial press. If they are realistic, they should know that they are dependent to a large extent on government for their news. Virtually all the information published by the journalists about government is derived from (and often validated by) some government-related person. Newspeople know almost nothing about public events and issues except what they obtain from external sources and authorities. If the media want to limit access to such sources, then they will stress their adversarial role; if they want to expand their sources of information, then they will stress their cooperative and friendly role. Adversaries, of course, are not friendly.

An adversarial role is often not even a responsible—or ethical—role. There is nothing sacred or intrinsically good about being an adversary. In fact, adversaries are more likely than not to deal in propaganda—to play games of disinformation and misinformation. Adversaries like to win—they are not comfortable with even-handed information, with attempts to inform thoroughly and fairly.

Let us not forget that in a real adversarial relationship government has the same right to "fight" as does the press. The government can, in such a relationship, try to withhold information, to have secret meetings, to distort information for its own advantage, to have its favorite reporters and reward them in various ways, to deal in disinformation and other propagandistic techniques, to subpoena journalists, and to restrict their activities.

In short, the government would be a true adversary.

In a real adversarial relationship the press no doubt would have the upper hand, unless the Constitution were changed. The press has the last word in any controversy with government. It also has the first word. The government really has no word at all, except that provided to it by the press. Any government official's voice reaching the public through the media is immediately thereafter subjected to analysis and interpretation by media figures: telling the American people who have just heard the official what the person "really" said and what he or she "really" meant. Instant analysis, as it is often called, might better be referred to as "instant bias" by which the press makes sure it has the last word.

The government's hands are largely tied. About the only way it can be an adversary of the press is through occasional verbal blasts at media practices. And these blasts themselves are subject to media management and to instant analyses and the "final word." The government, to be sure, does have one other weapon, a purely defensive one: secrecy in certain deliberations. Without a doubt it makes use of this weapon, but in the process it opens itself to more problems: the "leak" by disgruntled functionaries, escalated criticism by the press when it learns of such government operations, the felt need to justify government activities at every turn, and the helpless feeling of government people when the press fires its unanswerable barrages at them.

In a true adversarial relationship there is one thing the government could do (and should do) to help its position: It should involve itself more in the media business. It should cease permitting the press to be the informer of the people; it should itself actively inform the people, circumventing when possible the commercial press. When the government has no real voice, it is an unequal and almost helpless contender in this press—government fray. Perhaps the Hutchins Commission was correct in 1947 when it suggested that government might indeed have to get into the communications business. It is obvious that in any kind of rhetorical battle, the side without control of internal, public channels of communications is at a distinct disadvantage.

If the people are to know the maximum and to be exposed to the widest range of opinions, it would seem logical that government voices would be of help. In fact, the government probably has a responsibility to communicate directly to the people instead of allowing its messages to be filtered through the distorted and often biased lens of the American mass media system. Why should the press, any more than any other institution, be saddled with the awesome responsibility of providing government information to the people?

Surely my coauthor will contend—speaking, I am sure, for the great majority of press people—that the government has no right to compete with private media. But why not? Is not government competition implicit in an adversarial relationship?

Could not the government through its own publications, broadcast outlets, and other resources fill a multitude of gaps with information and viewpoints? Could not the government then have an instrument to compete with the private media? Could not the government then have a chance to set the record straight, or at least to tell in its own way what it has to say to the people? This activity would be consistent with the concept of pluralism to which free press people pay lip service. It would also make the adversarial relationship more equal. It would give a virtually voiceless entity (the government) a voice with which to speak directly to its constituency. It would help make it a real contender in this supposed adversarial relationship. An example is in Britain, where the British Broadcasting Corporation (BBC) competes with independent (private enterprise) networks and stands for quality while still being government-controlled, however loosely.

But, as has been noted, the press would not like this. In spite of its talk, the press does not really want an adversarial relationship with the government.

The fact that the press looks at itself as an adversary of government not only is theoretically questionable but leads to problems with ethics. The belief that the press must be a check on government, a critic of government, or a watchdog on government results in a hyperactive and contentious journalism. The adversarial role causes the press to dig and probe, snipe and snoop; it causes the press to speculate, to deal in gossip and innuendo in its attempt to unearth corruption in high and low places. This press concept is responsible for the press's accentuating the negative in governmental matters. It fosters the idea that the government is inherently evil and must be checked. And in this little game which the press sees itself playing, the press has appointed itself to keep the government honest.

Today, as an increasing number of voices are asking who checks the checker, the press falls back on its constitutional freedom guarantee, and when all the rhetoric is done, the answer from the press is essentially this: *Nobody* checks the checker. The press is nearly free from being checked. Is this answer consistent with the contention that the press and government are *adversaries*?

In conclusion, let me quote a reputable American journalist, James Reston, who ends his discussion in *The Artillery of the Press* by contradicting his "artillery fire" title: "Clever officials," he says, "cannot 'manipulate' reporters, and clever reporters cannot really 'best' the government. From both sides, they have more to gain by cooperating with one another, and with the rising minority of thoughtful people, than by regarding one another as 'the enemy'" (1967, 108). So Reston recognizes the mythology implicit in his book's title and in the whole concept of the adversary relationship of the press and government.

I repeat my position: In reality there is no adversarial relationship between press and government and there should not be one.

Argument summation: The media and government should not be adversaries.

The media and government are not adversaries—or at least they shouldn't be. Such a situation would assign to the press a role that would be in conflict with editorial self-determination. An adversarial relationship may well exist from time to time, but in a free and open press system such a relationship should be strictly ad hoc. Why should a free press feel it must be an adversary to government? Why not just as well be a friend? Some media at some times and in some circumstances may want to oppose the government in particular matters, but a generally assumed opposition to government is not only irrational but contrary to the basic tenets of a free and self-determining press.

RESPONSE

Dennis: The media and government should be adversaries.

Granted, *adversarial* may be an overly dramatic term to describe the ideal relationship between press and government, but the concept has come to have legitimate meaning and, in fact, as it is commonly understood, it is quite desirable. Adversarial means simply that the media should be critical, argumentative, and contentious in their relationships with government. The press may be the only organizations that have what Justice Potter Stewart called "structural rights," or rights that belong mostly to institutions, such as the press, as opposed to rights such as religious freedom that are both personal and institutional or structural under the Constitution. The primary function of the press under this legal arrangement is to provide the people with a free flow of information.

As anyone who has ever observed governments knows, they try to perpetuate themselves by managing and manipulating information. The press is one of only a few social forces that can challenge them. From the time of the divine right of kings to the present, government has realized that information is power and the control of information (at least to some degree) is essential to public support for its policies and mandates. This was the reason for the old press licensing and sedition laws in Britain against which American colonists and patriots such as John Peter Zenger rebelled. In modern times government secrecy, carried to the extreme, sometimes has deprived the American people of information they needed to be fully knowledgeable citizens. When the White House wanted to cover up the Watergate scandal, the press shouted "foul" and revealed for all to see that seamy chapter in the nation's history. Illegal domestic spying and wiretapping by the Central Intelligence Agency and the Federal Bureau of Investigation have also been uncovered by a vigilant press wary of government in the best adversarial tradition.

Several of my coauthor's arguments deserve close scrutiny. He maintains, for example, that under a libertarian theory of the press there is no adversary relationship between press and government. Indeed, the libertarian idea (not to be confused with the Libertarian Party) allows for multiple voices in the marketplace of ideas that can take issue with government or oppose it, but the greatest likelihood is a clash of values and controversial discussion. This often keeps the media as free as possible from government involvement. Of course, he is correct in saying that positions taken by the press are strictly up to editors or broadcasters. Although we do not live under a libertarian system today, when we did in the late eighteenth and early nineteenth centuries, the press fought hard against government strictures on information and helped establish the present adversary relationship. The idea of a libertarian press grew out of Enlightenment philosophy and posited notions about the free flow of information and opinion without censorship or other government interference or control. At the dawn of the nineteenth century, which journalism historians call "The Dark Ages of American Journalism," the government passed the Alien and Sedition Acts, which the press opposed with great fervor because they led to instances of outright censorship and the closure of some newspapers. Libertarian journalism brought us highly opinionated, partisan publications. Some were adversaries of government, others were house organs for political parties. All this ended with the rise of a mass press, which was brought about by a happy mixture of technology, education, advertising, and other factors.

Today, most media no longer follow the libertarian model, preferring a system of social responsibility and ethical imperatives. Exceptions are talk radio and opinion magazines, truly libertarian in their approach. While we no longer have a libertarian press system, we do have a press that shares the common value of a critical (or adversarial) posture toward government. We have a system of "social responsibility," wherein the press assumes certain rights and corresponding responsibilities or duties. One is the full and robust coverage of government. An adversarial posture is helpful if not essential to this arrangement. One of the only American newspapers I can think of that exemplifies the libertarian tradition is the *Manchester* (N.H.) *Union-Leader,* a feisty publication known for its biased reporting and vehement attacks on liberal political figures. This paper, operated for many years by conservative publisher William Loeb (and presently run much the same way by his widow), sometimes mixes its editorial and news functions. It is clearly a point-of-view newspaper that rejects notions of social responsibility, fairness, and balance. But even the *Union Leader* has an adversary stance with government, so much so that it can justly be called "antigovernment." To some extent, radio talk maestro Rush Limbaugh is libertarian in his outlook.

Although they may be somewhat trite, no discussion of the typically American media—government relationship is complete without international comparisons. In many countries there is a controlled press—not just in North Korea and China, but also in many developing and industrialized states. In some places it is not uncommon to have government ownership of the media. Government press councils and laws also limit press freedom. Even in Britain, the mother of democracies, harsh laws keep the media on a short leash. French journalists have rightly complained that they could not do vigorous investigative reporting because of the fear of government reprisal.

A call for greater freedom linked to an ambiguous relationship with government is really quite dangerous, even if well intentioned. As should be evident from such recurrent issues as book censorship by school boards, wherein freedom to read controversial works is challenged, freedom of expression is not something that is established on marble tablets and enshrined for all time. It must be continuously defended or it will cease to exist. Reporters who cover local government often lament their continuing battles with public officials over open meeting and open records practices. The laws regarding public access to meetings and records are on the books, but many government officials will ignore and thwart them unless challenged by the press. Without an adversarial press, it is unlikely that our "sunshine" laws would be used at all. When it comes to such basic rights as press freedom, we must "use 'em or lose 'em."

Typically during war or other great national crises press and government are quite cooperative. The press's coverage of wars usually supports the government. This accommodation is due both to a conscious practice by the press and to government censorship which makes coverage difficult and forbids release of such information as troop movements or air and naval maneuvers.

Within the framework of an adversary relationship a whole range of strategies and tactics can be employed by the press and, yes, by government. Washington correspondents, for example, are engaged in an adversarial process. They try to get information about a particular policy or agency. Some of the information is freely provided by helpful information officers; some that might be embarrassing to the agency is withheld. The reporter then develops a strategy to get the missing information. This is done through the use of leaks, alternate sources, or jealous politicians. In this adversary posture the press is suspicious of the actions of government and vice versa.

Who, in fact, really represents the public interest? Both press and government claim to do so. The government makes a strong claim, since it operates by the "consent of the governed." The press, on the other hand, also has some basis for asserting that it is a representative of the public. At least it makes this claim in many lawsuits where its motives are challenged. Thus through court decisions, terms such as "the fourth branch of government" and "the fourth estate" have gained real meaning with legal teeth. When the courts, for example, grant the press rights to enter a prison to interview inmates, a right that the rest of us do not have, this special privilege is extended to the press as a "trustee" of the people. Since we all cannot wander within prison walls to find out what is happening there, the press does this for us and is therefore our representative. Writing in *Saxbe* v. *Washington Post Co.,* Justice Lewis Powell agreed, saying:

> The people must therefore depend on the press for information concerning public institutions. . . . The underlying right is the right of the public generally. The press is the necessary representative of the public's interest . . . and the instrumentality

which effects the public's right. (1974, 417 United States, 843 and 864)

In another case, however, film producer Fred Wiseman was denied access to an institution for the mentally ill.

Professor William L. Rivers of Stanford University has documented in great detail the extent of the adversary relationship between press and government in two books, *The Adversaries* and *The Other Government.* He argues forcefully that the press is truly an adversary of government. We need to remember that government is not a single entity, but federal, state, and local units of executive, legislative, and judicial bodies. Columbia University law professor Vince Blasi argues that the press has a "checking value" in its relationship with government (1977).

The virtues of an adversary government between press and government are vividly demonstrated when one compares the news coverage of public affairs with, say, that of business or sports. While the coverage of government is by no means exhaustive (and it assuredly has many flaws), there is a conscious effort by the press, both nationally and in local communities, to cover important events—happenings and issues in legislative bodies, the courts, and public agencies. At the federal level the presidency is watched by a legion of several hundred reporters. A large contingent is assigned to Capitol Hill while very few cover the Supreme Court and the federal bureaucracy. Look at any local community and you will see the local press carefully watching the city council, the courts, and public agencies. This coverage includes some that is purely descriptive, some that is analytical, and some that tries to ferret out wrongdoing. All of it contributes to an adversary relationship. Generally, relationships between government sources and reporters are quite cordial. This cooperation is fine when government is running smoothly and the press is simply doing routine, descriptive coverage. The more contentious, adversarial stance is appropriate when things are not going so well and when the public ought to know about it.

Now consider press coverage of business. Business coverage has improved markedly in recent years, but for a long time it was a tedious treatment of commercial activity. Much of it was little more than the printing of publicity releases that various businesses and industries provided. The press took little interest in internal conflicts and controversies or in corporate strategies that led to a particular product line. In the 1990s many news organizations improved their coverage of business because the private sector has such a profound impact on individuals and their communities.

Sports is an area where the press has traditionally cooperated with sources to the extent of becoming boosters and promoters. Local papers typically support local teams, and coaches are lionized by reporters and columnists. Under such coverage many fundamental yet changing assumptions about sports in American life went undetected. Those included corrupt practices by teams and their owners, drug use by athletes, and others. Conflicts within teams and organizations were ignored. Sports reporters often acted more like advocates for teams or players than like journalists. They ignored embarrassing facts and helped make heroes. Today the adversarial approach is making inroads on sports pages, but progress has been slow.

Critics the world over agree that the adversarial relationship makes the U.S. media distinctive. For the most part the press in the United States is low key, but on occasion it can rise to greatness by taking on government with a ferocity that can emerge only when news sources are treated like enemies of full disclosure and free-flowing information. Of course, most of the time this extreme posture is not necessary, but most reporters would argue in favor of a fundamental distrust of government. They might not go as far as I. F. Stone did when he declared that "government always lies," but they would agree that government can obscure, distort, and mislead. The public needs an advocate to challenge, cajole, needle, and inquire. In America this is the job of an adversarial press.

Argument summation: The media and government should be adversaries.

The fluctuating government–media relationship can be characterized either as disagreement between friends or as occasional agreement between adversaries. The latter relationship is preferable in order to preserve a healthy, fundamental distrust of government among the media, which is essential to maintain the checking function of the press. American experience during the libertarian period of the media, when the press became spokesmen for biased views, confirms the power of the press to be used for partisan objectives. A nonadversarial relationship would lead to an erosion of press rights by governmental involvement. While government and media both represent the public interest and can cooperate, an adversary posture is needed to ensure a fundamental distrust of government that is critical to democratic society.

TOPICS FOR DISCUSSION

1. Should citizens have more trust in their press than in their government? Why? Discuss.

2. In what ways can the government have an adversarial role against the press? Which of the "adversaries" (government or press) has the advantage? Discuss the reasons for your answer.

3. It is argued that governments manipulate information. Could you say the same thing about the press? Give some examples from actual news stories.

4. Many persons assume that out of an adversarial relationship will emerge truth. Discuss this notion. If the adversarial press makes the U.S. press distinctive in the eyes of the world's journalists, would you consider this assessment to be an approbation or a criticism? Why do you think there are not more nations with such an adversarial press?

5. Discuss the advantages and disadvantages that are likely to accrue in a country from having a press that is an adversary to government.

TOPICS FOR RESEARCH

1. Do a study of a local governmental agency and how it relates to the press. It might be police, mayor, health department, or others. How much of the agency's press relations work is reactive? How much is proactive or initiative? What barriers does the press construct for the agency in getting its message to the people? What problems does the agency cause for the press in trying to get information? Is the resulting relationship characterized by conflict or consensus?

2. Find a public official or politician—locally or on the national scene—and research his or her relationship with the press. Is the relationship organized in a systematic fashion? How does the press treat the individual? If you were giving that person advice about improving or changing his or her image, what would it be?

3. Is there domestic censorship in the United States today? Who, if anyone, are the censors? What is the legacy of censorship of newspapers, books, films, and so on from the past? How much was the result of laws? What is the status of such censorship today? In assessing who cares about such censorship today, you might want to consult library journals and science publications as well as press and media studies and periodicals.

4. Prepare a comparative analysis of press—government relations in the United States and those of another country, preferable one where the press system is radically different.

5. What does press freedom mean in the following countries: the United Kingdom, North Korea, South Africa, and Singapore? How is the concept defined by laws there? What does government do to impair or enhance press freedom?

FURTHER READING

Anderson, David. "Media Success in the Supreme Court." Working paper. New York: Gannett Center for Media Studies, 1987.

Baker, C. Edwin. "Scope of First Amendment Freedom of Speech." *UCLA Law Review* 25, no. 5 (June 1978):264–1040.

Blasi, Vince. *The Checking Value in First Amendment Theory.* Samuel Pool Weaver Constitutional Law Series. Chicago: American Bar Foundation, 1977.

Cater, Douglass. *The Fourth Branch of Government.* Boston: Houghton Mifflin, 1959.

DeFleur, Melvin L., and Everette E. Dennis. *Understanding Mass Communication.* 3d ed. Boston: Houghton Mifflin, 1988. See especially Chapter 7, "The News and the Media," for a discussion of changing styles and standards of reporting, including an analysis of adversarial journalism.

Dennis, Everette E. "The Press and the Public Interest: A Definitional Dilemma." *DePaul Law Review* 23, no. 3 (Spring 1974): 937–60.

Friendly, Fred. *Minnesota Rag.* New York: Random House, 1981.

Hertsgaard, Mark. *On Bended Knee: The Press and the Reagan Presidency.* New York: Farrar, Strauss & Giroux, 1989.

Luedtke, Kurt. "An Ex-Newsman Hands Down His Indictment of the Press." *Bulletin of ASNE* 651 (May–June 1982): 16–17.

O'Neill, Michael J. *Roar of the Crowd: How Television and People Power Are Changing the World.* New York: Random House, 1993.

"The Presidency in the New Media Age." *Media Studies Journal,* Spring 1994. New York: Freedom Forum Media Studies Center.

Reston, James. *The Artillery of the Press.* New York: Harper & Row, Colophon Books, 1967.

Rivers, William L. *The Adversaries.* Boston: Beacon Press, 1970.

———. *The Other Government: Power and the Washington Media.* New York: Universe, 1982.

Rourke, F. F. *Secrecy and Publicity: Dilemmas of Democracy.* Baltimore: Johns Hopkins University Press, 1966.

Schudson, Michael. *Watergate in American Memory: How We Remember, Forget and Reconstruct the Past.* New York: Basic Books, 1992.

Chapter 3

MEDIA AND THE PUBLIC TRUST

As one encounters the procession of speakers in London's famous Hyde Park, it is clear that some know what they are talking about while others are fanciful, unreliable, even disturbed. We trust and believe some of them while we are wary of others. The same is true of our media. The unsupported and often abrasive views of some talk show hosts on radio and television or lurid headlines in supermarket tabloids may not inspire our confidence immediately (or ever), while network news, major newspapers, and other reliable media usually make an effort to gain public trust.

Discussions of the media and the public trust usually center on the relationship between the media (both individually and collectively) and their audiences. The nature of that relationship is summed up in the term *vox populi* or "voice of the people." In a democracy the press or media are said to function as the people's voice—expressing their concerns, providing the information they need, and allowing channels for discussion and debate. Will Rogers once said that a good newspaper was "a nation talking to itself," which expresses very well the idea of public trust. Public trust means that the media are believed and relied upon by the public, that they are the necessary representative of the people in much of the public discourse in this nation. In recent years the concept of public trust has been linked with credibility, believability, and trustworthiness. It is said that a news organization such as a newspaper or a television news program cannot succeed unless it achieves public trust, that is, unless most of its audience believe what they read, hear, or see in the content delivered by the newspaper or television station. An idealistic view of the media suggests that this is the main reason why media organizations exist and why people choose to work for them rather than for someone else. In this formulation the media mainly perform a public service in delivering news and information, opinion, and entertainment, and they also serve as a useful marketplace for goods and services. There is another view that says the commercial media in our society, at least, are capitalistic enterprises whose main concern is profit. In such a scheme any public service rendered in establishing a public trust relationship is done strictly for self-serving ends. But whatever the view, the media and the public trust is a much-discussed topic.

CHALLENGE

Merrill: The media chiefly desire to make profits.

Tradition, conventional American wisdom, and oft-expressed idealism combine to suggest that U.S. media are primarily in the business of communication to provide a public service. Certainly, it is said, if the media want to get and retain the "public trust" they will provide such public service.

It is not easy to challenge such an idealistic contention, but with profit making and competition being strong inclinations in a capitalistic society and supporting the basic American ideology, the contention must in fact be challenged. In the United States, regardless of flowery rhetoric at media conventions, the "bottom line" is the machine that drives media policy and is the main concern of media directors.

All we have to do is to consider the volume of paid advertising filling our media, spotted here and there with bits and pieces of editorial material, to get a panoramic view of the media's drive toward profit making. Surely the 65 to 75 percent of the average publication's space given over to advertising is not seriously thought of by media moguls as "serving the public interest." Such exorbitant attention to commercialism that fills the coffers of the media makes a very weak argument for providing the public with a substantial diet of nonpropagandistic content.

Let us agree that, under our media philosophy, profits are desired and necessary. The question, however, is whether the media need to make the exceedingly large profits that they do while sometimes skimping on the number of staff members and their salaries.

Where is the great concern for the public when media units are gobbled up by big media corporations, multimedia conglomerates proliferate, and national media spew forth the same low-level, common-denominator pabulum? Where is concern for the public when media managers—in newspapers as well as in broadcasting—make salaries in the six digits, many in the millions, while editors, reporters, and writers grind out their days with salaries of $30,000 to $50,000, and many even less?

Where is the concern of the media for public service when even small weekly newspapers in this country are on the selling block for millions of dollars? Where is the concern for the public when family-owned media, which have served their communities for years, are increasingly bought out for fantastic prices by absentee owners who care little or nothing about the communities? Is it the public these media people are concerned about, or is it lining their own pockets?

Shirley Biagi presents interesting facts about media ownership: The top ten newspaper groups own one-third of the nation's dailies; twenty corporations control about 60 percent of annual magazine revenues; twenty corporations account for more than 50 percent of radio revenue; 70 percent of all TV stations are network affiliates; and six book publishers receive 30 percent of all book revenue yearly (Biagi, 1988).

Admittedly these figures by themselves do not prove that media have no public concern, But they do prove that money and the increase of money through concentration of media power are very powerful in American communications. And they show that growth is what fascinates big media moguls of the United States.

Professor Biagi admits that making money is a goal usually supported by the American people, but it is the way these big media companies make this money that is the debatable question, she says. And she poses three interesting questions: "Does the legacy of First Amendment protection for news-gathering organizations mean that they have a special responsibility to provide the information people need in a democracy? Should entertainment-producing companies provide a diversity of cultural outlets for creativity? Will the adoption of corporate values benefit or harm the mass media industries?" (Biagi, 1988, 277).

Ben Bagdikian, a leading press critic, notes that "in the face of enormously increased interest in public affairs, newspapers have reduced their average space devoted to news" (1974, 9). Bagdikian goes on to question the press's concern for public service: Political coverage is poor; most papers are mediocre and many are wretched; most cities are dominated by one newspaper; advertisements increasingly eat into former news space; live news is decreasing; only about 3 percent of American cities have competing newspapers (in 1910 a majority did); and increasing amounts (probably one-third) of news are supplied by public relations outlets (Bagdikian, 1974, 8–17 passim).

In the world of newspapers the control of content is narrowing. Successful companies are getting bigger and more powerful. Note Ray Hiebert and his coauthors of a popular basic media textbook:

> The media, in general, have become more competitive in trying to capture the largest, most valuable audience available, instead of attempting to meet the special needs of all segments of society. (Hiebert, Ungurait, and Bohn, 1988)

CHAPTER 3. MEDIA AND THE PUBLIC TRUST

If this is true, does it sound like the media are concerned about the public interest?

Hiebert et al. say that broadcasters also are struggling to reach a mass audience and are neglecting specialized audiences. When specialized audiences are considered at all, can they be reached profitably? Hiebert et al. note that media investors are prone to take only mild positions on sensitive issues and that they seem sensitive only to "demands of the marketplace" (1988, 594–95).

Perhaps they do not have the "public be damned" attitude of a former time, but the average publisher and editor seem to care little about the real informational or intellectual health of the people who read their paper. Editorial prerogative is the watchword. "We will make the decisions we want to make. That's our job. You readers will take what we give you. After all, if you don't read us, who will you read?"

And when asked about responsibility for finding out what the readers want and trying to provide it, the typical editor responds: "We are journalists, and journalists develop the instinct to know what the readers want. In a real sense, what we want is what you want."

So what do readers and television viewers generally get? Snippets of gossip and speculation about Michael Jackson and Roseanne. Pictures of whales trapped in ice. Stories and pictures of congressional malfeasance. A rundown on the brutal rape-murder in smalltown America, with the grieving mother being asked by the reporter how she feels about her daughter's death. The picture of thousands of university students nihilistically awash in Beijing's main square. And as smoke is shown billowing from a U.S. city, the deep funereal voice of the TV anchor takes us "now to the scene of the devastating explosion that shakes man's faith in technology."

It should be obvious to the American media consumer that most of the messages are trivial, superficial, titillating, sensational, negative, crisis-oriented, and often flippant. Except in certain elite journals like the *New York Times, National Geographic, New Yorker,* or *Commentary,* the reader seldom gets any thoughtful, substantive information and analysis. And the TV viewer drifts about in a desert of crime, sex and shallow "situation comedies." Programs with depth and insight, such as those found on the Public Broadcasting System, are rare.

But business-oriented media managers will be quick to say: "Such programming aimed at the thoughtful and the educated is not *profitable.* The readership and viewership would be too small. Our nets must be cast wide and into shallow waters so that we may catch as many fish as possible." Is this "public service"? Perhaps. But it is a special kind—that which provides junk food for idle minds and lazy souls that undoubtedly inhabit vast expanses of the general public. So the motto of the media manager is generally this: "Give them pap, not what they really need." Or perhaps even better: "Give them what we hope they will accept because of its easy assimilation, so our circulation will increase and our ratings will rise—along with our profits."

The Commission on Freedom of the Press (chaired by Dr. Robert Hutchins), in its 1947 report *A Free and Responsible Press,* rendered the first large-scale indictment of the American press for not taking the public trust seriously, among other things. According to the Commission, one of the three main dangers facing the press was that the few people who ran the press had not provided a service adequate to the needs of society. Such a criticism, which is taken seriously even today by many critics, indicates that media are not concerned primarily with public service, but rather with private interest.

Jerome Barron, lawyer and media critic, has emphasized in *Freedom of the Press for Whom?* that the media do not serve the public interest because of their arrogant exclusiveness. Barron cites sources that indict the American media for normally accentuating the false and the irrational and for excluding small and powerless minorities from a media voice (1973, 78–79.)

But it can be said that media in the United States are businesses, and businesses are profit-making enterprises, with exclusionary privileges, and with financial growth and the "bottom line" as primary objectives. J. Herbert Altschull notes that in a commercial media system "the content reflects the views of the advertisers and their commercial allies, who are usually found among the owners and publishers." Altschull puts the final nail in the "public interest" question by asserting that "no newspaper, magazine, or broadcasting outlet exceeds the boundaries of autonomy acceptable to the paymasters" (1984, 254–55).

Marketplace theory is usually dragged out to justify the American profit-making system, as a recent volume on media freedom and accountability indicates (Dennis, Gillmor, and Glasser, 1989). In theory the system is supposed to increase message pluralism—as well as owner pluralism and unit pluralism—because of the natural desire of free people to compete and to make money.

But is it working that way? Many would argue—many do argue—that pluralism is really shrinking and that fewer and fewer voices are being heard throughout the land. Is not the desire to make bigger profits actually causing media directors to take fewer chances, to play it safe, to aim for the lowest common denominator? How does doing this serve the public adequately? It is obvious how it serves the personal financial interest of the media owners.

In this day when every survey shows that Americans are trusting and respecting the media less, the high-sounding shibboleths about the media's "recognizing a public trust" is ever more hollow. Perhaps it is time to cease this kind of rhetoric and honestly admit that the main purpose of the media is to make a profit—and that public service comes into the picture only to the degree that it fosters this primary objective.

Argument summation: The media chiefly desire to make profits.

The American media mainly desire to make profits. Any thought of public service is secondary. Advertising, dominating all the media, is a key to this emphasis, permitting media to make excessively high profits. Where is the public concern when media corporations are gobbling up increasing numbers of smaller media units? Where is the public concern when media executives earn salaries in the six digits, many in the millions, while staffers who actually produce the product earn salaries between $20,000 and $50,000? Where is the public concern when the media are aimed at the lowest common denominator, and where local, family-owned grass-roots papers are disappearing? Political coverage is poor, most papers are mediocre, most cities have only one newspaper owner, live and hard news is decreasing, and public relations is supplying about one-third of the news we do get.

RESPONSE

Dennis: The media mainly serve the public interest.

In recent years no issue has proved more captivating to the leadership of the American media than credibility and public trust. The terms have often been used interchangeably, although *public trust* is the broader and more inclusive formulation. Beginning in the mid-1980s such organizations as the American Society of Newspaper Editors, Radio and Television News Directors, the Newspaper Association of America (NAA), American Press Institute, *Times Mirror,* the *Los Angeles Times,* the Poynter Institute, and the Gannett Center for Media Studies have shared a common passion for understanding and improving the relationship between the media and the public. Why? At first, in response to the Grenada crisis during the Reagan administration, it became clear that the government could bar the media from a war zone and get away with it. There was no outcry from the public asking that correspondents be allowed to go to the scene of battle. Instead the public said (in polls), "Keep 'em out." This reaction shocked many within the U.S. media, and they were intrigued enough to look deeper into the matter. They commissioned studies, organized commissions, sponsored public forums, and engaged in other activities to search for an answer to a question raised by *Time* magazine: "Why does the public hate us?"

For several years there were credibility and public trust studies conducted by respected academic organizations and pollsters. There had been such studies before—indeed there is a fifty-year legacy of media–public attitude research—and the results were both good news and bad news. In studies cited in *Reshaping the Media* (1989) I showed that most of the public found the media credible and believable, though a sizable minority did not. A majority also found the press generally accurate and impartial, though again, there was a worrisome minority that had grave doubts. Happily, most Americans did want their media to be government watchdogs, although there was precious little understanding of the First Amendment and of press freedom.

The reason for all this consternation about the media and the public trust goes to the heart of John Merrill's arguments regarding profits. I believe that it is difficult to have significant media profits or any kind of economic success under our system unless there is first a climate of public trust. After all, the public is paying for a public communication system, and it stands to reason that it wants the resulting information to be competently gathered, accurate, and useful to them. This expectation is public trust at its best. The public also wants access to differing opinions and interpretations of public affairs, as well as entertainment, sports, and advertising. Some will argue about advertising, but many people do find it both entertaining and useful. Those who do not can push the mute button during the commercials.

I believe there is ample evidence to support the idea that a passion for journalism and a desire to serve the public come first for most people and organizations that make up the media business in the United States. This fact is clear both from many studies of American journalists and from personal experience. That is why press people react so strongly when their lifeline—the public trust—is challenged or threatened by libel suits, or by the misbehavior of reporters such as Janet Cooke of the *Washington Post* or Foster Winans of the *Wall Street Journal,* who both misused their positions and betrayed the public. The press may be defensive at times, but it will act quickly to correct situations that challenge credibility and believability. In fact, it was just such a crisis in the 1980s that made Robert MacNeil suggest that "there is plenty of evidence that [the crisis] is grave, evidence that the public trust at least at the moment, is an ebbing tide" (1985, 4). MacNeil was one of many leading journalists who joined in a constructive critique of such topics as the blending of news and entertainment, biased reporting, and factual inaccuracies. His concern and that of his colleagues was that public trust is essential if media are to command loyal audiences who find public communication both fair and useful.

It is clear that media people care deeply about the public trust and that they will take steps to see that the quality of their work warrants public support. In recent years, for some of the reasons Professor Merrill mentions, they have been pushed to do this with even more vigor by economic trends. There are today more media outlets seeking public attention and advertiser support than ever before. Cable television has opened up scores of new, competing channels; we have successful national newspapers; new electronic media networks including CNN, Fox, and others have emerged; new magazines emerge faster than we can count them; and the once-declining newspaper has stabilized. In this mix there is enormous competition—in spite of ownership considerations that will be discussed later—and with such competition the need for a credible and respected product is more vital than ever.

The issue raised by Professor Merrill is directed toward motivation of media people, both the working press and the owners. He thinks the worst of them: They are all money-grubbing individuals whose only concern is the bottom line. Certainly this is not true of most journalists, who are far removed from profit-making considerations. They are driven more by a love of public affairs, writing, and expression. There is also ego involved in bylines and other recognition. A similar case can be made for people who make television entertainment programs, edit magazines or books, or draw cartoons. And most journalists I know see themselves as engaged in a public service. Many could pursue other careers, but they do not because they find working for the media a compelling challenge.

Many media owners do make large profits, but for the most part their investments are in media rather than other enterprises. For most (not all) media companies, information and entertainment are the principal concerns. As a result, they generally are not investing in other high-yield enterprises or trying to diversify their holdings. They are, in short, committed to the media business, to producing a "product" that will find a receptive public. Any argument blaming the owners—people like Katharine Graham of the *Washington Post,* Arthur H. Sulzberger of the *New York Times,* Ted Turner of CNN, Rupert Murdoch of the News World Corporation—for taking advantage of general economic trends needs to be carefully examined. Most of the criticism of the growing concentration of ownership in U.S. media, where there are fewer companies owning the means of communication, suggests that this is somehow a unique condition caused by excessive greed. Not at all. Throughout American business there are fewer small firms and more larger companies. It is a fact of life, a trend that the media businesses are merely following.

To me there are two important questions that we ought to ask about those trends, both relating to the consequences of ownership. First, have the number of voices in the marketplace seriously decreased in a fashion that threatens diversity in communication? Second, has the quality of media fare suffered? To the first question, it can be shown that there are more accessible channels of information today than ever before. Until the 1980s, most American households received only four or five television channels. Today they get scores of them, all offering diverse fare. At the same time other media enterprises are prospering. While there are big companies, there are also thousands of newsletters published by individual entrepreneurs, courtesy of desktop publishing and the electronic revolution. The idea that there is not diversity in our media marketplace is questionable. Naturally, it is always healthy to watch these economic trends to see that diversity is not seriously threatened. For this task we need thoughtful critics such as Ben Bagdikian, although he joins a chorus of commentators, including Oswald Garrison Villard and Upton Sinclair, who since the 1920s have predicted that a handful of greedy owners would one day control all U.S. media. To date it has not happened, and I do not think it is likely.

To the second point—quality—the quality of American journalism has been on the rise. While there is always plenty of room for improvement, the quality of American journalism and entertainment is far better today than it was ten or twenty years ago, let alone at the turn of the century when there were 7,000 daily newspapers, compared with under 2,000 today. News coverage has improved enormously, partly helped by technology; writing quality is also up by most accounts, and design and graphics have improved a thousandfold in all media. There is more specialist coverage both in the print and electronic media and in databases. There has been, in fact, a communication revolution in the world, something Professor Merrill and his favorite media-bashing sources seem not to know.

The growth of media and the increased development and use of market research have made the media more responsive to its audiences. Media people know what their readers and viewers say they want. They receive almost continuous feedback in the forms of readership studies, television ratings, and other measures of the relationship between the media and the public. This feedback, made possible by market forces and reinvested profits, keeps the public trust vigorous and healthy. Without a trusting relationship between media and public and without opportunities for feedback, the tendency would be for media consumers, both individually and collectively, to stop watching some TV programs, cancel the newspaper, and fail to renew the magazine. This is not happening, and for good reason: The public trust comes first, the profits follow. Although the media people may not be saints, their motivations are not as venal as has been suggested.

Argument summation: The media mainly serve the public interest.

Journalists seek to serve the public interest, and that is why they react adversely when their credibility is threatened. Since the public trust is necessary to sell papers, profit motive takes a secondary role. Besides, the vast majority of journalists are far removed from the ranks in which profits are shared. Owners' profits stem mainly from the media themselves.

They seek to diversify ownership of the means of communication, not the message. As a result, centralization has not decreased the number of voices in the marketplace, while the quality of news has improved.

TOPICS FOR DISCUSSION

1. Is the desire for profit a sign that media evade public service? How would you define *public service* and the *public trust*?

2. Groups and organizations such as the NAA, The Freedom Forum, and the Poynter Institute are doing much to improve the media–public relationship. What do you think is their prime motivation in doing this?

3. Assuming that the argument is true that we have "enormous competition" in our media system, do you think competition implies public service and concern for the public trust?

4. Are the arguments of Merrill and Dennis, in which they give statistics on media and their audience sizes, in any way related to the question about the public trust and public service? If they are, how do they prove or disprove the contention that profits are the media's main concern?

5. Do you think that most citizens have faith in and admire the media? What leads you to your opinion? What have surveys said about this question?

TOPICS FOR RESEARCH

1. Document the public service activities and programming of a local broadcast station. Interview an official at the station to determine how he or she tries to carry out the FCC's mandate of "public interest, convenience and necessity." Have these activities changed over the past decade? Have they increased or decreased? Has deregulation of broadcasting had any impact?

2. Discuss broadcast ratings. Do they provide an index for the idea of public trust? What about newspaper readership studies? What do these kinds of studies tell news decision makers about the public and its attitude toward news media?

3. Do an analysis of media available to you in your local community. What part of their content deals with matters of public service and public trust? How does the content seem to reconcile the difference between

journalistic work that informs the public and that aimed more at generating a profit? Can both occur? If so, how?

4. Study the editorial policy of any newspaper or magazine. From the published editorials, determine how many are truly public service statements and how many are more self-serving, perhaps even pandering to a particular audience or group, such as politicians, sports fans, or others. Characterize the publication's editorial policy in terms of: (1) issues covered, (2) positions taken (pro, con, or neutral), and (3) audience to whom editorials seem directed (e.g., policy makers, the public, specific interest groups).

5. Examine "public service" advertising,—advertising that does not advertise specific products or firms but promotes public issues such as the Community Chest, AIDS research, ecology, and the like. To whom do these ads appeal? What is the motivation of the media in running them? Do you discern issues or causes that do not get public service support? Document your findings carefully, studying a specific magazine or broadcast organization.

FURTHER READING

Altschull, J. Herbert. *Agents of Power.* White Plains, NY: Longman, 1984.

American Press Institute. *The Public Perception of Newspapers: Examining Credibility.* The J. Montgomery Curtis Memorial Seminar. Reston, VA: American Press Institute, 1984.

American Society of Newspaper Editors. *Newspaper Credibility: Building Reader Trust.* Washington, DC: ASNE, 1985.

———. *Newspaper Credibility: 206 Practical Approaches to Heighten Reader Trust.* Washington, DC: ASNE, 1986.

Aronson, James. *Packaging the News: A Critical Survey of Radio, TV.* New York: International Publishers, 1971.

Associated Press Managing Editors Association. *Journalists and Readers: Bridging the Credibility Gap.* An APME Credibility Committee Report. San Francisco, 1985.

Bagdikian, Ben H. *The Effete Conspiracy and Other Crimes by the Press.* New York: Harper & Row, 1974.

Barron, Jerome A. *Freedom of the Press for Whom?* Bloomington: Indiana University Press, 1973.

Biagi, Shirley. *Media Impact.* Belmont, CA: Wadsworth, 1988.

Cirino, Robert. *Don't Blame the People.* New York: Vintage Books, 1971.

Clurman, Richard. *Beyond Malice.* New Brunswick, NJ: Transaction Publishers, 1988.

Commission on Freedom of the Press. *A Free and Responsible Press.* Chicago: University of Chicago Press, 1947.

Dennis, Everette E. *Of Media and People.* Newbury Park, CA: Sage, 1993.

———. *Reshaping the Media.* Newbury Park, CA: Sage, 1989.

Dennis, Everette E., Donald M. Gillmor, and Theodore Glasser, eds. *Media Freedom and Accountability.* Westport, CT: Greenwood Press, 1989.

Ghiglione, Loren. *The American Journalist: Paradox of the Press.* Washington, DC: Library of Congress, 1990.

Hiebert, Ray, Donald Ungurait, and Thomas Bohn. *Mass Media V.* White Plains, NY: Longman, 1988.

Lichter, S. Robert, Stanley Rothman, and Linda Lichter. *The Media Elite: America's Powerbrokers.* Bethesda, MD: Adler & Adler, 1986.

MacNeil, Robert. "The Mass Media and the Public Trust." New York: Gannett Center for Media Studies. Occasional Paper No. 1, 1985.

"Media and Public Life." *Media Studies Journal,* Winter 1985. New York: Freedom Forum Media Studies Center; see also "The Entertainment Age." *Media Studies Journal,* Summer 1995.

Weaver, David H. and G. Cleveland Wilhoit. *The American Journalist: A Portrait of U.S. News People and Their Work.* Bloomington: Indiana University Press, 1986.

Chapter 4

PEOPLE'S RIGHT TO KNOW

Members of a local school board exclude journalists while they discuss a motion to dismiss a teacher and void her contract. Later the board chairman urges a newspaper editor not to print the story. Here are two related instances of blocking what is often called "the people's right to know." In the first instance there is an effort to stop the gathering of information; in the second, its publication and dissemination. The right to know, as defined by many journalists and some legal scholars, is the right of the listener to information of public interest and importance. In order for this "right" to be functional, however, information must be acquired and published.

Although it is not specifically stated in the Constitution, there is a widely held belief among journalists and other media personnel that there is a "people's right to know." This "right" is usually defined as the right of the public to have access to information about government policy and decision making. The press sees itself as the conduit for such information, since the average citizen has neither the capacity nor the resources to gather continuing, detailed information about what the government is doing. The people, the argument goes, must have full information about what their government is doing in order to be knowledgeable voters and good citizens. Government secrecy is thought to lead to suspicion and a lack of confidence in public officials and their policies. The people's right to know is transformed, however imperfectly, from an abstract principle to a concrete reality in "sunshine acts," which require government bodies to hold open meetings and to have their records open for public inspection. Theoretically, government should operate in the open and should be accountable to the people, and the "right to know" would make that possible.

CHALLENGE

Dennis: There is no right to know.

The right to know is not an inalienable right guaranteed by the Constitution, but rather is something that was invented by journalists. For a number of years journalistic organizations have been badgering the courts and the legislatures in the hope of establishing their right of access to various confidential sources of information. This so-called right now has some modest basis in law, in that on occasion courts have said that under certain circumstances and in very specific areas there is a right to know. But this is something so conditional that it is not a right at all but a quite limited privilege that depends on the disposition of judges. What they give today, they can take away tomorrow. I believe that the right to know is a badly flawed concept that actually interferes with other rights and may do more to impair than to advance First Amendment freedoms.

The right to know is most often invoked when media people are asking for rights and privileges that the rest of us do not have. It is a justification for a vague category of corporate rights, because the right to know is not put forth as an *individual* right, but as an *institutional* right, and here is where the argument gets hazy. The First Amendment guarantees a "right to speak" that belongs to individuals. Advocates of the right to know say that this "new right" is derived from the "right to listen." Listeners (or anyone receiving the messages of free speech and press) are entitled to a flow of information—hence the right to know. It is notable that most of the rights enumerated in the Bill of Rights are for individuals, but our friends in the media would add a little corporate-institutional appendage.

According to Harvard law professor Lawrence Tribe, a leading constitutional scholar, right-to-know advocates would not differentiate between the "focused right of an individual to speak" and "the undifferentiated right of the public to know" (1978, 674). Professor Tribe says people who take this position argue that the First Amendment does not confer individual rights but protects a system of freedom of expression. "This view," he says, "unduly flattens the First Amendment's complex role" (1978, 675). Another leading scholar, Edwin Baker, agrees. A right to know, he says, is never more than a right to have the government not interfere with a willing speaker's liberty.

The right to know is something of a journalistic invention. It began in the early 1950s when the press felt increasingly thwarted by bureaucrats who were standing between them and government information. It began as a quest for access to records and meetings, the so-called sunshine laws, meaning government operations "in the sunshine," that is, open. These journalists wanted access to government records, documents, and proceedings at both the state and federal levels. This effort was called the Freedom of Information (FOI) movement. Its bible was a thoughtful, weighty tome called *The People's Right to Know—Legal Access to Public Records and Proceedings* by Harold L. Cross (1953).

The FOI movement had many positive consequences. It brought sunshine laws (open-meeting and open-record legislation) in most of the states, fostered the Federal Freedom of Information Act, and opened up many government meetings from which the press and public had previously been barred. The FOI movement was both necessary and desirable, but the journalists did not stop there. Many excesses followed.

Over the years the press claimed that it should have access to many classified government records, including some dealing with national defense and national security. Journalists also asked for greater immunity from libel suits, those brought by both public officials and private citizens. Some reporters asked for a right to rummage through the private papers of individuals to "pursue the truth" and frequently claimed that the right of privacy was an undue hindrance on the press and public.

So what if journalists argued for these things? If these positions were merely the mutterings of media people at the press club, there would be no problem. But all of these claims and many more were brought to the U.S. Supreme Court. In each case the rationale was the people's right to know. This approach is what Anthony Lewis calls "press exceptionalism": Special rights for the press that are not available for the rest of the public. This approach also introduces a conceptual problem, because the rest of the Bill of Rights applies to individuals, but the right to know is advanced as an *institutional* right.

Efforts were made to establish a broad constitutional right. And, as good lawyers will tell you, there is always "authoritative support" for any position if lawyers look hard enough. In this instance authoritative support was found in the writings of James Madison, who once said:

> A popular government without popular information, or the means of acquiring it, is but a Prologue to a Farce or a Tragedy; or perhaps, both. Knowledge will forever govern ignorance; and a people who mean to be their own Governors, must arm themselves with the power which knowledge gives. (1906)

Right-to-know advocates got support from Supreme Court justices Hugo Black and William O. Douglas. Douglas was particularly eloquent:

> The press has a preferred position in our constitutional scheme, not to enable it to make money, not to set newsmen aside as a favored class, but to bring fulfillment to the public's right to know. The right to know is crucial to the governing powers of the people. (Douglas, 1972, *Branzburg v. Hayes,* 408 United States, 665 at 713)

These words had a bittersweet ring for a number of publishers and broadcasters who are clearly in the communications business to make money and who have only the vaguest passing interest in the people's right to know, even though their rhetoric sometimes suggests otherwise.

Although the right-to-know leaders appreciated the support of Justice Douglas, they hankered for something more than mere rhetoric. They thought they had it when in 1974 Justice Potter Stewart gave a notable speech at Yale Law School. In that now-famous speech Justice Stewart said that the "Free Press Clause extends protection to the institution" (1975, 631). This was what the right-to-know advocates were waiting for: the First Amendment as an institutional right and mighty support for the idea of a people's right to know. But alas, Stewart's declaration seemed to have currency only at Yale. It was not a majority position of the Court (or even a minority view) and thus not the law of the land. The people's right to know was still in the realm of grand theory. Although it has been repeatedly pointed out that the Stewart speech had no standing in the developing law of the First Amendment, it is often invoked as though it were chiseled in stone and blessed by the framers. The Stewart speech, nevertheless, gave much fuel to hungry legal and journalistic minds seeking support for the right to know.

The next turn in the debate was a position put eloquently by Federal Judge Irving Kauffman, who said that freedom of the press was dependent on protection for three aspects of the communication process: acquiring, processing, and disseminating information. This makes perfect sense, and journalists argued vehemently that it is virtually impossible to disseminate information without acquiring it (through news-gathering methods) and processing it (by editing and preparing it for publication). This is logical reasoning, of course, but once again journalistic fancy was light-years ahead of legal reality. What Judge Kauffman posited was a theory of freedom of expression—and from my point of view a very desirable one—but one without a solid legal foundation: Most legal scholars agree that there is powerful constitutional support for the dissemination of information. Most First Amendment law centers on the right of people to speak and publish. But there is much less legal basis for acquisition of information and, in fact, much of the press's claim in this area is tied to a case that *denied* the press any special privilege to withhold names of news sources in court proceedings. In that case Justice Byron White offered a less-than-reassuring statement with a double negative construction, that "news gathering is not without its First Amendment protections" (White, 1972, in *Branzburg* v. *Hayes,* 406 United States, 655 at 707). He did not say what they were, however. On the matter of processing news or editing it, the law is quite thin. Rarely have courts been asked to give special protection to this aspect of media work, and not surprisingly they have not initiated it themselves. In a few instances when they were asked to grant "news-processing" rights, they declined to do so. The press has been inventive and resourceful in trying to establish the right to know as a provision of constitutional law, but to date it has not done so, and from all appearances this idea will have to percolate for a long time before it is allowed to raise conceptual havoc with the rather specific language of the First Amendment.

The right to know is a very limited privilege with many important exceptions, so many that to call it a right is misleading. One of the strongest advocates of the right to know is communication law scholar Franklyn S. Haiman, who says the public's right to know is a vital element of the First Amendment "because much essential knowledge is in the hands of agencies and officials of government who can thwart the democratic process by keeping relevant material secret" (1981, 368). Haiman says the right to know is based on the need of the public for information to exercise its responsibilities of citizenship; furthermore, he says:

> In a fundamental sense, data in the hands of government belongs to the public, having been collected through the use of taxpayers' money and for the exercise of authority derived from the people as a whole. (1981, 368–69)

All well and good, but then come the *exceptions* (which Haiman acknowledges and supports) to government disclosures that seriously undermine any "right to know." They are:

1. The need to protect the privacy and other legitimate personal interests of those about whom information is gathered.
2. The need to ensure candid deliberative processes.
3. The need to safeguard the public's economic interests.
4. The need to preserve the physical safety of society and its institutions. (Haiman, 1981, 369)

These broad and compelling exceptions blow a hole in the people's right to know, which need not be absolute but certainly must have a broader reach than Haiman and other scholars envision if it is to be a fundamental right that has real meaning. Rights are not "now you see them, now you don't" propositions.

The right to know, then, has a flimsy legal foundation, and that is reason enough to question whether it should be accorded the kind of status journalists want to confer upon it. But there are even more compelling reasons for viewing this so-called right with real trepidation. Journalist and screenwriter Kurt Luedtke, quoted elsewhere in this book, put it succinctly when he told the Newspaper Association of America that

> there is no such thing as the public's right to know. You made that up, taking care not to specify what it was the public had a right to know. The public knows whatever you choose to tell it, no more, no less. If the public did have a right to know, it would

then have something to say about what it is you choose to call news. (1982, 4–5)

Luedtke had it right. If the public really does have a right to know, it surely has a right to determine what information it truly needs to know and to demand that the press (as its surrogate) deliver that information forthwith. Out the window goes the right of the editor and broadcaster to edit and to decide what is news. And here the nightmare begins. If the press is to become the legal representative of the people under a general principle of a right to know, then it will certainly be told by the courts and legislatures that it has a duty to provide particular information to the public. This directive definitely would be a shocking intrusion on freedom of the press and is something that I hope no thinking journalist would advocate. New rights bring new duties, and I have serious doubts that the press will want the baggage that comes with the public's right to know, if such a right should be given full and complete constitutional protection. I say let well enough alone; stop making self-serving claims in the name of this public "need."

Argument summation: There is no right to know.

The right to know is not to be found in the Constitution, which preserves individual rights, not institutional rights. The right to know is, rather, a creature of statutory law and is therefore a privilege that can be taken away. Before rising to constitutional importance, it must take on more breadth than is presently recognizable. Originally the freedom-of-information movement achieved legitimacy by focusing on the need for access to government records, but it has since expanded its aims to include a general "right to know." However, even the right of access to government records is severely limited by exceptions such as privacy, candid deliberative processes, economic interests, social stability, and national security.

RESPONSE

Merrill: There is a right to know.

My coauthor contends that the right to know is not an inalienable right guaranteed by the Constitution, and that it is, rather, something invented by journalists. It is difficult to dispute either of these contentions. Such a "right" is not overtly in the Bill of Rights, and it does seem that only journalists have made much, if anything, of such a right.

Nevertheless, even after saying this, I must insist that a right to know for the citizenry of a libertarian society (free and open) does indeed exist—even if such a right is a philosophical right and not spelled out literally in the First Amendment.

It may well be that a people's right to know is not explicitly stated constitutionally, but journalists did more than "invent" it: They inferred from the freedom-of-the-press clause that a people's right to know existed. I suppose that by making such an inference, which seems quite logical to me, they did in a sense invent this right to know. But instead of feeling guilty for such an "invention," if such it was, journalists should be proud of the fact that they have seen this public right standing in the philosophical shadows supporting a free press.

Why, we should ask, should the Founding Fathers provide for a free press? Simply for the sake of having a free press? Just so future citizens could brag about such a provision? Obviously there was a pragmatic reason for the free-press (as well as the free-speech) provision in the Bill of Rights. And this reason revolves around what we now call the people's right to know. If the people of the republic (the sovereign rulers of the country) do not know about public affairs and government business, they surely cannot be good sovereigns; they cannot govern themselves well. Since their government is built upon the assumption that they will know, then in order to be consistent with their political purpose, they *must* know. They have a philosophical mandate to know. The very reason for a free press is that the people can know.

Someone will ask: If the people have a right to know, then does not the press share responsibility with government in letting them know? My answer is yes. If the press argues for such a right (and I maintain that the press in a free society, with its press freedom, *must* believe in such a fundamental right), then it must take very seriously its responsibility of providing knowledge about public affairs to the people. If there is such a public right to know, and I believe there is, then the press has an important responsibility to fulfill this right, to see to it that the people are able to know.

At this point the government enters the picture, for the press cannot let the people know what the press cannot get from government. I maintain that the people do have a right to know public business and that both the press and the government have the responsibility to let the people know. Certainly the people cannot know about their government without the cooperation of both press and government. The fact that both of these institutions from time to time fail to let the people know does not negate the people's right.

The concept of "the people's right to know" has been promoted mainly since World War II. Books such as Kent Cooper's (1956) *The Right to Know* and Harold Cross's (1953) *The People's Right to Know* as well as numerous articles have declared such a right and castigated government for infringing on it. No adherent to a libertarian theory of the press can but admire such anti-government broadsides, but the problem is larger than this.

Two other important factors are involved in this business of letting the people know: the people and the press. Too often they are left out of a discussion of this topic.

Frankly, the people either don't know they have a right to know or they don't take it seriously. It appears that they simply don't care. Such a right to know is certainly one of great importance—a civil right if there ever was one. Such a right is at the very foundation of American government, of public discussion, of intelligent voting, of public opinion, of the very essence of democracy. And yet the people appear to have little or no concern for this right. But unconcern does not do away with the right.

The only segment of our society that seems really concerned about the people's right to know is the press. Journalists criticize and agitate about government's infringing upon the people's right to know. They justify—rightly—their own press freedom by appealing to the public's right to know.

A problem with the press is that it places all the blame on government for denying the people this right. The truth is that the news media themselves participate in the denial of this right. Persons familiar with the typical news operation must recognize that only a very small portion of government-related information gets to the average citizen's eyes or ears. In effect, the news media are themselves guilty of the same sins of omission and commission that they point to in government.

Editors and news directors, while promoting the idea of a people's right to know, are busy selecting and rejecting government information. They leave out this story, that picture, this viewpoint. They are, in effect, censors—perhaps with the best of motives, but censors nevertheless. They manage the news just as government officials do. They also play their part in the restriction of the people's right to know.

Of course, editors call this practice "exercising their editorial prerogative." They see themselves as merely "editing" while they see the government "managing" and "restricting" public information. But the people's exercise of the right to know is being limited regardless of these semantic games. And all the while press people are hailing the right to know as indispensable for the country.

One who observes the editing operations of a newspaper or magazine is struck by the swiftness with which government news is discarded. While wastebaskets fill with information that the people presumably should be reading, there are few tears and little gnashing of teeth in journalistic ranks. These practitioners of journalism seem not to realize that they, like the government officials they criticize, are keeping back information that, in their own words, "the public has a right to know."

The public does have a right to know, of course. This right has always been in the American journalistic context, even though it has not been as popular traditionally as it has been since World War II. Now the emphasis is shifting from the press to the people, from journalistic freedom to journalistic responsibility, from institutional rights of the press to social rights of the citizenry. It is all part of the shift from "negative freedom" to "positive freedom"—from freedom *from* to freedom *to*. Part of the social responsibility theory of the press is an emphasis on what the press does actively, not what the press might be kept by government from doing.

The people's right to know is a logical outgrowth of this trend. I maintain that the philosophical rationale for press freedom (interpreted until recently as the *press's* freedom) all along has been that the people *need* to know. This need philosophically is translated into a "right" in our type of pluralistic, open, libertarian society where the people theoretically are the sovereigns.

So, in spite of the sophisticated arguments put forward by Dennis and others who deny this people's right, I again propose that such a right exists. However often it is denied to the people—by government and by the press—it is still there serving as the main underpinning of an American democratic society. It is the justification for press freedom and the absolute requirement for the political viability of the United States.

Argument summation: There is a right to know.

Certainly there is no explicit constitutional "right to know," but there is surely an implied or natural right to know. The concept of press freedom assumes such a right, for obviously the press would not have such freedom for no (or only a selfish) reason. The country's philosophy is based on the people as sovereigns; therefore there is a need for them to know, and this need is logically translated into a "right." Both the press and the government share in the responsibility to let the people know. The people may not think much about such a right, but they instinctively feel they have it, given their type of government. If they do not have such a right, then they see no real reason for a free press.

TOPICS FOR DISCUSSION

1. Think about the public's need to know, desire to know, curiosity to know—and consider these alongside a "right" to know. What are your conclusions?

2. If such a right to know is not in the Bill of Rights, where do we get such a right? Is it any more than a theoretical or idealistic right?

3. If it is a right of the people "to know," why do media themselves withhold information? How can a newspaper editor believe in such a people's right while refraining from giving a quote's source, naming a rape victim, or divulging the source of a government leak?

4. Can press freedom, which *is* in the Constitution, be equated with the public's right to know? Explain your answer. If the invention of the right to know came about in the early 1950s, why do you think it developed so late in American history if the principle on which it rests is valid?

TOPICS FOR RESEARCH

1. Write a paper about forces for and against the right to know. Who have the pro-right-to-know spokespersons been over the years? Who have been their opponents?

2. Prepare a study of the origins, present status, and probable future of the federal Freedom of Information Act.

3. Write a review essay about three or four major books or articles on privacy from the perspective of the right to know. When do privacy rights take precedence over the media's desire to know something?

4. What is *intellectual property*? How is it connected to the law of copyright? Why is copyright law included in the U.S. federal law as part of the U.S. Code? How do copyright and protection of an individual's or author's rights impair the people's right to know? Should anyone care?

5. Why is there a debate over the right to know? Why is it that journalists believe it exists and lawyers don't?

FURTHER READING

Anderson, Jack. "We the People: Do We Have a Right to Know?" *Parade*, January 30, 1966, pp 4–5.

Boyer, John H. "Supreme Court and the Right to Know." FOI Center Report 272. Columbia: University of Missouri, November 1971.

Cooper, Kent. *The Right to Know.* New York: Farrar, Strauss Cudahy, 1956.

Cross, Harold L. *The People's Right to Know—Legal Access to Public Records and Proceedings.* New York: Columbia University Press, 1953.

Dennis, Everette E., D. M. Gillmor, and David Grey, eds. *Justice Hugo Black and the First Amendment.* Ames: Iowa State University Press, 1978.

Douglas, William O. *The Right of the People.* New York: Doubleday, 1958.

Haiman, Franklyn S. *Speech and Law in a Free Society.* Chicago: University of Chicago Press, 1981.

Kurtz, Howard. *Media Circus.* New York: Times Books, 1993.

Luedtke, Kurt. "An Ex-Newsman Hands Down His Indictment of the Press." *The Bulletin of ASNE* 65 (May–June 1982):16–17.

———. "The Twin Perils: Arrogance and Irrelevance." Speech at annual meeting, American Newspaper Publishers Association Convention. San Francisco, May 1982.

Madison, James. *Writings of James Madison.* G. Hunt, ed. 1906.

Merrill, J. C. "Is There a Right to Know?" FOI Center Report 002. Columbia: University of Missouri, January 1967.

———. "The People's Right to Know Myth." *New York State Bar Journal* 7 (November 1973):45.

———. "The Press, the Government, and the Ethics Vacuum." *Communication,* 1981, p. 6.

Rourke, Francis E. *Secrecy and Publicity: Dilemmas of Democracy.* Baltimore: Johns Hopkins University Press, 1966.

Stewart, Potter. "Or of the Press." *Hastings Law Journal* 26 (January 1975):631–38.

Sunstein, Carl. *Democracy & the Problem of Free Speech.* New York: The Free Press, 1993.

———. "The People's Right to Know: How Much or How Little?" *Time,* January 11, 1971, pp. 16–17.

Tribe, Lawrence H. *American Constitutional Law.* Mineola, NY: Foundation Press, 1978. See especially Chapter 12, "Communication and Expression," pp. 576–736.

Whalen, Charles W., Jr. *Your Right to Know.* New York: Vintage Books, 1973.

Williams, Lord Francis. "The Right to Know." *Twentieth Century,* Spring 1962, pp. 6–17.

Chapter 5

PUBLIC ACCESS TO THE MEDIA

A woman believes that the local newspaper is essentially sexist, both in its use of news sources (mostly men) and in its trivialization of women's issues. She wants the newspaper to be more sensitive to women and to publish her views critiquing the paper on a regular basis. The paper refuses, and she asserts that she and thousands of like-minded people have been denied "access" to the public through the public media. She may have a point, but to date there is no constitutionally guaranteed "access to the media."

The principle of public access to the media is based on a positive interpretation of the press clause of the First Amendment. The clause ("Congress shall make no law . . .") is, of course, stated negatively. Under a positive interpretation it is often claimed that the public has a right to freedom of the press through access to the media, that is, through a right to publish opinions and be heard in the printed press and on broadcast stations.

It is maintained that the public has no real freedom of the press without this right of access; only those who own the means of communication have freedom of the press. (The counterargument is that in order to have freedom of religion, speech, or assembly, one need not own a church, a public platform, or a street.) The theory of access posits that the First Amendment grants protection to all persons, not just those who own the mass media. The right of reply to newspaper and broadcast material and the right to buy advertising have been suggested as corollaries to the right of access.

While guaranteed public access to the print media—such as the right of reply to an editorial or the right to run an advertisement—has generally been denied by courts, the electronic media present a different case. Largely because the regulation of broadcasting has been based on a theory of scarcity—that is, there are a limited number of broadcast (not cable) frequencies, so not everyone can operate a radio or television station—the government has granted a number of privileges to citizens who want to respond to broadcast editorials and other electronic content. With the electronic media the public does have a limited and prescribed right of access; not so with the print media.

CHALLENGE

Merrill: The public has no right of access.

Many critics of the press during the last several decades have proposed that the First Amendment should be reinterpreted to force the mass media to give space and time to individuals and groups wanting to present "minority" points of views. One key leader in this crusade for a right of access to the press has been legal scholar Jerome Barron. He has argued that the First Amendment prohibition of government restraint does not forbid the government from acting to enhance citizens' opportunities to exercise their freedom to the press. He has argued vigorously in favor of a legal right of access to the mass media by citizens.

In the June 1967 *Harvard Law Review* and subsequently in many other articles and speeches, Barron has proclaimed that the main interest of media owners and controllers is to maximize profit, not discussion. Only with a right of access to the press, Barron argues, can the voice of the people be heard. What he and others are advocating is a new interpretation of the First Amendment whereby the courts can mandate that the press use material from individuals and groups.

This key passage from Barron's *Harvard Law Review* article provides the thrust of the "access" position:

> Our constitutional theory is in the grip of a romantic conception of free expression, a belief that the "marketplace of ideas" is freely accessible. But if there . . . [ever was] a self-operating marketplace of ideas, it has long ceased to exist. The mass media's development of an antipathy to ideas requires legal intervention if novel and unpopular ideas are to be assured a forum. (1967, 1641)

So far the courts have not been impressed with Barron's arguments, although the topic has become popular in public and journalistic debates. The firmest rejection of Barron's arguments came in the case of *Tornillo* v. *The Miami Herald*. In the fall of 1972 Pat Tornillo, Jr., a candidate for the Democratic nomination in a Florida state legislative primary, sought to use a 1918 state law that a newspaper assailing a candidate's character had to give that candidate a chance to reply free of charge. *The Miami Herald,* having carried a critical editorial about Tornillo, nevertheless refused to provide free space to Tornillo to answer. Tornillo and Barron, who was Tornillo's legal counsel, convinced the Florida Supreme Court of their position, but the U.S. Supreme Court took the view that editorial decisions were to be made by editors, not courts.

If an individual citizen (such as Tornillo) should have the right of access to a newspaper, why should not the government have a similar right? Why should not President Bush, for example, have the right to force the *Washington Post* to print his answer to a critical editorial? Why would not any government official have such a right to get his or her (or the relevant agency's) side into the press? It is hard to imagine the chaos that would result from such a situation, with editorial decisions of this type being made in the already overloaded courts. The editors of the country would find themselves mere figureheads, making no editorial decisions—or feeling the chilling effect of such a legal system to a degree that they would fill their columns with material from those they most feared would take them to court.

Barron may have seen his suggestion as a new interpretation of the First Amendment. I see it as a perversion or abdication of the First Amendment. It so obviously takes away editorial freedom or determination by the press that it should strike any reasonable person as a travesty of the concept of press freedom. In essence, if individuals could force their opinions into newspapers, newspaper editors would lose their freedom to use or reject an article; any editorial determination would obviously be gone.

No one will deny that there are persons who would like to have access to the large audiences reached by the major mass media. Naturally I have certain opinions I would like to see made public in a newspaper like the *New York Times* or my local daily. Naturally a certain limitation is placed on me if I cannot get my opinions published. I still can *speak* my opinions, however, whether or not my voice reaches all the listeners I might like it to reach. My right of free speech is not negated just because I do not have as large an audience as I would like. The fact that there is a freedom-of-speech clause in the First Amendment, as well as a free press clause, indicates to me that the writers of the Bill of Rights intended to separate the two: that there should be the press's freedom to print *and* the people's freedom to speak. If not, there would have been no need to state both rights in the First Amendment.

It is, in fact, relatively easy today for people with something to say to get at least some of their ideas before the public or portions of it. But, say the access proponents, the problem is getting a big audience for the message. The important thing, they say, is getting one's message into the mass media—newspapers, magazines, radio, and television. I agree with Ayn

Rand in her position on this matter. She is in opposition to those, like Barron, who would redefine the First Amendment as giving "the people" some kind of inalienable *right* to have someone else publish their opinions. The right of free speech means that a person has a right to express his or her ideas without danger of suppression, interference, or punitive action by the government. It does not mean that others must provide this person with a lecture hall, a radio station, or a printing press through which to express his or her ideas (Rand, 1964, 97).

With Rand, I believe that there are no "rights" for consumers of journalism if no journalist chooses to produce the particular kinds of journalism that certain consumers want. There is only the right of citizens to be journalists and produce them, or for them to try to get the kind of journalism they desire, or try to get their ideas into the media.

"Remember," writes Ayn Rand, "that rights are moral principles which define and protect a man's freedom of action, but impose no obligations on other men" (1964, 98). A case in point would be Rand's own book in which these words appear: She had the freedom to write, but it was a publisher who decided that her views were of sufficient interest to warrant publication.

Let us consider a basic question: *Who* are the editors or editorial decision makers in the American press system? Who *should* be? Are they persons working for (or owning) private newspapers, or are they some outside authority? This is a question that cannot be turned aside with idealistic arguments about some theoretical "people's freedom," the desire on the part of individuals to have their opinions published. The concept of *people's freedom* suggests the socialist world's emphasis on a *people's press*. Even a cursory knowledge of the press of a country like the Soviet Union exposes what happens to press freedom and pluralism when the rhetoric of a people's press is actually put into practice.

I fail to see how the Founding Fathers had in mind any concept of the people (nonprinters and nonpublishers) having freedom of the press. The concept is far-fetched, both from philosophical and from linguistic perspectives. When the First Amendment was written, in the post-colonial period, the writers had in mind prohibiting the control and suppression of the press by a government such as that then prevailing in England. They wanted *the press,* not the government, not the courts, to make editorial decisions. They were trying to head off any a priori press censorship or control by government.

I believe that when the Founding Fathers spoke of the press, they meant *the press*, not the people. When they wanted to talk about the people, they spoke of the people. If they had considered the Barron contention that the people should have a right of access to the press, they would have clearly placed that "right" where it belonged—in the Bill of Rights. Certainly they would not have obscured such an important right under the free-press right. If the people were to have the right to force their messages into the papers of the states, this right would have had to be listed in the Bill of Rights.

If one looks at this complex issue as having to do only with ensuring minority opinions a fair hearing, it is little wonder that a proposal such as Professor Barron's would be considered salutary and perhaps even long overdue. This, however, is not where the problem ends. If such a proposal were taken seriously by enough powerful people to bring it into practice, a whole new bag of troubles would be opened in regard to protecting a free press. Even as "freedom of the press" implies the freedom to be heard—a freedom for the consumer—we must not forget that it also implies the freedom to print or not to print—a freedom for the publisher.

The First Amendment provides that federal government will not pass any laws that abridge press freedom. Although press freedom is not defined in the Bill of Rights, an explicit concern with not passing laws that might diminish it appears to be quite clear. When any group—even government seeking to remedy certain ills it believes it detects—tells a publisher what he or she must print, it is taking upon itself an omnipotence not far removed from authoritarianism. It is restricting press freedom in the name of freedom for an individual to have an outlet for his or her messages and in the name of freedom to read.

This paradox brings up the interesting point that *freedom of the press* should not be used synonymously with *freedom of information*. It is obvious that the press can have freedom to print anything it desires without making available to the reader everything it has available to print. Its freedom, in other words, imposes an implicit restriction on the reader's freedom of access to every bit of information or point of view.

If one looks at the issue in this way, it is not difficult to see that press freedom does not imply freedom of information. The latter term refers to the right of the reader to have all material available for reading, while the former term denotes the right of the publisher to publish or not to publish.

Perhaps the problem is that we try to make the term *freedom of the press* cover too much. If we were to understand it narrowly, in the sense clearly indicated by its syntax, we would emphasize the *press* and its *freedom* in the context of information flow. This would mean that freedom belongs to the press. The press alone, in this definition, would be in the position of determining what it would or would not print. The press would have no prior restrictions on its editorial prerogatives; this would be *press freedom*. Those who favor an interpretation of the First Amendment that protects *freedom of information* would hardly agree to a definition that deemphasizes the rights of the people.

The person who is concerned about what is not in the press does not appear to be concerned primarily about the *freedom of the press* to make editorial decisions. However laudable this person's concern may be, we must recognize that such a position is potentially authoritarian, just as the existing libertarianism of the press is potentially restrictive.

Those who would compel publication justify their position by using terms such as "the public's inherent right to be heard," and the "public's right to know," and "press responsibility." Such people put what they regard as the social good above what individual publishers consider their right of editorial self-determination.

Few thoughtful individuals would quarrel with the position that "the good of society" or "social responsibility" is a laudable concept that should be served by the press. However, trouble comes when these theoretical concepts are applied to the actual workings of the press in society. The *what* of the concept presents considerable difficulty. What, for instance, is the best way to do the most good for society, and what is the best way to be socially responsible? There are many who would feel very strongly that forcing opinions (especially certain opinions) into a newspaper would be very harmful to the social good, and that doing so would be the epitome of social irresponsibility.

The *how* of the concept adds further complications. How would decisions be made about what would or would not be printed? What would be a rational manner of making such determinations if we were to take them out of the hands of individual publishers and editors? A federal court? A federal ombudsman? A Federal Press Agency organized on the lines of the Federal Communications Commission?

Among all the minority positions in a given community or in the nation, which would have a right to be published and which would not? Which spokesperson for any one minority would be published as a representative of the whole minority? Or would all of them—or many of them—be published, since undoubtedly there is a pluralism in minority opinions even on a single issue? These are basic and important questions that would constantly plague the authority charged with making such decisions.

We would end up with the same situation that exists today. Somebody has to make the editorial decisions about what to use, be it editor or court or other entity. Viewpoints that one authoritative body would deem worthy of publication might, to another authoritative body that is equally perspicacious and dedicated, seem inane, irrational, or otherwise lacking in value. Undoubtedly, even among the staunchest advocates of minority rights there is preference for some minorities over others. How will decision making in such a system differ in any substantial way from that presently done by editors? One thing is certain: Not every opinion can be used. Therefore always there will be the charge that someone is not being given the proper exposure for his or her opinions.

There is still another perplexing, closely related problem. What emphasis should various minority views receive in the press or even in a single newspaper? Would this be determined by the proportion of the total population that this particular minority comprises? Would it be decided on the basis of the intrinsic value to society of the particular viewpoint? If so, how would such worth be ascertained? Would it be decided on the basis of the economic or political pressure a particular person or group might bring to bear on the power structure? How would a nonpress decision on what will or will not be printed have any real advantage over pluralistic editorial decisions made by the press itself?

Many persons will reply that these are unimportant and theoretical questions that should not be permitted to interfere with the serious consideration of a forced publishing system. "Sure there will be problems and weaknesses," they will say, "but we must push on, in spite of obstacles, toward a New Journalism in which all opinions receive equal and just airing and in which no minority group or aggrieved individual can feel slighted by the treatment received in the press."

I maintain that proposals for the right of public access or for a legally forced publishing concept, in spite of idealistic objectives, are extremely naive in view of the practicalities of day-to-day journalism and the explicit language of the Bill of Rights.

Argument summation: The public has no right of access.

A public right of access to the media contradicts both the idea of press freedom and the principle of editorial self-determination. Either the media determine their content or some other group or person does. In a capitalist society, where the press's freedom is constitutionally protected, the idea of a people's right of access is preposterous. Such a "right" has even been rejected by the Supreme Court (*Tornillo* v. *The Miami Herald*, 1972).

It is impossible to imagine the U.S. press being forced (a necessary situation for such a right to exist) to publish the many news items and opinions that would seek exposure in the media. Courts, presumably, would have to turn into editors, and as a result editors would be powerless, mere technocrats and functionaries in court-run entities.

RESPONSE

Dennis: The public has a right of access.

On its face this position may seem to be a difficult if not impossible one. However, it is not. Many opponents of the right of access say the issue has already been decided in the *Tornillo* case. Did the U.S. Supreme Court demolish access in its 9-to-0 decision striking down the Florida law? No, not quite, but unfortunately for access advocates, Jerome Barron, an attorney for plaintiff Tornillo, used the case, albeit a weak one, to test the theory of access. He lost, but that loss does not forever pull the chain on the right of access. Public access to the media is based on a quite simple and, I believe, just assumption: that when the framers of the Constitution wrote the First Amendment, they meant that *all* the people have a right to freedom of the press, not just the *owners* of the media. Professor Barron worries that a "romantic and lopsidedly pro-publisher" (1973, 12) view of the First Amendment does not necessarily benefit the public. When we look closely at other features of the First Amendment, the interpretation that only the owners of the media can enjoy press freedom seems strange indeed. Press people often forget that the First Amendment also says something about religion, speech, and assembly. Consider freedom of religion, for example. No one would sensibly argue that only organized religious groups or churches have freedom of religion. On the contrary, we understand that both individual and institutional rights (those of churches) to freedom of religion can be accommodated under the First Amendment. The religious rights of individuals have been tested repeatedly in the courts and, over time, a substantial legal basis for them has been developed.

Very few cases involving individual rights to press freedom have gone to the courts, and there is little formal legal foundation for a people's right of access. This void should not deter us from pursuing the case for access. After all, there was no legal assurance for a right of privacy in 1890 when Samuel D. Warren and Louis Brandeis wrote a famous law review article proposing it. In time, the right of privacy was articulated in statutes, court decisions, and philosophical treatises. Today few would question that there is such a right. Indeed, there is both a tort(s) of privacy and a constitutional right of privacy. Similarly, Professor Barron is ahead of his time in arguing for a legally protected right of access.

While it is true that the framers did not specify people's rights, it can be argued that they did intend the provisions of the Bill of Rights to apply to individuals. Institutional rights (such as those extended to the press as an institution) are granted because such institutions have responsibilities to individuals, such as to citizens who can benefit from the activities of the press. The role of the press, then, is to deliver press freedom to individuals, communities, and the country. A country is the sum of its parts, and its parts include individuals. The framers expected the press to promote the free flow of information. Is that free flow one-way only or should the press be responsible to its audience? Should it meet people's informational needs? Should it reflect and report on their opinions and ideas? The answers, I think, are a resounding "yes." But just how this should be accomplished and whether a right of access is the best way are questions that need considerable analysis and study.

In spite of some harsh things said about him, Professor Barron is hardly a dangerous radical. A law school dean and distinguished legal scholar, he simply believes that all people should have a legal right to buy advertising and be able to reply to editorials that either mention them or affect them directly. This is a modest request and a step toward allowing the public to talk back to the media in an age when mass communication plays a central role in their lives.

Barron and others in the access movement would not turn the news media over to a howling mob and strip editors of their legitimate right to make editorial decisions. Barron's two proposals would require enabling legislation in states and perhaps in Washington. That legislation would then no doubt be tested for constitutionality by media groups opposing it. If it met the test, there would be a guaranteed public right of access.

It has long been assumed that through the granting of freedom to the *issuer* of communication (the media), quite naturally the *user* (the public) also had press freedom. This was the view of the distinguished philosopher William Ernest Hocking, a member of the Commission on Freedom of the Press. "There are," he wrote, "two distinct interests ... only one of them needs protection; to protect the issuer is to protect the consumer." Freedom of the press, he suggested, "has always been a matter of public, as well as individual importance. Inseparable from the right of the press to be free has been the right of the people to have a free press" (1947, 164).

It seems to me that this is a specious position. There can be a press that is perfectly free but so elitist that it speaks to and for only a limited segment of the population. Indeed, in America today market researchers advise media executives that certain people are not worth communicating with because they are unlikely to buy the products being promoted through advertising.

For years minority persons in the United States were "the invisible Americans." Their views, problems, and concerns were simply not covered by major media. This lapse became quite evident during the demonstrations, marches, sit-ins, and riots of the 1960s and to a lesser extent in the 1990s when many disenfranchised people took to the streets. As a result of the upheavals, American media leaders agreed to provide (1) more complete and extensive coverage of minority communities and (2) jobs in the newsroom for minority persons.

During the social upheaval of the 1960s there were several reports criticizing the media for turning their backs on the problems of minorities. In the early 1980s a Brookings Institution report pointed out that some of America's most popular tourist cities—Boston, Philadelphia, and St. Louis—were in worse shape than less glamorous places such as Detroit and Newark. How could this be? Two distinguished researchers, Floyd Mattson and Jim Richstad, assert that not only are people entitled to freedom of the press, but that there is an inherent "right to communicate." Other scholars agree that communication is one of the people's basic needs, and it would follow that there ought to be some mechanism for this in a civilized society.

It would also seem that there will be a great benefit to society if people's sense of powerlessness can be reduced and partially satisfied by letting them have a forum for their ideas, complaints, and frustrations. There are some opportunities, of course, in newspaper letters to the editor and radio and television call-in shows, but they are minimal, given the potential demand. If we can agree that there is a fundamental right to communicate and that the Constitution means everybody should enjoy freedom of the press, then it should not be impossible to develop a regime wherein such freedom of expression could be encouraged. It could occur in at least two ways:

1. Through natural forces of the free marketplace.
2. Through government intervention and mandatory access where appropriate and necessary.

In the first instance, I would see advocates of access in the private sector mobilizing information campaigns to help people use the available channels of expression, those mentioned above and others. In addition, it may take reminders from access leaders to leaders of the media to point up both the commercial and social value of staying in touch with all aspects of the community.

Individuals and institutions or neighborhoods systematically or routinely ignored in news coverage should fight back by competing for their fair share of media attention. They can do this through various strategies and regular information campaigns. The commercial advantage to the media of staying in touch with particular market segments, as well as the social obligation to reach out to all elements of the community, can be emphasized. Many editors would respond affirmatively to such an approach, and they would likely provide space on the editorial page for occasional columns and commentaries. The same could be done with television and radio.

Perhaps the most significant development on the public access front is cable television. As America is wired for cable in the 1980s and 1990s, many local cable operators are providing public access time for use by local citizens. In cities where public access has been tried, it has enjoyed a degree of success. *Access* in this instance is an umbrella term for free, noncommercial channel time that a cable operator makes available for public agencies, nonprofit organizations, and private citizens. Under most franchise agreements the cable operator provides studio facilities, cameras, and editing equipment. Cable public access has existed in New York City since 1970, and there is a track record of high use by individuals, especially persons from the black community, who had a difficult time getting on commercial television. Public access gives ordinary people a chance to participate in the marvels of the electronic age as well as to be heard by their fellow citizens. Public access channels, however, are not particularly popular with commercial cable television operators, who would rather put revenue-producing fare on the channel and thus make more money.

In broadcasting there is already a strong access tradition, although it can be said that it is not as effective as it ought to be. There is a right of reply to personal attack that permits individual and institutional response to broadcast editorials and news coverage, as well as a right to equal time in political broadcasts. There was formerly a legally required procedure for ascertainment whereby attitudes of community leaders are sought out. These opportunities for access do not at present affect a large percentage of the population, but they could be used more judiciously by those in the access movement.

Two other mechanisms for access are public opinion polls and two-way television, made possible in some cable systems. Polls, if conducted properly, give all citizens an equal possibility of having their views aired. Of course the chance of being chosen is quite small, since sample sizes for national polls are tiny. A better job needs to be done also in polling on questions that truly concern the American people, rather than those of interest solely to political figures and educators. Alex Edelstein of the University of Washington has been a leader in calling for public opinion studies that emphasize "salience information," that is, information of direct concern to people as ascertained in open-ended personal interviews. This method, he says, is superior to having individuals rank the five most important issues in the country, based on some preconceived list developed in the offices of elitist pollsters.

There have been experiments with interactive television for a number of years. In some interactive systems viewers can make choices and do such things as home shopping and banking. One experimental system called QUBE, in Columbus, Ohio, also unsuccessfully tried a "town meeting" approach to citizen choice on a number of public issues. Some television stations also use 1-900 telephone numbers to get feedback from viewers, but these efforts are quite unscientific and only partly successful. However, the prospect of interactive television still exists and could have an impact on our ability to talk among ourselves while talking back to the media. At present the most effective interactive communication comes through personal computers.

Attempts to force the print media to provide greater public access will no doubt be thwarted by political forces at the legislative level and by the courts, where the judiciary is wary of prior restraints or special requirements for the press. Still, as the press continues to ask for more and more special privileges based on its social role of "representing the people," imaginative citizens and lawyers will probably look for an opening. (This is, in fact, one of the reasons why I said earlier that it is dangerous for the press to ask for rights that the rest of us do not have.)

A public right of access does not guarantee a perfect situation where people will be satisfied all the time. It is not feasible to give every single citizen air time on television or a guest column in the newspaper. Thus it may be necessary for the media to try to select representative views and citizens to stand in for the rest of us who cannot be heard. This selection is already done to a limited degree with letters to the editor.

Naturally, no one is required to listen to anyone else's views, and in many instances getting a listener, whether in print or electronic media, will require the speaker to make compelling and persuasive presentations. We live in the real world, and while communication might become an inherent human right, individual voices will need to live within realistic limits. There is nothing inconsistent about this limitation, though. To argue that the right of access might be limited to time, place, and circumstances or offered up to the channel capacity of available resources does not diminish its importance. After all, freedom of the press itself lives with many constraints and barriers.

Professor Barron has done us a favor by making his case in law review articles and in the courts. Just because he did not prevail in a rather weak case is no reason to doubt that access would benefit individuals and society in many ways. Ayn Rand can have her "virtue of selfishness." Selfishness and greed are not the basis for a coherent and successful society, although such a society can tolerate within limits these essentially negative forces. Nor am I persuaded by "red-baiting" references to a "people's press" in the Soviet Union or China. No one in the access movement is suggesting that the people take over the traditional media, wresting control from professional editors and managers. Instead, they are asking for a chance to be heard, to contribute to the community and to national dialogue, to be represented in the media that claim to represent them and serve as public trustees. The question is one of truly participative media wherein all of us have some chance, however small, of being heard.

Argument summation: The public has a right of access.

The First Amendment must apply to all Americans, not just media owners. The Constitution provides institutional press rights because the media have responsibilities to individuals. Public access does not mean stripping editors of their control; rather it would provide for the right of individuals to buy "advertorial" space to express their views and to respond to editorials that mention them. A right of access is required to give the disenfranchised a means to actualize their right to communicate and to prevent wealthy press owners from ignoring poorer segments of society. Access can be achieved either through more effective utilization of existing mechanisms or through legislative requirements.

TOPICS FOR DISCUSSION

1. Do you think the writers of the First Amendment meant that all people have a right to freedom of the press? What does such an idea mean? Can people have freedom *of* the press, or must they have freedom *to* the press?

2. Do you think the press's role is to deliver freedom to the people, or do you think its role is to deliver information and opinion to the people?

3. Consider the possible scenarios if the right of people's access to the press were upheld by the Supreme Court.

4. Explain how such a right of access can be logical in a privately owned media system.

5. Can you think of ways the media can be more representative of people's opinions and news, other than enthroning such a people's legal right to access?

TOPICS FOR RESEARCH

1. Do an analysis of the 1972 Supreme Court case *Tornillo v. The Miami Herald,* relying on periodicals that covered the conflict. Why has this case remained a benchmark? To what extent did the press (news magazines, newspapers, trade journals, scholarly publications) explain and explicate the *right of access?* How did that case distinguish the *right* from the *law?* Does the right of access have any future?

2. Do a study of letters to the editor of a local newspaper. Who writes such letters? To what extent do they counter the paper's position? Are they an "access channel" for the public or not? Connect your observations with published articles about letters to the editor from the scholarly literature of media studies.

3. Prepare a paper on the public's right of reply to television and radio stations. Interview local station officials and ask them to discuss how often, if at all, the right of reply has been exercised by local citizens or organizations.

4. If you have a local cable system with a public access channel, do a study of that channel and its use. Who uses it? What kinds of programs do they offer? What positions are put forth? Can you characterize the public access channel?

5. Write a short paper on C-SPAN, the congressional cable service. How does it give the public access to meetings and events not available in full in other news reports or sources? Does C-SPAN accomplish access? If so, how?

FURTHER READING

Barron, Jerome A. "Access to the Press—A New First Amendment Right." *Harvard Law Review* 80, no. 8 (June 1967):1641–78.

———. *Freedom of the Press for Whom? The Right of Access to Mass Media.* Bloomington: University of Indiana Press, 1973.

Dennis, Everette E. "The Press and the Public Interest: A Definitional Dilemma." *DePaul Law Review* 23 (Spring 1974):937–60.

Dennis, Everette E., Donald M. Gillmor, and Theodore Glasser. *Media Freedom and Responsibility.* Westport, CT: Greenwood Press, 1990.

Gross, Gerald, ed. *The Responsibility of the Press.* New York: Simon and Schuster, Clarion Books, 1971.

Hocking, William Ernest. *Freedom of the Press. A Framework of Principle.* A Report from The Commission on Freedom of the Press. Chicago: University of Chicago Press, 1947.

"Media Freedom and Accountability." A conference report. New York: Gannett Center for Media Studies, 1986.

Murray, Edward. "The Editor's Right to Decide," *Seminar,* March 1970, pp. 23–26.

Patterson, Thomas E. *Out of Order.* New York: Alfred A. Knopf, 1993.

Rand, Ayn. *Virtue of Selfishness.* New York: New American Library, 1964.

Rubin, Bernard. *Media, Politics, and Democracy.* New York: Oxford University Press, 1977. See especially Chapter 4, "Popular Participation and Media."

———. *Small Voices and Great Trumpets: Minorities and the Media.* New York: Praeger, 1980.

Schmidt, Benno C., Jr. *Freedom of the Press v. Public Access.* New York: Praeger, 1976.

Wicklein, John. *Electronic Nightmare: The New Communications and Freedom.* New York: Viking Press, 1981.

Chapter **6**

MEDIA BIAS AND POLITICAL LEANINGS

While a free and independent press is almost universally regarded as essential to democracy, there is considerable argument about the political leanings and potential bias of reporters, editors, and others engaged in gathering the news. People of a conservative political persuasion—from commentators like William F. Buckley to radio talkmeister Rush Limbaugh and Speaker of the House Newt Gingrich—strongly argue that the press is liberal, tilted to the left, and often biased and unfair. This view is widely disseminated by various media critics, foundations, and study centers that are tilted to the political right. On the left, commentators and critics using the same terms but different definitions say the press and news media are too conservative and oriented to support the status quo and establishment organizations. Critics like Jeff Cohen of Fairness and Accuracy in Media (FAIR) promote this view and ruthlessly attack PBS's *MacNeil/Lehrer NewsHour* as a right-leaning, establishment-oriented program. Ironically, critics on the right consider this program and much of public television as liberal. In the middle are journalist-critics who regard themselves as fair-minded, nonideological professionals, guided by standards and practices learned in journalism schools and in the nation's newsrooms, which always warn against too much political involvement and against becoming an actor. Still, some of these people will readily agree that much of the news media does tend to tilt in a political direction, and which way depends on whom you talk to. Fred W. Friendly, the legendary CBS and PBS giant, once said, "Of course the press is liberal," but then admitted that he was talking mostly about the major newspapers and networks that he knew well. Richard Clurman, former chief of correspondents at *Time* magazine and the author of several leading media books, including *Beyond Malice* (1988), agrees, even though he himself would be regarded by many as an establishment figure who is left of center.

Pollsters and various survey organizations and study groups have also weighed in on the matter. The Center for Media and Public Affairs in Washington, D.C., is headed by social scientist Robert Lichter, whose findings often support a liberal bias in the media, although his critics point out that much of his work is supported by conservative organizations. The Accuracy in Media group, headed by conservative activist Reed Irvine, also documents what Irvine terms "liberal and radical abuses in the media." John Corry, a columnist for conservative *American Spectator,* agrees and says that journalism is sometimes a status game wherein a liberal ideology is required for success.

Sociologist Herbert Gans and a number of other scholars dismiss the idea of political bias of the media, saying that, if anything, the media are essentially apolitical, that few reporters play a direct political role while most jealously guard their impartiality. Media critic Edwin Diamond once characterized America's reporters as "the best and the blandest," noting their essentially neutral role in public life and in the media industries. Journalism educators David Weaver and G. Cleveland Wilhoit, authors of the respected study *The American Journalist* (1986), also document an essentially apolitical press corps, albeit with more journalists identifying with the Democratic Party than with the Republicans, but they find no evidence of heavy-handed political bias. Certainly anyone who is a student of the international media finds the American press to have what *Nation* editor Victor Navasky calls "an ideology of the center," and one of the authors of this book once told an international audience: "Look—forget about political bias and a party press in America. If anything, objectivity is our ideology, even though we really don't believe in any pure form of objectivity."

This debate notwithstanding, when most Americans are asked whether they believe that the press does have a political agenda and ideological leanings, whether liberal or conservative, they answer yes. Thus in a society where the free flow of information and opinion are at the core of democratic values, the integrity of the media is severely challenged by the belief in the notion of political bias in the media.

CHALLENGE

Dennis: The news media are not biased.

This rather stark statement may seem to lead the author on a fool's errand, since so many Americans instantly assume that the news media are filled with political bias and often reflect the personal politics and outlook of its practitioners, whether newspaper reporters, television anchors, or other communicators. Let me begin by removing from the argument opinion journalism and commentary. Of course the views expressed on editorial pages, on op-ed pages, in television commentary that is clearly so labeled, and on talk radio have a point of view—it is in that sense biased, but not necessarily prejudicial. The best commentary sifts through evidence and offers conclusions. That is its function and, of course, commentators tend to come from a section of the political spectrum and to reflect their own experience and self-interest. That is opinion journalism, a form practiced throughout newspapers in many countries of the world, especially in Europe.

But what we're really talking about here are the news columns and the news delivered on television, which for better or worse are often more descriptive than interpretative and are laden more with facts than with ideas or opinions. Much of American journalism is simply descriptive, some is analytical, and some gets involved in interpretation. As we argue in Chapter 9, journalistic objectivity is a style of presentation wherein information is organized to answer certain questions: What happened? Who was involved? When did this occur? Did it make any difference? While surely there will be different answers to some of these questions, the idea that this approach constitutes political bias is nonsense.

A look at history demonstrates how the political bias argument evolved. President Franklin Delano Roosevelt, knowing that more than 80 percent of the nation's newspaper publishers opposed his administration, courted reporters whom he guessed were younger and more liberal than their then-conservative bosses. He also made an end run around then-traditional media by giving his own "fireside chats" on radio, where he could present his point of view. To Roosevelt the press was both conservative (in its editorial expressions) and occasionally friendlier to him—and apparently more liberal—in its news columns, not because reporters were cheerleaders for his administration, but because they played the news straight. Years later Adlai Stevenson, the Democratic candidate for President, called the American media a "one-party press," by which he meant a conservative, anti-liberal press. Since that time virtually every U.S. President has had strong views about the press, which was typically tough on them and their administrations, thus giving rise to charges of bias—either conservative or liberal, depending on the time and the administration.

Herbert Gans, in a detailed analysis in *Columbia Journalism Review* (1985), has dissected claims that the press is too liberal, challenging the assumptions of conservative researchers and urging them to make their data available for others to assess. Robert and Linda Lichter and Stanley Rothman, in their book *The Media Elite* (1986), make the case for a biased, left-leaning media but point mostly to major media outlets such as the news magazines, networks, and big-city newspapers. A counterargument is made by Weaver and Wilhoit, who, using a national sample, suggest that journalists are not driven by political ideology and bias nor are they joiners of organizations. And as Gans and others have pointed out, affiliation with a political party—as long as one is not an activist—does not prove that the individual colors the news to suit his or her fancy, any more than one's religion precludes one from writing fair-minded reports on other people's religions.

The reason I side with this view is professionalism. The employees of news media organizations are trained professionals and there are many checks and balances to keep them from using the news media for their own personal or political ends. Journalists are either trained or initiated into methods of gathering information, sorting out sources, and synthesizing reports and documents into a coherent news report. While there is less newspaper competition city by city than was once the case, you can bet that a biased report in the *New York Times* would be quickly challenged and savaged by the *Wall Street Journal* or even by network television. There are scores of news organizations in television, print, cable, and even cyberspace gathering and disseminating information, and these serve as a check and balance on each other. There are also ways for the public and for sources to talk back—through letters and by lodging personal complaints; they appeal to other media to tell their story as they see it, and they can and do sue for defamation when their reputations have been unfairly sullied.

While the U.S. media system is far from perfect—it has many flaws, from tabloid sensationalism to overemphasis on sex and violence, not to mention lack of continuity in coverage—it is not a political press in the sense that other nations' media are. That is, we rarely have a pro-government newspaper or network, one that is uncritical of those in power. If anything, we have an anti-authority press that is always suspicious and critical of the status quo and of those in power. The press and other news media are largely, although not entirely, negative in their news judgments, portraying society's warts more often than they do its strength and triumphs.

Increasingly too, politicians looking for the friendly reporter who is biased in their favor—whether Democrats or Republicans, liberals or conservatives—are disappointed. Luckily, reporters ready to write up biased reports are rare, and media organizations deal effectively with those who are found to be unethical or prejudicial in their work. Of course, much that is poorly reported, weakly reasoned, and ineptly edited does get in the American media, but not because of bias.

Louis D. Boccardi, who as president of the Associated Press presides over the world's largest news-gathering organization, refuses to say whether he belongs to a political party and who he might have voted for. Boccardi is so well regarded as an exemplar of impartial news judgment, that he makes a strong case against any kind of deliberate (or accidental) political bias in his organization, which is a major supplier of news to print and electronic media.

The media, of course, have a strong vested interest in not succumbing to political bias: credibility and believability, their most valuable asset. Without credibility, which comes with impartial, professionally gathered and edited news, the news media lose their franchise with the public. That's why so many news groups and scholars have regularly studied credibility. The self-correcting nature of the press in regard to deliberate political bias is swift and unforgiving, just as it is for fabrication, uncaring sloppiness, or other factors that contaminate what the Hutchins Commission called "fair and accurate presentation of the day's news." I reject the simple-minded idea that the news media, who have so much to lose if they contaminate their own product, can be accused of biasing the news, whether in a leftward or rightward direction. If anything, the American news media often err on the side of blandness, bending over backwards to be fair in delivering a truthful account to their readers and viewers, who they hope will return again and often.

Argument summation: The news media are not biased.

Bias and deliberate distortion are rarely found in the U.S. news media. Forces of professionalism on the one hand and fear of litigation on the other make it highly unlikely that the news media will engage in deliberate bias or allow the political leanings of a reporter to overly distort what he or she is writing about. Some critics are fond of accusing the media of having a liberal or a conservative bias, but in fact the news media in America have more of a centrist approach and try very hard to hew a neutral line rather than take sides. Of course opinion media and editorial pages often argue a strong point of view and do have ideological leanings, but the news media for the most part (and compared with the media of other countries) not only are not biased per se but are often rightly accused of blandness, so cautious is their coverage.

RESPONSE

Merrill: The news media are biased.

Ev Dennis must have his tongue in cheek when he contends above that the news media are not biased. He admits that most people believe they are biased, but he seems to put this perception down to a kind of populist ignorance. But to Dennis's credit, he does explain that he is not talking about opinion aspects of the media, but only about news columns and TV news. Editorial pages, op-ed pages, and television and radio commentary, he says, naturally are biased, as is most opinion journalism.

So now we have a focused statement, somewhat different from the debate topic. Dennis is really talking about this proposition: *The news segments of the news media are not biased.*

This new formulation of the debate question notwithstanding, I must take the position that even the news in the news media is biased. Of course this statement is not easy to prove. Bias is a complex concept, almost impossible to ascertain and measure. Often one sees bias, or the lack of it, through the lenses of one's own biased perceptions.

But it seems quite evident to me that a reporter's reality strainer (one's own subjective value system or perception) projects or reflects reality from a personal and biased perspective. A liberal reporter and a conservative reporter will report the same issue or event differently. A black reporter will report the Los Angeles riots differently than a white reporter, other factors being equal. A reporter who is a member of the Branch Davidian religious sect would report the 1993 Waco episode differently than an Episcopalian liberal. A woman reporter will report the spousal abuse story differently from a male reporter. An Arab reporter will report the Israeli-Palestinian confrontation in a manner different from that of a Jewish reporter.

Dennis says that journalistic "professionalism" protects the journalist against biased reporting. He speaks of many checks and balances keeping reporters from biasing their stories. And he maintains that one newspaper will savage another quickly if a report is biased. This may all be true in an ideal journalistic world, but the present one falls short of that. Look at any complex and controversial story carried, for instance, by a liberal and a conservative paper. Notice who is quoted, what quotes are selected for use, what pictures are used, and so on. It is not too difficult for the reader to tell which is the liberal and which is the conservative paper. Bias is there, all right, even if it gets in through emphasis and deemphasis of portions of the story or through the sources chosen to be quoted.

Dennis goes on to support his media-are-not-biased contention by saying that the United States does not have a political press, that seldom do we have a pro-government newspaper or network. "If anything," he says, "we have an anti-authority press that is always suspicious and critical of the status quo and of those in power." Well, if this is so, doesn't this fact indicate a bias? A bias against authority? A bias against the status quo? I agree with Dennis that the media are largely negative in their news judgments. And this, for me, indicates a *negative bias,* certainly not a *balanced or neutral* concept of news.

Another point made by Dennis to show a lack of bias is that when stories are poorly reported, weakly reasoned, or ineptly edited, that is the result of ineffective reporting and sloppiness rather than bias. Well, maybe, but how do we know? Dennis also says that bias is lacking in the media's news coverage because the media have credibility and believability; this, he says, is their most valuable asset, and they must keep it.

If public faith in the news media is indeed correlated with lack of bias, I would propose that this fact shows only too clearly that the media *are* biased. Why? Because all surveys show that the media are *not* very credible with the public.

Dennis says that politicians looking for a reporter to bias stories in their favor will be disappointed. This is another reason, he says, that news stories are not biased. But cannot a reporter bias a story *unintentionally*? And is this not still bias? Maybe what we should be debating is the topic of *intentional* bias. Do reporters intentionally bias stories? Well, maybe and maybe not. Sometimes, perhaps. But whether bias appears in the news media intentionally or naturally, bias is still there. It would be difficult for any student of the press to conclude that the media's news coverage is bias free.

Finally, Dennis seems to wish the media were more biased, for he says, "If anything, the American news media often *err* [my emphasis] on the side of blandness, bending over backwards to be fair in delivering a truthful account to their readers and viewers." Admittedly much of what is found in the media is bland, but this blandness does not indicate a lack of bias. Bland bias is still bias, and even a newspaper's bias against bias is still bias.

Argument summation: The news media are biased.

News reporting by the media is largely biased, especially when dealing with political news or other social news of controversy. This bias is natural and stems from the individual reporter's value system and culture. It also is derived from other factors such as the reporter's education, religion, social class, gender, party affiliation, political ideology, and a whole bevy of personal biases. The reporter filters the story through this personal subjective bias and, although doing so may be largely unconscious, biases the story in some way. Even the reporter who is most biased against bias will bias the story out of an overcompensating attempt to be balanced, accurate, and fair. So the news media are biased. In fact, they simply represent (or reflect) the bias of their reporters and editors. And the bias may be unintentional, but it is still bias; it may be unconsciously woven into the fabric of the story, but it is still bias. Bias is natural. It permeates the media—even the news stories.

TOPICS FOR DISCUSSION

1. Take the dictionary definition of *bias*—a preference or inclination that inhibits impartial judgment—and consider how this might apply to the news media. How would you recognize bias in the news? How would you offer evidence of bias from your own viewing and reading?

2. Delving into journalism history, consider the differences between the "biased" party press of the early Republic and the corporatized news media today. Do the media have a political agenda? Can they?

3. Compare and contrast the opinion magazines' view of the world and that of major newspapers and magazines. For example, how is the President of the United States portrayed in the news columns of *Time, Newsweek,* and the *Wall Street Journal* versus an essay in *The Nation, American Spectator,* or *National Review*?

4. How can a news medium best make the case with the public that it is unbiased and impartial with regard to politics and elections?

5. How does political coverage differ on NBC or CBS versus CNN or C-SPAN? What about MTV News: What are its politics?

TOPICS FOR RESEARCH

1. Do a study of news coverage of a major state or national political figure in newspaper, magazine, or television sources, assessing each story as "positive," "neutral," or "negative." How did you develop your definitions for each category and how well did the medium you picked for study (for example, your local newspaper or a television evening news program) do?

2. Examine the criticisms of the news media by public officials: the President, Speaker of the House of Representatives, and others. Do they charge "bias" or "unfairness?" If so, what are their specific complaints? Act as an investigator and substantiate or discount their claims.

3. Interview a reporter or editor on political bias. What does this person think it is? How does the person guard against it in his or her news organization? What does the person think of the performance of other media, including his or her competitors, regarding bias?

4. Many of the critics of the media come from institutions such as business, education, labor, medicine, and others. They sometime charge bias and misrepresentation with regard to the treatment their fields get. Take up the proposition that the media are "anti-business" or opposed to some other institution or group. What are your own conclusions?

FURTHER READING

Benjamin, Burton. *Fair Play: CBS, Westmoreland and How a Television Documentary Went Wrong.* New York: Harper & Row, 1988.

The Commission on Freedom of the Press. *A Free and Responsible Press.* Chicago: University of Chicago Press, 1947.

Dennis, Everette E. *Of Media and People.* Newbury Park, CA: Sage, 1992.

"The Fairness Factor." *Media Studies Journal,* Fall 1992. New York: Freedom Forum Media Studies Center.

Gans, Herbert. "Are U.S. Journalists Dangerously Liberal?" *Columbia Journalism Review,* November/December 1985, pp. 29–37.

Goldstein, Tom, ed. *Killing the Messenger: 100 Years of Media Criticism.* New York: Columbia University Press, 1989.

Henry, William A. III. "Are the Media Too Liberal?" *Time,* October 19, 1992, pp. 46–47.

Lichter, Robert S., Stanley Rothman, and Linda S. Lichter. *The Media Elite.* Bethesda, MD: Adler & Adler, 1986.

Manoff, Robert Karl, and Michael Schudson, eds. *Reading the News.* New York: Pantheon, 1986.

McQuail, Denis. *Media Performance: Mass Communication and the Public Interest.* Newbury Park, CA: Sage, 1992.

Protess, David L., et al. *The Journalism of Outrage: Investigative Reporting and Agenda Building in America.* New York: Guilford Press, 1991.

Sabato, Larry J. *Feeding Frenzy: How Attack Journalism Has Transformed American Politics.* New York: The Free Press, 1991.

Schudson, Michael. *The Power of News.* Cambridge, MA: Harvard University Press, 1995.

Weaver, David H., and G. Cleveland Wilhoit. *The American Journalist: A Portrait of U.S. News People and Their Work.* Bloomington: Indiana University Press, 1986.

Chapter 7

POWER OF THE MEDIA

Political candidates, television evangelists, advertising executives, and rock stars probably agree on at least one thing: that the media are powerful and do have considerable influence. There are scholars and critics, however, who doubt this power, asking for specific evidence that it was press or media influence, not personal contact or institutional forces, that fostered a particular belief or influenced a political or consumer decision.

Whether and to what degree the mass media have power has been widely debated. For many years the concept of the "power of the press" was a given, documented by historians, propaganda researchers, and others. That the press, and later other media, could move minds and goad people to action was widely believed. However, in the 1940s in study after study this popular public view was severely challenged by empirical evidence. A more modest view of the power of the press evolved and, especially in the scholarly community, a theory of "minimal effects" of mass communication has been in vogue. The press and other media, this view contends, have the power mainly to reinforce what people already believe, the power not to move the public mind but to influence some opinion leaders. Other forces such as the family, social groups, religious beliefs, and political parties have greater impact on the individual than do the mass media. Texts in psychology, political science, sociology, and other fields clearly downplayed the power of the press, saying that media operate in a nexus with other factors. The jury is still out on this question of media power and, in one form or another, the issue continues to be debated.

CHALLENGE

Dennis: The media are quite powerful.

If at first this statement seems obvious, I can assure you it is not. The reason is that for years new journalism and communication students have been cautioned about overestimating the impact of the mass media. The conclusion was that the media were not really very powerful after all. Now that view is changing. Now it is not unusual for scholars assessing the media to conclude that the impact of communications needs real scrutiny.

The 1981 publication of the *Annual Review of Psychology* (volume 32) occurred without notice in the press and with less than a resounding ripple among media scholars in the United States. Yet one chapter had a message of profound importance for media professionals and students of mass communications. In measured language, researchers Donald Roberts and Christine Bachen wrote, "The past decade . . . has witnessed a revival of the view that the mass media exert powerful influences on the way people perceive, think about, and ultimately act in their world" (307–8).

To some this may not seem such a startling statement. We are rarely without graphic examples of the alleged power of the media, whether in foreign policy (where government leaders sometimes play to the media), in national politics (where some critics claim that television has taken over the role once played by political parties), or in social behavior (where we worry whether sexually suggestive advertisements for designer jeans are corrupting the values of youth). Concern about the media clearly extends beyond the halls of academe and into everyday life, as terms such as *media event, hype,* and *image* become commonplace in our language.

The media have been replete with such examples for many years. Naturally this emphasis has led to the popular conception that media institutions have influence, impact, power, and, yes, effects. While it is true that these terms were never defined to everyone's satisfaction, there is an almost universal belief that mass media institutions shape our thinking, influence our attitudes and opinions, and contribute toward particular behavior such as voting and buying certain goods.

Mass communication was an invention of the nineteenth century, but it did not attract much scholarly attention until after World War I. From that time until the mid-1940s the yield of scholarly studies contributed to the conclusion that the media had enormous power. During this period the scholarly view and the lay view were virtually congruent. Of course there was no universal agreement about just what the media could and could not do. The interpretation depended on whether one was listening to a critic, an empirical social scientist, a media practitioner, or the uninitiated layperson. Still, at the simplest, most basic level there was considerable agreement with a hypodermic-needle model of media effects, wherein the media infused the minds of individuals directly with powerful messages.

This shared perspective changed under the scholarly and professional leadership of sociologist Paul Lazarsfeld (1944) and a generation of empirical researchers. By trying to isolate questions that could be probed by social researchers, Lazarsfeld and company narrowed the focus of the media effects discussion to provable impact as demonstrated by specific, short-term studies. Looking mainly at attitude and opinion change in electoral campaigns, these researchers brought us the two-step flow and a model of personal influence, wherein mass communication was not necessarily a central and dominant force, but instead operated in conjunction with interpersonal communication and various socializing influences. When empirical researchers were asked to explain media power, they used vague qualifying language and said they thought the earlier view of a powerful press was probably wrong. Thus came the idea of minimal effects of mass communication. This view, prominent among social scientists, had a strange and fragmenting influence on scholars' perceptions of mass communication. At the same time, the public's view of media power did not change. Even in instances when one might have doubted the power of the press to change voting behavior, for example, plausible common-sense explanations were found. When it became evident that newspaper editorial endorsements for presidential candidates did not have a direct effect on the voting public, people often chose to believe that this fact did not really challenge media power. After all, we were told, reporters are liberals and their favorable treatment of liberal candidates drowns out stuffy, conservative endorsements on the editorial page.

The notion that the media had little direct influence on people led to much confusion and outright disbelief in the researchers. This disbelief fostered anti-intellectualism and a deep chasm between practitioners and scholars, especially in journalism education, where students received mixed messages. Students received a minimal-effects indoctrination in their mass media classes and also in economics, political science, sociology, and history. Some social science teachers, in their desire to simplify and explain, too often presented the great researchers as purist scholars who sneered at any notion of powerful media effects. Rarely did they suggest that thoughtful people using different assumptions and different methods might come to quite different conclusions. No wonder students found themselves in a conceptual muddle. Consider, for example, the journalism student who is told by a public opinion teacher that the media have minimal effects only to discover that the reporting teacher thinks newspaper stories can have powerful consequences. In the everyday world, then, the student watches television and perceives quite rightly that advertisers act as though media can encourage people to buy goods.

While it is difficult to doubt the scholarly benefits that came with the minimal-effects perspective, it did tend to fragment our understanding of mass communication and appeared to set practitioners against researchers. Contrasting the powerful-effects approach with the minimal-effects view does provide useful background for the continuing debate over media effects, especially now when people are arguing for a return to the concept of powerful media with some modification.

One of the main reasons we study media effects is to get a handle on our own thinking, to trace our own intellectual history and chart increments and obstacles in its development.

Whether the dramatic shifts in research findings (as noted by Roberts and Bachen) truly represent what the historian of science Thomas Kuhn in *The Structure of Scientific Revolution* (1962) calls *paradigm change* or complete change in our thought process is not clear, but scholars increasingly think this might be so.

The first stirrings of the apparent shift in communication research came not in a new and startling book or theory, but in the shared views of a number of scholars, some of whom were well established while others were just beginning their careers. The distinguished researcher Wilbur Schramm urged study of the "quiet, continuing effects" of mass communication which, he said, were largely ignored and might yield important findings. Melvin DeFleur and Sandra Ball-Rokeach, authors of *Theories of Mass Communication* (1982), said we should explore the role of mass communication in the enlargement of people's belief systems, a study that they thought might seriously challenge the narrow conclusions of earlier studies. The German researcher Elisabeth Noelle-Neumann called for a return to belief in the concept of a powerful mass media. "The fact is," she wrote, "the decisive factors of mass media are not brought to bear in the traditional laboratory experiment" (1973, 67). Adding to the discussion, several other scholars agreed that *what people learn* from communication activity is a more rewarding topic for media effects research than is *attitude formation* or change. Offering a striking observation in his studies of media bias in electoral campaigns, John P. Robinson wrote that evidence now exists that under certain conditions the media can have political impact. Robinson was one of the first to challenge seriously the minimal-effects perspective, asking rhetorically in his 1972 *Journalism Quarterly* article, "Can the Media Affect Behavior After All?" Agenda-setting studies by Maxwell McCombs and Donald Shaw (1972) concluded that the informational-learning role of the media was its most important effect. This means that the media will tell people not *what to think* but what to *think about.* The above scholars were quite careful and understated in their new view of media power, but others were not so quiet. Sociologist Todd Gitlin denounced the Lazarsfeld (minimal-effects) tradition in an article that accused researchers of failing to "put the crucial questions" because of "intellectual, ideological and institutional commitments" (1978,

205). Said Gitlin, "behind the idea of the relative unimportance of the mass media lies a skewed, faulty concept of importance, similar to the faulty concept of power" (205). To Gitlin, that approach had the effect of justifying the existing system of media ownership, control, and purpose:

> By its methodology, media sociology has highlighted the recalcitrance of audiences, their resistance to media-generated message, and not their dependency, their acquiescence, their gullibility. It has looked to "effects" of broadcast programming in specifically behaviorist fashion, defining "effects" so narrowly, microscopically, and directly as to make it very likely that survey studies could only show slight "effects" at most. It has enshrined short run effects as "measures" of "importance," largely because these "effects" are measurable in a strict, replicable, behavioral sense, thereby deflecting attention of larger social meanings of mass media production. (203–6)

This view comes mainly from humanistic reasoning and observation. However, Roberts and Bachen (1981) reached a similar conclusion on the basis of a review of several areas of research, including patterns of media use, probes of children, and media studies of uses and gratifications, information transmission and processing, the knowledge gap hypothesis, the cultivation of beliefs, attention and comprehension, responses to advertising, political socialization, antisocial behavior, pro-social effects, and sex role socialization. This research raises new questions and expands the arena for investigation well beyond the old targets into the largely uncharted realm of cognitive effects. It is here that many studies, with striking and distinctive findings, are encouraging researchers to consider a modification of the minimal-effects doctrine. Several recent texts about media effects also make this point. It is not surprising that one of the most articulate proponents of a new view, the German researcher Noelle-Neumann, says there are clues in research that have not been considered to any great extent before:

1. *Ubiquity of the media*—the ability to be everywhere, to dominate the information environment. The media are so ubiquitous at times that it is difficult to escape a message.

2. *Cumulation of messages*—frequent repetition of the message that tends to reinforce its impact. One should look beyond the individual, fragmented messages to the cumulative effect over time.

3. *Consonance of journalists*—remarkable agreement and demographic similarity among journalists and other media professionals, leading to a sameness in newspapers and newscasts and limiting the options the public has for selective perception. (Noelle-Neumann, 1974, 67–112)

Similarly, communication researcher James Lemert (1981) attacks what he calls the "simple reductionist model" of the minimal-effects school, which measured media influence mainly through attitude change. This, he says, is too simple an explanation because it uses only one measure—behavior—to ascertain effects. Lemert would have us discard the idea that attitude change is either necessary or sufficient for public opinion change. He believes that minimal-effects researchers attempted to explain society with limited information about individuals. The mass media, he says, can have a powerful impact on the information given to decision makers. Lemert proposes integrating research on public opinion with the role of decision makers and journalists, in studies that would take effects research beyond "simple reductionism." More important, he recognizes that we must first understand the prevailing research patterns in order to use their strengths and avoid their limitations. Like Noelle-Neumann and others, he is concerned with the news media as collectors of attitude information and with the context of attitude information and change.

Many media people are reluctant to brag about it, but they are also aware of their power. Theirs is the only institution that really gets no policing; it falls back on the Constitution when occasional darts begin to come close. In protecting its power, every mass medium paints its critics as uninformed cranks who would repeal the First Amendment and censor the press.

Richard Harwood, columnist for the *Washington Post,* pointed up media power: "Newspapers and other media enterprises . . . have acquired considerable wealth, influence and perhaps real power in this century" (1989, *World Media Report,* May–June, 3). Harwood is, of course, being modest when he says "*perhaps* real power." He and other journalists know full well that media are powerful and have far too few checks on their power. This is the very reason he thinks newspapers should have ombudsmen such as he.

When the dust is settled on the present media effects debate, I believe that a true paradigm shift, in Kuhn's (1962) term, will be evident. We have, in fact, seen an integration of all the stages of change that accompany paradigm change. There has been incremental change, as represented in the empirical scholarship wherein researchers are framing new questions that take them beyond the limitations of short-run effects studies and into cognitive areas. This change has come about through a useful collaboration between people interested in the largely externally oriented social impact and those caring more about individuals and their attitudes as well as those who care about media organizations. In the early stages of some of this research, findings that conflicted with prevailing patterns and widely held beliefs were often seen as change by exception. As these findings recurred, however, they eventually replaced the earlier view. Some scholars say there has been a pendulum shift and they decry the "errors of the past." If research really does tell us that we need a new view of media power, such a view may be due to studies that probe such issues as the social construction of reality and long-term cumulative effects. Notably, research of this kind is no longer confined to a small group of theoretical researchers in mass communication or social psychology and related fields. Persons from within mass communication with interests in history, law, institutional analysis, economics, and other topics are also working diligently on questions often central to media impact, influence, and effect. Even these terms are getting more precise definition as scholars raise new questions and try to make more refined calibrations.

Ironically, we proponents of the media as powerful have gotten some new allies in recent years: students of critical theory led by such commentators as Stuart Hall, Todd Gitlin, and others who write about the cultural hegemony of the media and argue that it is powerful indeed, although they draw their evidence from different kinds of observations and analysis than do social scientists. These commentators score the media for helping to maintain the existing power structure and for their support of capitalism. They believe that the media play a decisive role in contributing to what is an unequal society.

All of these factors will help us understand the impact of mass communication with greater sophistication than before. We will not return to the point of having uncritical awe of so-called media power, but we will understand better how mass communication works in the context of other social forces without underestimating its importance. Clearly, the media are powerful.

Argument summation: The media are quite powerful.

The general perception that the media are a powerful force in society is correct. The research of social scientists who revealed a limited impact of media on formation of opinions only fragmented our understanding of the power of the media. Today more balanced research is leading to a growing recognition of media power. The difference is how the importance of the media is measured. Modern researchers feel that the impact of media power is in telling people what to think *about,* not what to think. The behavioral focus of early media sociologists led them to ignore the broader social impact of mass media by measuring its importance only in narrow, easily definable areas. It is now accepted that the power of the media comes not from single messages but from the cumulation of messages and from the media's domination of the information environment. Attitude change is not necessary for a change in public opinion; hence earlier studies failed to account for the power of the media. As relevant terms get greater clarification and more precise definitions, the power of the media will become increasingly evident.

RESPONSE

Merrill: The media are not so powerful.

I take issue with the contention that the media are all-powerful. Still I am in good company, as even my coauthor will agree, since he points out that for years there have been researchers who have maintained that the impact and influence of the media have been overstated. Thus this topic is, in spite of its fuzzy nature, quite controversial.

I am put in a difficult position, however, by the very wording of this proposition. I really cannot maintain that the media have *no* power and that their impact is *nonexistent*. It is all too obvious that media have some power and that their influence on society cannot be denied. Advertisers, pragmatists and realists that they are, recognize the power of the media. Sociologists have documented various trends started and maintained by media attention. Politicians have contended that their careers have been helped or ruined by attention or neglect by the media. Panics have been precipitated by the media. Riots, demonstrations, skyjackings, and acts of terrorism are thought to be stimulated by media publicity. The "contagion" aspect of events is obviously connected with public exposure.

I cannot and will not, therefore, deny that the media have some power. But the question really is: Do we know for certain that the media are *in themselves* powerful? Or are they simply secondary factors, triggering mechanisms if you will, which have various impacts in society under certain circumstances?

Let us admit immediately that some media, under some conditions, with some people, have some effects or impact. Media, however, do not work in a vacuum. Certainly Paul Lazarsfeld and his colleagues (1944) were right when they concluded that the mass media operate in conjunction with many social forces to bring about certain results. The implication of much of this "effects" research is that mass communication is influential but not central or dominant in the model of personal influence.

Let us say a candidate for office is elected. Did the media put him in? The answer must be, "No—but they probably played their part." The candidate appeared to many voters in person, as an individual without media help. He conversed; he debated; he answered questions. He used the telephone. He and his family and friends knocked on doors and handed out flyers. He spoke at the Rotary Club and at the county fair. He was an individual, as well as a media, event. At the national level think of Newt Gingrich. Do you think the media favored his election to Congress or to the Speaker's chair?

In addition we must recognize that the candidates themselves (exclusive of the power, presumed or real, of the media) had talents, effectiveness, charisma, a friendly and trustworthy smile, and other personal attributes that made them popular and electable. The media themselves did not give them these attributes. The media may have served as channels whereby the public or portions of it were exposed to these attributes—but they were personal, not media-induced. How can researchers seeking to perceive the impact of the media separate personal "power" from media "power"? I do not think they can. There is no evidence, to my knowledge, that can show that all other impacting factors can be separated. So the conclusion is that the media have no more than tangential or minimal impact.

Journalists, of course, like to think that they and their media have great power and that they are movers and shakers in society. It is satisfying to them to think that they are king makers, agenda setters, corruption unearthers, society improvers. Of course they are not quite so sure of their power when someone points out that the negativism, violence, sensationalism, and sexploitation permeating the media might be having a deleterious effect on society. They seem to see themselves as having only "positive" power and seldom, if ever, "negative" power.

Although Dennis alludes to many communications scholars, such as DeFleur and Noelle-Neumann, who call for more research of media impact in the real (nonexperimental) world, hardly any research of this nature has been done. How does one perceive the impact of the media when trying to study them in a total social symbiosis? How does one separate or isolate purely media effects from other effects? These questions have been addressed, of course, but have not been satisfactorily answered. When scholars such as Max McCombs and Don Shaw (1972) conclude that agenda setting by the media is an important role and has "power" in that it tells people what to think *about,* they have stated an obvious informational principle, but they have come no closer to specifying the real power of the media. Of course, I will generally think more about news events that I read much about and see prominently on the TV screen than I will about those that are ignored or minimally treated by the media. Nobody can deny that I may be aware of these events or even think about them because of their media attention, but the question still remains: What impact does such consciousness have on me?

A locked front door to a building may cause me to go around to a side door to enter. In one sense the lock has power and has caused a change in my activity; it has modified my interaction with my environment. But how has it affected me? Studying the lock will not answer the question. Neither will a study of the quantitative aspects of my new and more elongated journey to another door. Only an in-depth psychological study will cast some light on the impact on me of the locked front door.

What I am trying to say is that our lives are constantly affected by a multitude of factors—some of which are messages reaching our brains—and these factors are so complex and intertwined as to defy clear determinations as to the impact of each. What we think obviously has some kind of effect on our lives. What we do is also important. But what we do is not always determined by what we think, so we cannot say that if we have certain information we will act in a certain way on the basis of that information—or, in fact, that we will act at all.

John P. Robinson (1972) says that evidence now exists "that under certain conditions" media can have political impact. That is almost like saying that under certain conditions an Alpine valley town can be destroyed by an avalanche of snow. Of course media can have political impact. I can just as well say that under certain conditions media can *not* have political impact.

My coauthor cites James Lemert's (1981) attack on the "simple reductionist model" of minimal effects, which measures media influence mainly through attitude change. Lemert says, according to Dennis, that the mass media can have a powerful impact on the information given to decision makers. I would go even further: Mass media can have *total* control and impact on the *information* given to decision makers. (Impact on the *information:* Now here is a new concept!) At least this would certainly be true of the information given to the decision makers by the media. Earlier I maintained that people (including decision makers) get much information from sources other than mass media.

What we need in this debate about media power are some clear definitions. I do not think most researchers and students in this area are really sure of what they are talking about. What do they mean by *power*? What is meant by *minimal effects*? Or *maximal effects*? Just how powerful (by any definition) would the media need to be to be considered powerful or effective?

Are there not different types or forms of power? Providing information (regardless of the impact) is one kind of power. Another power is the effect of such information on the *mind.* Still another power would be the effect of such information on the *actions* of a person. Most often the distinctions among these kinds of power are ignored or minimized. I would postulate the following:

1. Media are most powerful in furnishing information and setting agendas for members of a public.

2. Media are next most powerful in impinging on the thoughts, opinions, and attitudes of members of a public.

3. Media are least powerful in affecting actions of members of a public.

In conclusion, I agree that media are powerful sometimes and to some extent. Just when they are and to what degree are questions crying out for more research. At present we know very little about media *power.* It may well be that media are really more powerful than media power proponents think—but then again they may be far less powerful.

I cannot say in good conscience that media are not powerful, but I can say in good conscience that what power they have is shared with innumerable forces in society. I also say that, so far as I am able to learn, media in themselves are not nearly as powerful (in any of the aspects of power) as journalists and other media people generally contend.

Argument summation: The media are not so powerful.

We usually assume the media are powerful, but we have very little evidence. Naturally media have some power, but it is usually overblown. Secondary factors have various social effects on audience members in certain circumstances. We do not know how *much* power media really have, because we cannot isolate their impact from other influencing factors, such as conversations, peer pressure, family, school, and church. It is most likely that media have the most power in focusing our attention in certain directions—*attention power,* if you will—but that is quite different from power to cause action.

TOPICS FOR DISCUSSION

1. Assuming media have powerful effects in society, what does this suggest for (a) education of media people, and (b) ethics of media people?

2. Why do you think the issue of media power has such a fascination for communication scholars? Do you think media practitioners are "power hungry"?

3. Why do you think *what* people learn from mass media has significant effect upon them or indicates that media are, or are not, powerful?

4. When scholars say that "under certain conditions" media can have impact, are they supporting or minimizing the powerful-effects theory of the media?

5. Explain why advertising and its large expenditures argue for powerful effects of media. Also discuss why many politicians who get more exposure than their opponents often lose the election.

TOPICS FOR RESEARCH

1. Write an essay about the academic—professional disputes over media power. Compare the perceived power of the press in the 1930s and 1940s

with that in the 1950s and 1960s. What is the prevailing sentiment today? Do academics and media professionals agree or not? Why?

2. Compare ideas about the power of the media to deliver consumers through advertising, as presented in economics textbooks versus mass communication or advertising texts. What differences in interpretation and analysis do you find?

3. Some media researchers doubt that the media can do much to change people's attitudes, opinions, and behavior in elections. Campaign managers and politicians themselves seem to doubt this, or they certainly act as though they do. To what extent do media influence (or not influence) the outcome of elections?

4. Do a profile of a leading media consultant who works on political campaigns. What do we know about the person? How does he or she work? What evidence does he or she marshal in deciding what communications resources to deploy in a campaign? How do we know whether the strategy worked?

5. Write a "biography of an idea," that of *agenda setting*. What does the term mean? Who originated it? How did it come to be known as "an important media effect"? What have studies of agenda setting shown? Review, especially, twenty-fifth anniversary treatment in various journals. How would you explain the agenda-setting hypothesis to a lay audience?

FURTHER READING

Altschull, J. Herbert. *Agents of Power: The Role of the News Media in Human Affairs.* White Plains, NY: Longman, 1984.

Babb, Laura L., ed. *Of the Press, by the Press, and Others, Too.* Boston: Houghton Mifflin, 1976.

Bogart, Leo. *Commercial Culture.* New York: Oxford University Press, 1995.

Cohen, Jeremy, and Timothy Gleason. *Social Research in Communication and Law.* Newbury Park, CA: Sage, 1990.

Comstock, George, et al. *Television and Human Behavior.* New York: Columbia University Press, 1978.

Davis D. K., and S. J. Baran. *Mass Communication and Everyday Life: A Perspective on Theory and Effects.* Belmont, CA: Wadsworth, 1981.

DeFleur, Melvin L., and Sandra Ball-Rokeach. *Theories of Mass Communication.* 4th ed. White Plains, NY: Longman, 1982. Also see 5th ed.

DeFleur, M. L., and Everette E. Dennis. *Understanding Mass Communication.* 3d ed. Boston: Houghton Mifflin, 1988.

Dennis, Everette E. *The Media Society.* Dubuque, IA: William C. Brown Publishers, 1978.

———. *Reshaping the Media.* Beverly Hills, CA: Sage, 1989.

Gitlin, Todd. "Media Sociology: The Dominant Paradigm." *Theory's Society* 6 (November 1978):205–53.

———. *The Whole World Is Watching.* Berkeley: University of California Press, 1980.

Jamieson, Kathleen Hall, and Karlyn Kohrs Campbell. *The Interplay of Influence.* Belmont, CA: Wadsworth, 1983.

Klapper, Joseph T. *The Effects of Mass Communication.* New York: The Free Press, 1960.

Kraus, Sydney, and Dennis Davis. *The Effects of Mass Communication on Political Behavior.* University Park: Pennsylvania State University Press, 1976.

Kuhn, Thomas. *The Structure of Scientific Revolutions.* Princeton, NJ: Princeton University Press, 1962.

Lazarsfeld, Paul, et al. *The People's Choice.* New York: Duell, Sloan & Pearce, 1944.

Lemert, James B. *Does Mass Communication Change Public Opinion After All?* Chicago: Nelson-Hall, 1981.

McCombs, Maxwell, and Donald Shaw. "The Agenda-Setting Function of Mass Media." *Public Opinion Quarterly* 36 (1972):176–87.

Mills, C. Wright. *Power, Politics, and People.* New York: Ballantine Books, 1962.

Noelle-Neumann, Elisabeth. "Return to the Concept of Powerful Mass Media." *Studies of Broadcasting* 9 (1973):67–112.

Reeves, Richard. "The Press's Great Threat." *Esquire,* August 1, 1978, pp. 10–13.

Roberts, D. F., and Christine M. Bachen. "Mass Communication Effects." *Annual Review of Psychology* 32 (February 1981):307–56.

Robinson, John P. "Can the Media Affect Behavior After All?" *Journalism Quarterly* 49, no. 2 (1972):239–46.

Rogers, Everett M. *A History of Communication Study.* New York: The Free Press, 1994.

Rubin, Bernard. *Media, Politics, and Democracy.* New York: Oxford University Press, 1977. See especially Chapter 5, "Media and Election Trends."

Schramm, Wilbur, ed. *The Process and Effects of Mass Communication.* Urbana: University of Illinois Press, 1954.

Schramm, W., and William Porter. *Men, Women, Messages, and Media.* New York: Harper & Row, 1982.

Schudson, Michael. *The Power of News.* Cambridge, MA: Harvard University Press, 1995.

Small, William J. *Political Power and the Press.* New York: Hastings House, 1972.

———. *To Kill a Messenger: Television News and the Real World.* New York: Hastings House, 1970.

Stein, Robert. *Media Power: Who Is Shaping Your Picture of the World?* Boston: Houghton Mifflin, 1972.

Chapter *8*

QUALITY OF MEDIA CONTENT

For decades critics of mass communication have hammered away at the quality of media content. Whether one is discussing the information, opinion, or entertainment functions of the mass media, the quality of the fare offered to the public is often at issue. The standard view in communication history is that the press has become stronger, freer, and better over the course of time. We have come to think of newspaper articles, movie scripts, and television scenarios as increasing in quality. To some, media content of two decades ago or earlier seems not only dated but of somewhat primitive quality compared with what is offered today. Others disagree. Criticism of media content usually focuses on (1) the substantive information or entertainment material being presented, and (2) the style or form of presentation. Often it is argued that audience preferences and tastes offer little support for quality, and television programs, news content of newspapers, and magazines give the public what it wants. This argument convinces some but not others.

CHALLENGE

Dennis: Media content is generally of poor quality and getting worse.

Evaluating media content is a difficult task. If we have low expectations, almost anything will seem better than it could have been. If we have high standards and measure what *is* against what *might be,* we are likely to be disappointed. Frankly, I am in the middle. I look at today's media content against a standard of what is reasonable, and on that basis I am unimpressed by what I see in almost all of the mass media in the United States. True, there are rare pockets of quality in some of the so-called opinion and literary magazines and on public television, but for the most part the performance of the American media can be termed only a major embarrassment.

Questions of quality almost always are equated with matters of elitism versus egalitarianism: It is assumed that quality is synonymous with a wealthy or highly educated audience, which would make an intellectual assault on what the people really want. I would argue that this is not the case. I believe that the American people have too often been subjected to low-quality media content, not because they want it but because media professionals have an inaccurate understanding of public tastes.

The major motivating force for quality in the American media is only the self-esteem of directors, producers, editors, broadcasters, and others. People who want to distinguish themselves from the commonplace have the motivation and interest to strive to produce something distinctive. These people, however, are often thwarted by their industry's perception of what the market will bear.

What distinguishes a quality performance by the media from one that is mediocre or poor? Contrary to the view of some egalitarian critics, appealing to rich or snobbish people is not the essential element. Instead, it is the following:

1. *Attractiveness* as expressed in design, presentation, and format.

2. *Literary style* as expressed in writing either for print or for electronic media.

3. *Universal appeal* in terms of those elements that touch the heart or mind and have a lasting impact.

4. *Impact* as seen in the long-term contribution of the material that is produced.

Finally, in my mind an elevating influence is being able to say that this is the best that can be done; it is better than what has come before, and it can be clearly distinguished from earlier work, more primitive efforts, and less informed approaches.

While I do not believe in the full-throttle theory of Excelsior (upward, onward ever), I do think there is a difference between stagnation and forward movement in media content.

Look at the newspaper, for example. Is today's newspaper better than the one that existed a few years or decades ago? By what measure do we answer this question? First I would look at the quality of writing. Is it more vital, more lively, more readable than earlier writing? Next I would consider the substantive information conveyed. Is it accurate? Is it complete? Is it compelling? Does it have proper context? I would also look at the methods reporters use in their work. Are these tools—in interviewing, use of documents and records, corroboration of sources—an improvement over those used decades ago? If so, how and why? If not, why not? I would ask whether the newspaper is in touch with its audience. Does it resonate the concerns that people have? Does it understand its readers and calibrate material to their interests and needs?

When we address these questions squarely, the American newspaper is a quite deficient product. Few critics assert that the writing in the American press is sterling. Good writing is the exception, not the rule. Tom Winship, the former editor of the *Boston Globe,* has excoriated the American press for its lack of attention to writing:

> Newspapers are dying, in part, because they are dull and predictable. If we are going to attempt good writing we won't be able always to play it safe; we'll have to try new forms, new subjects, new voices, stories written and reported at new distances, stories that are shorter than usual and longer than usual. Some of them won't work for good writing is always experimental. (1982, 22)

Experimental is the key word here. Most newspapers simply will not tolerate experimentation. They play it safe, and what they produce results in what New Journalist Tom Wolfe calls a "paralyzing snoremonger" syndrome. Few critics think the writing in American newspapers is anything but mediocre. The newspaper is not the home of America's best and most gifted prose. It could be, though. Literary giants of the past such as Hemingway, Faulkner, and others began their careers at newspapers and produced strong nonfiction prose that is memorable today. When the brilliant sports writer Red Smith died in 1982, a number of publications produced samples of his writing. This work was notable mainly because it was so unlike the turgid copy that usually appears on the modern sports page.

Writing, of course, is only one aspect of media performance. What of the methods, tools, and techniques of the journalist? Is there evidence that today's interviewing methods are significantly better than those of yesteryear? Are reporters more systematic, more meticulous, more competent in seeking out information for a wide variety of public records and documents? In spite of the surge toward investigative reporting in the early 1970s, it can rightly be said that today's reporters are guilty of journalistic primitivism. They are ignorant of their craft's history and frankly do not care about it.

Consider one example from investigative reporting. When Bob Woodward and Carl Bernstein did their Watergate investigation in the early 1970s, they were hailed as culture heroes. They were credited by some with bringing down a government and giving journalism a place at center stage again. But for journalism historians who compare this work with that of the great muckrakers at the turn of the century, the Watergate duo and other modern investigative reporters do not measure up very well. By contrast, Lincoln Steffens, Ray Stannard Baker, and Ida Tarbell, the original muckrakers, were world-class performers. Their prose was stronger; their investigative techniques, about the same; the time they devoted to their projects, greater. Students will find their work, plus histories and criticism of it, in any library. After a close inspection of the performance of the 1980s investigative reporters and those of the early 1900s, I would have to give the nod to the folks at the turn of the century. This fact in itself is not particularly noteworthy, but it is sad that in eighty years American journalism has progressed so little. If American medicine or science or even cooking methods had made as little progress, we would be terribly distressed, but we accept this sluggish performance by the media without much complaint. Indeed, the methods of a profession are often the best indicator of its progress.

One of the principal concerns of communicators is knowing and understanding the audience. Since the turn of the century there have been breathtaking advances in market and survey research and other forms of audience analysis. Audiences can be examined for the intensity of readership and in other highly revealing ways. What does the average American newspaper know about its audience? The advertising department probably knows quite a bit, but little of this information filters down from the editors to reporters in the field. Reporters of the 1980s are probably more ignorant of their audience than were their counterparts in the nineteenth century. In fact, there is evidence that contemporary reporters are hopelessly out of touch with the reader because reporters tend to be part of an elite class. Researchers at Michigan State University reported that "mobility, long working hours, and an attitude that news people are different from their readers contribute to journalists feeling out of touch" (Burgoon, Burgoon, and Atkin, 1982, 5). This study and others indicate that American journalists are not only insular, but are also quite contemptuous of their audience, referring to readers and viewers as "bozos" or "Joe Sixpack."

You might ask, why should we expect today's reporters to be more knowledgeable or better informed than their predecessors? The answer is simple: research, computers, and techniques for examining the audience with real precision. I recall with much disappointment the results of a study I did with science editors on daily newspapers. They were an elite group of reporters and had a better grasp of research than almost any of their counterparts had. Yet when they were asked about the audience they were writing for, their responses were incredibly unscientific as they confessed that they thought they were writing for "the Kansas City milkman." Many knowledgeable reporters genuinely thought they were writing for "everyone in the community" rather than for the highly specific and defined audience that exists today. They were not making any practical use of the research data readily available to them to stay in touch with the reader.

What of commercial television content? Few would argue that the soap operas which dominate daytime television are the best dramatic performances that we Americans are capable of producing and sustaining with advertising. Heavy-handed, melodramatic programs are the order of the day in the soaps. Evening programming is a little better, but not particularly noteworthy. Over the years some of the best-quality programs have been dropped. Nearly every season some of the shows that are taken off the air are among the best. In their place we may see such fare as sensational news and talk shows, sometimes called *trash television,* or the next generation of tasteless, violent fare introduced in autumn 1989, with ice skaters and gladiators competing in dangerous contests and games, appropriately called *crash television.*

Television is probably the best example of the "great leveler" theory of mass communication, which posits that one must appeal to a vast, homogeneous audience in order to succeed commercially. In the early 1960s the chairman of the Federal Communications Commission declared that television was a vast wasteland. Since then the situation has not improved. Television programs are banal, silly, and generally poor in quality. Those of higher quality usually are destined for the trash bin.

Television news is also worth examining. In recent years the most notable thing about TV news has been the addition of the news consultants, who have had an enormous effect on program content. These "outside contractors" are hired by stations to do audience research and propose solutions that will boost ratings. They are sometimes called "news doctors." Their contribution has led, not to more serious and thoughtful coverage of the public arena in a fashion that people will find interesting, but to "happy talk" news in which newscasters reflect a kind of jovial idiocy as they make jokes between reports about plane crashes and bloody coups in foreign lands. There is more emphasis on the hairstyle of the anchorperson than on the substance that person presents on the evening news. There are certainly some pockets of good performance in television news as compared with radio news, which is still a headline service and an even vaster wasteland than television.

Television news has justifiably been called "chewing gum for the eyes." It emphasizes trivial events that have a visual component regardless of their importance; it is biased toward the spectacle instead of the more subtle trend; it misleads the public by following the visual cue to the exclusion of deeper meaning.

Across much of the media the economic glue that holds things together is advertising. And what of advertising? Is it of high quality? Does it elevate the American people? Do we admire it for its ethical sensitivity? For its fairness? For its devotion to truth? Of course not. These questions cannot even be put seriously. Advertising content is better than it was in the days of patent medicine shows and quacks, but it is hardly befitting a modern society. Advertising is self-serving; it is biased and it misleads. Even comparative advertising, in which one advertiser compares its wares with those of another, is less than desirable and hardly a serious consumer service. Without some supervision by the Federal Trade Commission and other government agencies, advertising would no doubt be worse than it is. Still, the end product of advertising agencies today can hardly be called admirable.

Many of the points made here about newspapers and television could be made for other media, but I will not develop an endless laundry list. Instead I will return to the criteria suggested earlier as points of comparison among the media. If we consider them seriously, we find some intriguing, if depressing, answers. I recognize, of course, that any criticism of media content subjects the critic to charges of elitism. Fair enough. Measures of quality are necessarily subjective, although I have tried to offer some support that goes beyond personal conjecture. My views may differ markedly from those of others. However, I would note that the American people, on the one hand, vote with their pocketbooks, and in so doing they continue to support the present output of the media. Yet when they are allowed to make qualitative judgments, they are singularly unimpressed by media content. In 1981 the Public Agenda Foundation, working with the pollster Daniel Yankelovich, conducted one of the most exhaustive surveys of public attitudes toward the media. The principal finding of that survey was a general public dissatisfaction with the media. The vast majority of Americans criticized the media for lacking fairness and for the growing trend toward sex and violence on television. Other studies of public confidence in the media as an institution also gave low marks to American journalism. It is true that these studies are somewhat limited and that the respondents often have little basis for comparison except their own personal standards. Still, the public is smart enough to know what it does not like.

As for social consequences, I believe that the media have a more important and sustained role. They give us a common frame of reference, possibly because they seek the lowest common denominator audience, thus giving everyone a common experience. The media, both print and broadcast, do have an influence deemed important and potentially powerful. Is this power exercised to the greatest possible good? Does the press generally serve the public interest, as opposed to its own narrow commercial interests?

The portrait of the content of the American mass media is not what it could be, even if it is better than the norm of international standards. I personally believe that the American people are intelligent, have standards, want quality, and decry the kind of brain candy that demeans and denigrates the human spirit. To date, the American media have not received this message.

Argument summation: Media content is generally of poor quality and getting worse.

Judged by a reasonable standard, not a utopian "what might be," the American media are still of embarrassingly low quality. To measure the quality of the media, it is necessary to evaluate the progress they have made over time. In the case of newspapers, this is minimal. Writing is of extremely low quality. An examination of investigative reporting reveals that the methods, tools, and techniques of journalism have failed to improve since the turn of the century. Despite improved techniques for examining the audience, elitist attitudes among reporters leave them ignorant of their readers. Commercial television is no better, as quality programming is dropped in favor of talk show and tabloid news programming. Finally, advertising has improved only slightly since the days of medicine shows and quacks, but it is still biased and misleading. Mass support for the media should not be misconstrued as a vote of confidence, for, while Americans vote with their pocketbooks for current programming, when asked to make qualitative judgments they are singularly unimpressed by media content. After all, they have little real choice.

RESPONSE

Merrill: Media content is generally of good quality and getting better.

Everette Dennis has admitted that evaluating media content is a difficult task. I would certainly agree but would add that pointing out negative aspects of the media and concluding that general quality is poor are much easier than accentuating the positive. Media critics such as Eugene Methvin in a *Quill* article on "destructive journalism" normally stress the weaknesses and, by and large, ignore the strengths.

The very nature of the mass media in America opens the door to a criticism that depreciates the general media picture, points up the rather low common-denominator quality of the media, which must appeal largely to the masses, and approaches media criticism from an arrogant and elitist perspective. *Generally,* of course, U.S. mass media are not paragons of quality; they do not reflect the basic characteristics of the very mass audiences they seek to serve. This is quite natural and it is also intelligent.

Again, as we have seen in other debates on mass communication, we find ourselves squarely in the middle of a semantic thicket. Imprecise definitions and the whole concept of relativity circumscribe such debates as this one and cause the discussion to be devoid of the precision and lucidity that we might wish.

For example, we are talking about "media content." But we are not sure just which *medium* we are talking about, nor are we certain about what specific *content* we are referring to. Beyond this, what do we mean by "generally poor" or "good" quality? Even though we have such questions as these, we can feel some justification for the discussion because the subject constantly thrusts itself into the public forum. The American media system is an important social force, and it is useful to ask questions about its quality and about the direction in which it seems to be going.

As I have reviewed a wealth of critical literature about the press in recent years, I have been struck by how poorly the press fares. Not uncommon at all are statements similar to this harsh one by Cecil King, publisher of London's *Daily Mirror:*

> I have to say that, in spite of all your modernization, the American newspaper is the shabbiest product in a land which has shown the world how the best designed and most elegantly finished goods can be produced for the masses. (1967, 19)

King's indictment of U.S. newspapers goes far beyond this generalization about shabbiness into considerable specificity. It is a rather good summary of common criticisms of the American press. Even though King's criticism is from an earlier decade, his words reverberate today. Indictments are heard on every side: about TV programs with no substance, about design and printing quality of newspapers and magazines, about sloppy writing and deficient grammar and spelling—about almost every aspect of the modern American mass media.

My coauthor says that, when we measure American media content against what it *might be,* we are likely to be disappointed. Undoubtedly, if we measure anything against what it might be, we are likely to be disappointed. I think we should be more realistic in our expectations; we should measure American media content against media content in the mass media of other countries and against the media content of past times in American history. If we do, I think we shall see that our media are very good indeed—that they are relatively vigorous, thorough, competent, literate, appealing, and useful. Any American who travels much throughout the world and has a chance to read magazines and newspapers, listen to radio, and view television will recognize that, in spite of weaknesses of American media, the overall media system is quite good. My coauthor feels the American media can only be termed "a major embarrassment." I have found that generally they can be termed a source of pride. I am not thinking about what they *could* be but am considering them in historical and worldwide contexts. Dennis extols the great muckrakers at the turn of the century and finds that modern reporters such as Woodward and

Bernstein come off poorly by comparison. Dennis sees as superior to today's journalism the "good ol' days" of American journalism, when "world-class performers" such as Ida Tarbell and Ray Stannard Baker produced prose and devoted great amounts of time to their projects.

Dennis thinks that American journalism has progressed very little, if at all, since the turn of the century. I accept this view as an opinion, but I have really seen no evidence of the superiority of earlier journalism. Dennis mentions the "strong prose" of earlier journalists like Lincoln Steffens, but which modern journalists are being compared with Steffens? Scotty Reston, George Will, William Buckley, Norman Podhoretz, Nicholas von Hoffman, Tom Wicker? We are not told. We can, of course, pick certain journalists from *any* age and use them to make the case that journalism of that age was superior to another. But this approach is not very convincing.

There was, perhaps, a certain sophistication and low-keyed charm to the journalistic prose of yesteryear. But is that journalism therefore better than today's journalism? You might find examples of good, forceful writing at the turn of the century or during the exciting Civil War period, but you will also find notable examples of sloppy interviewing, gap-filled stories, liberties taken with the facts, instances of fictionalizing, personal reportorial involvement and obvious bias, questionable ethics, and on and on. Certainly the American people were not informed as thoroughly and continuously at earlier periods as they are today. Journalistic quality cannot be limited simply to writing style or "forceful prose" attributed to a small sample of journalists.

From my study of elite newspapers and those aspiring to be high-quality, news-oriented newspapers, both in the United States and abroad, I am convinced that the United States has a sizable group of serious, well-edited newspapers with staffs of considerable sophistication motivated to great public service. I believe that the number of such reputable, qualitative newspapers is larger than ever before. And I know of no other country in the world with such a high proportion of reputable middle-level or mass newspapers. The reader of a daily newspaper in a city of 50,000 in the United States gets at least four times as much news as a counterpart would get in a similar city abroad. The United States has nothing to be ashamed of *generally* (and note that "generally" is part of the proposition for debate) when compared with media in other countries or at other periods.

I invite the reader to take a trip abroad and look at the media situation. Do not just go to Paris, London, Tokyo, Frankfurt, or Zurich. Go to some towns of 10,000 to 20,000. Watch TV. Read the local newspapers. Note the superficiality of news treatment. Notice how few pages the publications have. Compare the information you are getting there with what you would be getting in the United States—wherever in the United States you might be.

Go to a city in an advanced European country such as Switzerland or West Germany; visit a city comparable to Louisville, St. Petersburg, Dallas, or San Jose. See what kind of journalism you are exposed to. You will come away with a more positive feeling toward the media system of the United States. We need to remember that familiarity often breeds contempt and that quaint foreign practices do, indeed, often have undue appeal. This is why foreign media often seem more to our liking (at least in the short run) than do our own media. But it does not take long for an American foreign traveler returning from abroad to realize U.S. media superiority.

In his "challenge" Dennis sets up four criteria for quality performance by the media. Let us briefly look at these four which he has used to conclude that the U.S. media system is an embarrassment:

1. *Attractiveness* (as expressed in design, presentation, and format): Is Dennis's determination that the American media system is of poor quality and getting worse based in any sense on the concept of beauty? If so, he presents no evidence of faulty design, presentation, and format.

2. *Literary style* (as expressed in writing either for print or for electronic media): Is Dennis's determination of low quality really based on evidence of poor literary writing? If so, he presents no evidence of poor writing generally (or even in specific cases). He gives some opinions on certain aspects of this (dealing with muckraking) but really makes no comparisons.

3. *Universal appeal* (in terms of those elements that touch the heart or mind and have a lasting impact): Is the American media system of poor quality, in Dennis's opinion, because it has no elements that "touch the heart or mind and have a lasting impact"? Certainly some "hearts" or "minds" are touched by messages emanating from our media system. Sociologists and psychologists—not to mention pragmatic advertising specialists—would maintain that the American media have as much universal appeal as ever and certainly as much as can be found in the media systems of any other country. No evidence can be found to show that this appeal, even if it is not increasing, is diminishing. For our media system to be getting qualitatively worse, as Dennis contends it is, it would have to show that, among other factors, the universal appeal is diminishing.

4. *Impact* (as seen in the long-term contribution of the material that is produced): Impact of the media, like universal appeal, has evidently been inferred by Dennis and others who hold that this is a determinant of media quality. Certainly no evidence of lack of impact or even of lessening impact, has been given in Dennis's "challenge." I think that almost anyone familiar with the scope and potency of American mass media would be inclined to assume great impact (and even growing impact) by these media. Just what Dennis means by "the long-term contribution of

the material that is produced" is unclear, but I would suggest that "long-term" implies that the contemporary American mass media cannot be faulted in this respect yet. Critics like Dennis will have to wait for the long term to see what contribution today's media material *will* make to society.

Dennis puts good writing very high in his criteria of quality, and he finds the American press deficient. "Good writing," he says, "is the exception, not the rule." I would agree with this, but I would add that it is the exception *everywhere,* not just in American journalism. And only an unrealistic person would expect the best writing to be found in the *mass* media; less than the best writing is almost implied in the mass media concept. It appears to me unfair and unreasonable even to expect consistently good writing in the American press. As is true everywhere, some writing is good, some is not so good, and some is poor. Writing for the mass media is obviously not as consistently good as it could be, but I can just as well say that it is not as consistently bad as it could be either.

Tom Winship, former editor of the *Boston Globe,* is quoted by Dennis to give evidence that writing in the American press is poor. Good writing, says Winship, "is always experimental." Just what does that mean? Would not such a statement simply be based on (have meaning because of) what one means by *experimental?* How is such a statement helpful in identifying good writing? Winship says that journalists need to try new forms, new subjects, new voices, stories written and reported at new distances, and stories that are shorter than usual and longer than usual. When does a "new" form become old? How often do new forms need to come along before the old ones cease being good writing? How do new subjects and new voices determine good writing? How does the distance at which stories are written contribute to quality? Dennis does not let Winship answer such questions, nor does he attempt answers himself.

If media critics are expecting Faulkners and Hemingways to be writing the run-of-the-mill journalistic pieces for print and broadcasting today, they are of course living in a fool's paradise. If this is what they expect, it is easy to see why they think the American media content is generally poor.

What we need in this country are media critics who are realistic in their criticism. It does no good to insist that an impossible "literary" face be given to the American press and that outstanding literary stylists produce the general contents of the country's media. This has never been the case and it never will be. The modern mass media comprise a greedy giant that consumes writing at such a pace that it is logically impossible for the highest literary quality to be generally maintained. This fact would seem to me to be self-evident.

Argument summation: Media content is generally of good quality and getting better.

In spite of much criticism, information about basic and important aspects of society is available in the media. And it is presented in an interesting and understandable way. Exceptions are rare. Admittedly, media messages are aimed at the masses and are not of the highest literary or intellectual quality. However, much so-called journalism is in time anthologized as literature. Media writers are usually well educated and serious about their work. It is unfair to judge American media content, as Dennis does, by what it *might* be. We need to judge it against media content in other countries or against such content in the past. If we do, it looks very good—and it is getting better.

TOPICS FOR DISCUSSION

1. Discuss what you mean by *quality* media content. Does it refer only to message quality? What other aspects of media quality can you think of?

2. Suppose that TV programming is basically "chewing gum for the eyes." Does that refer to poor quality or does it mean that the selection of messages should have been different?

3. Does the mere fact that content is part of mass media automatically make this content poor? Can mass audiences sustain quality media?

4. How is media *message* quality related to media quantity? As media become more prosperous, what is the tendency in the proliferation of quality content?

5. Are newspapers duller and more predictable today than in the American past? Compare a typical U.S. newspaper of today with one at the turn of the century or during the pre–Civil War period.

TOPICS FOR RESEARCH

1. Write an essay defining quality in media content. Who has been involved in this debate? By what standards do they judge media quality—either in information, entertainment, or opinion? Are there different standards of quality for elites versus the mainstream of the population?

2. Discuss the idea of media quality—indicating which standards you are

using—by contrasting an entertainment program on commercial (network) television or cable with one on public television. What conclusions do you draw?

3. Discuss the quality of three major newspapers of contrasting types or approaches, such as the *Wall Street Journal, USA Today, New York Times, Washington Post, Christian Science Monitor,* or others. Evaluate the papers you choose on the basis of quality of content, design, reliability, or other criteria you wish to use. Defend and document your positions.

4. Write a paper on "quality media for the underclass," wherein you indicate how people with limited income can still get quality information, opinion, or entertainment at minimal cost. Are there communication channels from which this part of the population is excluded? Which ones and why?

5. People sometimes refer to the "quality" magazines, meaning publications such as the *Atlantic, Harper's, Smithsonian,* the *New Yorker, Scientific American,* and others. Select a quality magazine and study its content over several months. What sets it apart from other publications with larger circulations and more mass appeal? Does it have a distinctive character and approach? If so, what? What do its advertisements tell you about the audience it is seeking? Do this evaluation systematically, so that you can generalize from your results. Document the work carefully.

FURTHER READING

Bagdikian, Ben. "The American Newspaper Is Neither Record, Telegram, Examiner, Observer, Monitor, Mirror, Journal, Ledger, Bulletin, Register, Chronicle, Gazette, Transcript, Nor Herald of the Day's Events . . . It's Just Bad News." *Esquire,* March 1967.

Barbato, Joseph A. "What Is a Good Newspaper?" *The Quill,* October 1965, pp. 24–25.

Burgoon, Judee, Michael Burgoon, and Charles Atkin. *What Is News? Who Decides and How?* A Report of the Newspaper Readership Project, Michigan State University, 1982.

Curran, James, Michael Gurevitch, and James Woolcott, eds. *Mass Communication and Society.* Beverly Hills, CA: Sage, 1978.

Fiske, John. *Introduction to Communication Studies.* New York: Methuen, 1982.

Gans, Herbert. *Popular Culture and High Culture: An Analysis of Taste and an Evaluation of Taste.* New York: Basic Books, 1974.

Hulteng, J. L. *The News Media: What Makes Them Tick?* Englewood Cliffs, NJ: Prentice Hall, 1979.

King, Cecil H. "An English View of American Newspapers." *Editor & Publisher,* April 29, 1967, pp. 19, 98–99.

Lemert, James. *Criticizing the Media: Empirical Approaches.* Beverly Hills, CA: Sage, 1989.

Luedtke, Kurt. "An Ex-Newsman Hands Down His Indictment of the Press." *The Bulletin of the ASNE,* May–June 1982, pp. 16–18.

Lyons, Louis M. "A Commentary on the Press." *Neiman Reports,* June 1972.

Markel, Lester. "Why the Public Doesn't Trust the Press." *World,* August 15, 1972.

McQuail, Denis. *Media Performance—Mass Communication and the Public Interest.* London: Sage, 1992.

Merrill, J. C. *The Elite Press.* New York: Pitman, 1968.

———. "'Quality' Daily Journalism: An Analytical Discussion." *Gazette* 15, no. 1 (1969):51–56.

Merrill, J. C., and Harold Fisher. *The World's Great Dailies.* New York: Hastings House, 1980.

Methvin, Eugene H. "Mephisthophelean Journalism." *The Quill* 77, no. 4 (April 1989):38–40.

Weber, Ronald. "Journalism, Writing, and American Literature." New York: Gannett Center for Media Studies. Working Paper No. 5, 1987.

Williams, Raymond. *Communications.* Harmondsworth, England: Penguin, 1976.

Winship, Thomas. "The Care and Feeding of Writers." *Nieman Reports* 36, no. 2 (Summer 1982):19–22.

Chapter 9

JOURNALISTIC OBJECTIVITY

If there is a most important tenet of journalistic practice in the United States, it is the concept of objectivity. To some, objectivity does not mean clinical or scientific precision but instead an effort by journalists to produce news stories and newscasts that are emotionally detached and that separate fact from opinion. Objectivity in journalistic practice is often associated with the inverted pyramid news story (news organized in a descending order of importance) and with the 5Ws and H (who, what, where, why, when, and how), or with other systems of sorting out the facts necessary to convey the essence of an event or issue in an orderly fashion.

Objectivity to many means factual reporting, straightforward descriptive presentation. In recent years, though, objectivity as a theory of journalism has also included analytical reporting that goes well beyond simple description. Objectivity is a distinguishing feature of American journalism, especially in comparison with journalistic content in other countries and cultures. At least that is what the proponents of objectivity believe, and it has become the standard wisdom. While some of the world's newspapers engage in polemic and opinionated essays, the U.S. approach generally has been to keep the views of the journalist segregated from the story of an event and to keep factual news on the news pages and opinion on the editorial pages.

Most critics of journalistic objectivity, as well as its defenders, agree that objectivity is a high-minded value. Some see it as a helpful goal; others see it as an unrealistic and even harmful one. Many of the so-called "new" journalists and "existential" journalists scoff at this formulation of objectivity. Still, even they would argue that American journalism generally is journalism without ideology, where method goes far toward dictating factual presentation.

CHALLENGE

Merrill: Journalistic objectivity is not possible.

Many readers may think that my position—that journalistic objectivity is not possible—is like building a straw man and then proceeding to demolish it. They will say that nobody contends that journalistic objectivity is possible, and that such a "debate" simply turns into an exercise of semantic frustration.

First let me say that I sympathize with such a position just attributed to "many readers," but I believe that we cannot ignore such an important journalistic concept. If we did, we would be doing an injustice to a legitimate concern of those who are involved with modern journalism—all of us. Second, many journalists and others talk and write as if they believe in journalistic objectivity. If they do not believe in it, then I propose that they stop using the term.

Perhaps the concept of journalistic objectivity is a straw man to those who seriously think about it, who are sophisticated, and who are realistic about the realities of journalism. But I contend that such persons are not legion and that, generally, laypeople and journalists alike actually think that a news story can be objective or that there are objective reporters out there who can be identified as different from other reporters. Certainly we hear the term used often: "I wish he had written an objective story of that speech" or "Scotty Reston—now *there* was an objective reporter."

Let us consider "objective reporting." It would be reporting that is detached, unprejudiced, unopinionated, uninvolved, unbiased, omniscient—and infallible, I presume. Where do we find this? The objective report would, in effect, match reality; it would tell the truth, the whole truth, and nothing but the truth. Where do we find this kind of reporting? No reporter knows the truth; no reporter can write a story that can match reality, for as the general semanticists like S. I. Hayakawa point out, the "map is not the territory." The story, in other words, is never what it purports to be; it is always much bigger than its verbal image.

All reporters, in addition to being limited in their objectivity by the inadequacy of language, are also *conditioned* by experience, by physical state, by education, and by many other factors. They do not come to their stories as blank slates on which the reality of events is to be written. They may want to be unprejudiced, balanced, thorough, and completely honest in their reporting, but they simply cannot be.

Many believe that reporters are objective when they are *detached* from the event being covered. The problem here, of course, is what is meant by detachment. Detached in the sense of being outside the event being reported? Detached in the sense of being uncommitted to any of the positions involved in the event being reported? Detached in the sense of being uninterested (or disinterested) in the event except as something to be reported? Detached in the sense of holding one's self aloof from the event? Detached in the sense of making sure the reporter's point of view does not impregnate the story?

The obvious answer to all of these questions is that it is really impossible to be detached, that the reporter's subjectivity—values, biases, interpretations, and news judgments—always enter into the production of the story.

Let me briefly mention short remarks by three journalists on this subject; they abjure any pretense of a nonsubjective viewpoint:

David Brinkley: "If I were objective, or if you were objective, or if anyone was, we would have to be put away somewhere in an institution because we'd be some sort of vegetable. Objectivity is impossible to a human being."

Frank Reynolds: "I think your program has to reflect what your basic feelings are. I'll plead guilty to that."

H. L. Mencken: "We talk of objective reporting. There is no such thing. I have been a reporter for many years, and I can tell you that no reporter worth a hoot ever wrote a purely objective story. You get a point of view in it."

These brief opinions are representative of some journalists, but I doubt that very many journalists really would say such things, at least for public consumption. If journalists do not really believe in objective reporting, they should stop talking and writing as if they do. They should talk more about being accurate, about being as thorough as possible, about trying to keep overt or obvious opinions or judgments *of theirs* out of their stories. In other words, they should show that they are really *aware* that "objectivity" in journalism does not exist.

Sociologist Michael Schudson has said in his *Discovering the News* (1978) that journalistic objectivity is a faith in facts and a distrust of values—and a commitment to their segregation. Bernadette Parker-Plummer of the University of Texas believes that most working journalists operationalize objectivity by insisting on *verification* and *attribution.* But this researcher found that there is more rhetoric here than fact. In a study of the *New York Times* and the *Los Angeles Times,* Parker-Plummer noted that there had been a "dramatic increase over time of anonymous sources in the news" (1988, 62). If two of our so-called elite dailies cannot even provide attribution (so as to make verification possible), then there is little meaning left for the concept of objectivity.

So even if we apply a rather measurable and realistic definition to journalistic objectivity, we can see that it is really nonexistent. And when we submit the concept to more challenging epistemological standards, it tends to evaporate altogether.

As Michael Schudson notes, while attribution is valued by the media, it is sometimes compromised because of other factors. For example, the reporter may plead ethical motivation for withholding names of sources (or even principals in the story). I understand this constraint and will even grant that this is a correct action in some cases. But it doesn't change the fact that objectivity suffers because of it (if in fact objectivity could be said to exist in the first place).

Of course there may be some who think that objectivity is possible in journalism, although how they come to such a belief baffles me. They seem to think that if a reporter checks the facts, verifies all statements, eliminates all first-person pronouns, makes an attempt to present "both sides" (as if there were only two sides) of the story, then the story is objective.

The actual state of affairs is this: Every journalist—reporter as well as editorial writer—goes beyond descriptive facts into interpretation. Journalists cannot be objective, even if they would like to be. Every article, every sentence, every newscast, every movement before the camera, every voice inflection on radio is *subjective.* Even the so-called straight news reporter subjectivizes the story, which is always judgmental, value loaded, incomplete, and distorted as to reality. That is the nature of journalism. In fact, that is the nature of *any kind* of communication.

News reporters, even those wanting to be as aloof and neutral as possible, are caught in the natural trap of subjectivity. They involve themselves, their ideas, and their values in the story—even though they may ostensibly (verbally) keep themselves out. They are there nevertheless. They decide what aspects of the story to put in and which to leave out. They decide on the emphasis to be given various parts, which quotes to use, which parts of quotes to use, or whether to use quotes at all. When they paraphrase instead of using direct quotes, they in essence become *translators* and their interpretive powers come into play. Although this reporting is not objective, however, there is really nothing intrinsically wrong with it.

Michael Novak, writing about the journalist and objectivity, makes the following pertinent observations:

> The myth of objectivity leads to . . . misunderstandings in American journalism. There are no facts "out there" apart from human observers. And human observers become not more, but less astute when they try to be neutral. . . .
>
> Reporters and newscasters know that if they aim at objectivity, at presenting "the facts" without editorializing, they run the risk of giving dignity to nonsense, drivel, and outright lies. What really happened in an event is not, they know, discovered by some neu-

tral observation machine, not even by a camera. Events are not events until they are interpreted by human beings. . . . To list statistics, or outwardly observable happenings, or quotations from witnesses, is to give a very narrow view of the human world. It is to offer interpretation and editorial comment of a very misleading sort. Reality does not come divided into "facts" and "interpretation." (1971, 40)

Novak's remarks are in the tradition of other thinkers and critics such as Paul Tillich, Martin Buber, and, in the existentialist camp, Jean-Paul Sartre, who have great respect for subjectivity. They have attacked the emptiness of empirical and pragmatic objectivity beloved by Americans especially. They have said that not only is this belief in objectivity contrary to linguistic philosophy (and they could have said also to the principles of general semantics), but it demeans and devalues the individual and the concept of intersubjectivity.

The business of journalism is subjective from beginning to end, and reporting is no exception. There may be an image of objectivity in some stories—a linguistic aura of objectivity—but behind this aura is the reporter's subjectivity. Reporters are not mindless, soulless automatons who roam about, without values, opinions, and preferences, simply soaking up reality and spouting it out completely. They have their prejudices, their biases, their values, their favorite topics, their heroes, and their villains. We may wish that there were some robotized, completely unbiased and bland reporters who could report "objectively," but they do not exist.

As Donald McDonald said in a seminal article, a reporter's values are necessarily injected into the story.

> The value judgments [the journalist] must make at every critical stage in his investigation and interpretation of the facts must reflect the values he already holds. Again, these values flow from his personal history. They are products of his education, his religious experience, his childhood, family life, social and economic background, friendships and associations, national ties and culture, as well as his emotional life and experiences, and his reason. (1975, 71)

The context in which a story happens cannot be fully reported. But the reporter's inability to explicate the total context keeps a story from being objective. In a story about a political speech, not only the words that a speaker speaks, but how the speaker says those words is part of the story of the speech. What the speaker thinks while speaking is part of the story—a part unavailable to the reporter at the time of the speech. To speculate about it would be "subjective." To leave it out is to fail to be "objective."

Audience reaction, speaker movements, gestures, smiles, and the like form part of the objective story. The *totality* of the story is the true story.

But the reporter cannot give all this truth, so he or she sifts the objective portions of the story through a mental, emotional, and psychological sifter and thereby presents the audience with a necessarily subjective account of "what happened."

Journalists are selective. They are forced by the nature of their craft to select certain facts to report, certain quotations to bring to light, certain individuals to interview, certain perspectives to give, certain aspects of an event to expose. And what happens to the other facts, individuals, perspectives, and aspects in a story? Are not they also part of the objectivity of the story? The answer to the question is that many parts of the story are ignored, or they are slighted, deemphasized, or distorted in some way that keeps them from fulfilling the objectivity of the story.

There may be something that can be called *verifiable journalism.* If as a reporter I write, "John Doe stole six cows from W. H. Arden of Winchester," and if this is indeed what happened, then that sentence is factual and verifiable. That one aspect of the story is true, in the sense that it has no overt errors in it. But when that sentence is put into a context with other sentences to make "a story," then its nonobjective nature is exposed. Then we must begin looking at the story and not just at the sentence.

What are the gaps in the story? What is the totality of the story in the context of reality, and what has it become in its verbal nature in the story? In essence, what happened in reality that is left out in the story? Is there a correlation between the real event and the verbal picture of the event?

Also harming the reportorial objectivity is bias. Many recent commentators (for example, Rothman and Lichter, 1986, and William Rusher, 1988) have criticized the news media for ideological bias in its news presentation. Like-minded others say the press has departed from traditional sentiments and principles of the people and is substantially to the left of most Americans.

Many persons will say that journalistic objectivity is not meant to be total, that partial objectivity is what is really meant by those defending objectivity. When we consider such a "partial" concept, however, we run into trouble immediately: Just how partial can objectivity be? At what point will it cease being objective?

A British provincial editor, Arnold Hadwin of Bradford, has said that total objectivity might well be impossible but that "most people recognize and welcome objectivity that is less than total" (1980, 29). People may welcome *something* that is "less than total" but it is not objectivity. Objectivity *is* total. And one wonders how Mr. Hadwin knows that *most people* recognize and welcome such partial objectivity. Why would people—especially most people—recognize objectivity that is less than total? Is it recognizable in *any degree* less than total? Let's say that I read a news story and say to myself: "I recognize less than total objectivity here." What have I said about objectivity or about the nature of the story?

Nothing—or perhaps that I know that journalism is always less than objective. And if it is *less than objective,* it is *not objective.*

Armand Mattelart, a French Marxist sociologist, calls objectivity the "golden rule of journalistic practice, the cornerstone of its professional deontology, and the equivalent of the Hippocratic oath" (1980, 39). But he does not believe in the concept. He questions it by saying: (1) The concept presupposes on the part of the journalist certain perceptive powers capable of penetrating reality and determining what is important and what is not; (2) the concept postulates that the description of facts (which are *what they are in themselves,* not what the journalist *sees* them to be) goes no further than the facts themselves; and (3) facts are isolated by objectivity-oriented journalism, "cut off from their roots, deprived of the conditions which would explain their occurrence, and detached from the social system which endows them with meaning and in which they possess an intelligible place" (Mattelart, 1980, 39). Many writers excoriate those who, like Mattelart, maintain that journalistic objectivity is a myth. For example, John DeMott, a journalism professor at Memphis State University, speaking at the Defense Information School at Fort Benjamin Harrison, called such people naive, foolish, and lacking in imagination. He even hinted that such persons might be subscribers to Communist theory. But H. L. Mencken took much the same view as Mattelart, and he was certainly no Communist.

Professor DeMott, like many of those who claim to believe in journalistic objectivity, seems to subscribe to a belief in the relativity or the incompleteness of objectivity. He seems to be an absolutist—except when it comes to objectivity; then, he begins using all sorts of modifiers (like *greater* objectivity and *superior* objectivity) to weaken or lessen journalistic objectivity. Tell the whole truth and nothing but the truth, Professor DeMott concluded in his speech: "That's objective reporting—journalistic objectivity, pure and simple." Pure and simple? Good! When I find a journalist who gives the *whole truth* and *nothing but the truth,* I will capitulate and admit that there really is journalistic objectivity after all.

Argument summation: Journalistic objectivity is not possible.

Objectivity may be a worthy goal, but it is unrealizable certainly in regard to the press. In no way can a journalist be detached, unprejudiced, unopinionated, unbiased, and omniscient. The journalist must *select,* organize, and manipulate facts; that is the nature of journalism. From beginning to end, journalism is a *subjective* enterprise. No reporter knows the truth; certainly he or she cannot report it. A story of an event is no more than a partial (and poor) image of the real event out there in reality. Journalists are subjectivists, personally conditioned, and are able to provide audiences no more than superficial maps of the real territory.

RESPONSE

Dennis: Journalistic objectivity is possible.

There is considerable irony in this debate, because the prevailing view of objectivity today—shared by journalists and critics alike and persuasively summarized by John Merrill—was heresy in the 1960s. At that time (and for a thirty- or forty-year period) objectivity was the dominant philosophy that guided most of the nation's newsrooms. Those who criticized objective journalism as a myth that was beyond human capability were hooted down by defensive editors who declared that impartial and balanced reporting could be achieved and that true objectivity was a noble goal.

With great pride, Alan Barth of the *Washington Post* wrote in 1950 that "the tradition of objectivity is one of the principal glories of American journalism." Nineteen years later Herbert Brucker of the *Hartford Courant* agreed, writing: "We can do a good job . . . as long as we keep the flag of objectivity flying high. That will give a more honest and more accurate view of this imperfect world than trusting a latter day Trotsky, or any partisan on any side, to tell us what's what." His essay reviewed some of the reasons that objectivity became an object of scorn and derision. Critics declared that "everyone is subjective and journalists have no magic powers to be otherwise." And almost everyone who had ever taken a psychology course agreed.

Sometimes we forget that objectivity is merely a method and style of presenting information. Its defenders, who led the press out of a sorry period of partisan sensationalism in the 1920s, said it had three principal characteristics:

1. Separating fact from opinion.
2. Presenting an emotionally detached view of the news.
3. Striving for fairness and balance, giving both sides an opportunity to reply in a way that provides full information to the audience.

What is wrong with this straightforward set of goals is that they are too simplistic and assume that complex situations can always be reduced to a balanced presentation with two alternative views. Such an approach leaves little room for ambiguity.

Beyond the underlying philosophical problems associated with objectivity was the operational difficulty in the *inverted pyramid* story, which was the mode by which objective accounts were presented to the public. In its pristine form, objective news reports contain the 5Ws and the H, and they organize information in a descending order of importance. This journalistic style was often criticized as cold and lifeless. It was also said to obscure the truth. It was what the sociologist Gaye

Tuchman called a *strategic ritual,* wherein journalists used four procedures to lay claim to objectivity:

1. Presentation of conflicting possibilities.
2. Presentation of supporting evidence.
3. The judicious use of quotation marks.
4. Structuring information in an appropriate sequence.

Objectivity came under attack most significantly during the 1960s and 1970s when there was a flurry of new journalistic styles and standards. Although some of them were not altogether unknown before, they constituted a journalistic movement that expressed dissatisfaction with the status quo and brought change. At the center of this movement was a vigorous assault on the concept of objectivity. Some of the developments in journalism were these:

1. *The New Journalism*—with writers using such literary devices as extensive description, dialogue, interior monologue, and others previously discouraged by spare-prose 5W editors.

2. *Advocacy journalism*—With its unabashed support for particular issues and causes by journalists opposing the impartial, objective tradition.

3. *Investigative reporting*—which took an adversarial stance and sometimes proposed solutions to problems as it uncovered corruption and moved well beyond the scope of disinterested, stenographic reporting.

4. *Service journalism* or the marketing approach to news—which employed a different definition of news, emphasizing what is commonplace and of interest to the greatest number of people, rather than what is unique and new. With this approach both the selection of material covered and the unity of style aim at identifying closely with the audience. Stories aim at all homeowners, not just unusual ones. This form of journalism (discussed in Chapter 10) relies heavily on market research.

5. *Precision journalism*—which is the use of social science methods, including survey research, as reportorial tools to determine what is happening in the community.

6. *Public journalism*—a journalistic movement (see Chapter 13) that posits that the press should engage citizens and be more of an activist in helping a community set its agenda and seek policy solutions, as opposed to doing impartial reporting.

All of these approaches claimed to be more *objective* than traditional objectivity. New journalists said they provided greater tone, texture, and feeling than in cold, lifeless objective reports. "What we have here," said Tom Wolfe, "is a subjective reality. It is really more objective than traditional reporting." Advocacy journalists also claimed that they came closer to the truth than their more conventional colleagues. "We all have a point of view," they said, "so why not admit it—up front." Journalists all too often presented facts but missed the truth, wrote a 1960s critic, Raymond Mungo. Marketing approach journalists said, "We're giving people what they want. Our news is more pertinent and relevant." And precision journalists added: "We move beyond the limits of intuition. We use computers and statistics to give the most representative picture of the community that is humanly possible within the constraints of a news organization."

In the face of such criticism, support for objectivity crumbled. While much of the criticism of objectivity as it was articulated and understood in the 1950s and 1960s was warranted, I think that it went too far. As is often the case when a prevailing mode of thought is abandoned, those who push the new view feel a need to drive a stake through the heart of the old one. In this case it does us no service. The wave of new styles and reportorial approaches has definitely enriched American journalism, but it is time once again to look carefully at objectivity before abandoning it altogether. Objectivity fell out of favor because it was seen as an impossible goal. Maybe that judgment was too hasty. Objectivity deserves another chance. What is objectivity, anyway? According to *Webster's Third New International Dictionary, objective* means:

> . . . publicly or intersubjectively observable or verifiable, especially by scientific means . . . independent of what is personal or private in our apprehension or feelings . . . of such a nature that rational minds agree in holding it real or true or valid . . . expressing or involving the use of facts without distortion by personal feelings or prejudices.

Is this so wild a dream? No one would argue that journalists can achieve perfection, but is it impossible within the context of human frailty to try to be disinterested, not meaning *uninterested* or *indifferent,* but *impartial?* Is it impossible to observe and report those perceptions so that others can verify them if they choose to do so? Can we not reach some consensus about what is happening in our neighborhoods or communities and still leave room for differing interpretations and speculative views? To all of these questions, I would answer with a resounding "yes."

I believe that journalistic objectivity is possible if we adopt methods that lead to systematic decisions. We can borrow from some of the admirable new styles that have emerged in recent years and use the tools of rational decision making. This need not be a complex scholarly endeavor that is beyond the daily resources of the media, but is a practical strategy that will make journalism better and more reliable. I would do this in three ways: first, through strategic planning in the reporting process; second, through the use of systematic tools to analyze communities and gather information; and third, through the clear delineation of the presentation form used.

STRATEGIC PLANNING

For a number of years American corporations have engaged in strategic planning. Corporate strategies involve an agreed-upon approach, an understanding of the major decision-making points, and a well-calibrated effort to make the best possible choices. The relation of benefit to cost is always a central concern. Practical decisions are made with the expectation that they will yield the best possible results. What we can learn from this approach in journalism is that news gathering and news making involve choices that can be made on a rational basis. They need not be purely subjective. Writer Ronald Buel says that news is essentially data that must be made into a product. This process involves a series of interrelated decisions. (Buel's framework is paraphrased in italics below.)

1. *Data assignment: What is worth covering and why?* This will depend on the type of publication and its purpose. If the purpose of a newspaper is to cover the whole community as adequately as possible, it is not difficult to inventory various components of community life. This categorization may mean moving away from the old beat system that emphasizes what happens in public buildings (the courthouse, etc.) and to consider such issues as lifestyle, the workplace, business, fads and trends, and the environment. Within the paper's particular definition of news, it is not difficult to make rational decisions that can be defined and justified. For example, in the coverage of a political campaign, the paper should be able to explain how it covered various candidates and why some were deemed more important than others. These explanations ought to result in a view of the race with which other observers would concur if given the paper's original assumptions about news. They would also take into account such economic factors as staff size.

2. *Data collection: When has enough information been gathered?* This too is a matter of definition. But there are reasonable standards by which trained reporters know when they have assembled enough information to answer the key questions that make a complete story. Again, outsiders looking in ought to be able to understand the basis for decisions. The test here is whether, within the goals of a particular story, all of the critical questions have been answered with evidence from appropriate sources. This standard of "reasonable completeness" is frequently used in defense against libel suits, and news organizations are increasingly being asked to explain their thresholds for finished work.

3. *Data evaluation: What is important enough to be put into a story?* Once information is gathered, typically only part of it can be included in the story. What part? And why? Sometimes new reporters make a priority list, especially if they are asked to cut a long story to meet the space demands of an editor who cannot accommodate their first submission. This decision ought to be rational. If, for example, a reporter is covering a trial, it is not difficult to list basic facts, key sources, and interpretations. If this

list must be reduced markedly, the real test is what is essential to full and accurate presentation.

4. *Data writing: What words and images will be used?* Good writing means imaginative writing, which involves interpretations that are not always verifiable. Writing adds tone and complexity of perception. Still it is not difficult to write in such a way that the writer's impressions, legitimately expressed, are distinguished from purely factual information. This technique will provide a somewhat subjective portrait, of course, but still it ought to come close to what an average reader might have ascertained had he or she been on the scene. After all, journalists writing for mass media (as opposed to literary or specialized publications) should use words and images that are generally understood.

5. *Data editing: Which story should get a big headline and go on the front page or begin a broadcast, and which stories should be buried, which ones should be changed, and which ones should be cut?* Again, we return to the corporate strategy of the news organization. What is most vital to the audience? Once that is understood, decisions can be made about cutting material or providing emphasis. The underlying policies of media organizations are based on values. For example, news of government may be deemed more important than that of business because it affects more people. Nonetheless, it is important that orderly, consistent decisions be made so that readers have a clear understanding of the rules of the game. Naturally, values always play an important role. It is not possible to have universal answers to the questions raised in the Buel framework for all societies. The appropriate response in Lagos, Nigeria, will not be the same as that in Austin, Texas.

MODE OF PRESENTATION

There are at least three general types of journalistic presentation that ought to be considered.

Descriptive stories can easily be verified. Certain facts are presented and can be corroborated, even if there is disagreement about details.

With analytic stories we can usually inventory possible sources on a given topic. They can be listed and individual views set forth. The reporter brings an interpretive or sense-making perspective to the story, but this can be discerned by anyone who reads the story carefully. Also, if the reporter omits a possible source, the reader should be able to see this omission and evaluate accordingly.

Consequential stories are trickier, but they too can be presented impartially as statements of conjecture and speculation.

Armand Mattelart would no doubt see this process as astoundingly presumptuous, with journalists assuming superhuman powers to penetrate reality. But then, the very act of being a journalist, of presuming to report what is happening, is by definition presumptuous. However, this process is the social function of journalism and it can be done systematically in a manner that withstands examination. The true test is whether reasonable people in the same cultural setting would have similar, if not always the same, perceptions of the event or issue if they had done their own reporting. Certainly a highly trained lawyer will see a trial differently from the average person, but this difference does not negate the fact that mass communication aims at the mass audience and tries to make connections with a norm. The press is the surrogate of the people in our society—it represents them as their eyes and ears—and it has an obligation to present intelligent and understandable reports that give a reasonably representative picture of society. Objectivity in journalism or science does not mean that all decisions do not have underlying values, only that within the rules of the game a systematic attempt is made to achieve an impartial report.

Argument summation: Journalistic objectivity is possible.

Objectivity is merely a method or style of presenting information. During the 1960s and 1970s new styles of journalism led to an assault on objectivity, which fell out of favor as an impossible goal. However, impartiality is not beyond the capabilities of the modern journalist if procedures are followed providing for systematic decisions. This process should include strategic planning in the reporting process, the use of systematic tools to analyze communities and gather information, and clear delineation of the presentation form used. Following such guides would allow the reporters to report impartially on their communities or, at worst, properly distinguish subjective conclusion from fact. The goal should be to present the story so that individuals reading the report would have had the same perspective if they had been present themselves. That objective is not impossible in modern journalism, but it does require a systematic attempt to provide an impartial report.

TOPICS FOR DISCUSSION

1. How can a person—a *subjective* entity—write or present an *objective* story?

2. What do you think most journalists mean by "journalistic objectivity"? According to this meaning, do you think journalists are (or can be) objective?

3. Is it possible to give the truth, the whole truth, and nothing but the truth in a news story? How does truth relate to objectivity?

4. If a reporter refrains from naming a source of a quote in the story, or decides not to give the name of a juvenile offender, can the story be objective?

5. The New Journalism of the 1960s was said by its adherents to be more objective than Associated Press–type journalism. Similar claims are made for public or civic journalism in the 1990s. What do you think they mean? Do you think they are right?

TOPICS FOR RESEARCH

1. Compare and contrast objectivity in science or social science with objectivity in journalism. How do they differ in concept and practice? Indicate how a clinically objective scientific investigation might differ from a report a journalist would call objective. Use specific examples by comparing a research article in *Science Magazine* or some scientific journal with a news report in a publication such as the *Wall Street Journal.* How do the investigators' methods differ? How much evidence is offered? What of interpretation?

2. Write an essay about the concept of fairness. What is it? How is it defined and operationalized in the media? How would you advise laypersons about how they might judge the fairness of the media in covering a particular story or event? Assess, if you like, two or three different accounts of the same event from a standpoint of fairness.

3. Discuss advocacy journalism. What is it? How does it differ from objective journalism?

4. Write a personal essay about how you would try to be objective (if indeed you would) in gathering information about any controversial subject you choose. Be specific and indicate how you would decide which sources to contact, which to quote, how to sum up.

5. Write an essay that takes the middle ground somewhere between Merrill and Dennis on objectivity. Assume that both are giving you their best-case advocacy position. On what points do you agree, disagree?

FURTHER READING

Cohen, Stanley, and Jock Young, eds. *The Manufacture of News.* Beverly Hills, CA: Sage, 1973.

DeFleur, M. L., and E. E. Dennis. *Understanding Mass Communication.* 5th ed., 2d printing. Boston: Houghton Mifflin, 1996.

Epstein, Edward Jay. *Between Fact and Fiction: The Problem of Journalism.* New York: Vintage Books, 1975.

Gans, Herbert. *Deciding What's News.* New York: Pantheon, 1979.

Hadwin, Arnold. "Objectivity Is Crucial—But Is It Possible to Be Objective?" *Journalism Studies Review* (Cardiff, Wales: July 1980).

Hayakawa, S. I. *Language in Thought and Action.* 5th ed. New York: Harcourt Brace Jovanovich, 1990.

Hunt, Todd. "Beyond the Journalistic Event: The Changing Concept of News." *Mass Communication Review* 1 (April 1974):23–30.

Korzybski, Alfred. *Science and Sanity.* Lancaster, PA: Science Press Printing Co., 1933.

Lichter, S. R., S. Rothman, and L. Lichter. *The Media Elite.* Bethesda, MD: Adler & Adler, 1986.

Manoff, Robert Karl, and Michael Schudson, eds. *Reading the News.* New York: Pantheon, 1986.

Mattelart, Armand. *Mass Media, Ideologies, and the Revolutionary Movement.* Atlantic Highlands, NJ: Humanities Press, 1980. See especially discussion of objectivity, pp. 37 ff.

McDonald, Donald. "Is Objectivity Possible?" In *Ethics and the Press,* J. C. Merrill and Ralph Barney, eds., 69–72. New York: Hastings House, 1975.

Merrill, J. C. *The Imperative of Freedom.* New York: Freedom House, 1994.

Merritt, Davis. *Public Journalism and Public Life: Why Telling the News Is Not Enough.* Hillsdale, NJ: Lawrence Erlbaum, 1995.

Novak, Michael. *The Experience of Nothingness.* New York: Harper Colophon Books, 1971. See especially discussion of objectivity, pp. 37–40.

Roshco, Bernard. *Newsmaking.* Chicago: University of Chicago Press, 1975.

Rubin, Bernard. *Media, Politics, and Democracy.* New York: Oxford University Press, 1977. See especially Chapter 1.

Rusher, W. A. *The Coming Battle for the Media.* New York: William Morrow, 1988.

Schudson, Michael. *Discovering the News.* Cambridge, MA: Harvard University Press, 1978.

Tuchman, Gaye. "Objectivity as Strategic Ritual: An Examination of Newsmen's Notions of Objectivity." *American Journal of Sociology* 77, no. 4 (January 1972):660–67.

Chapter **10**

DECIDING WHAT IS NEWS

What is sometimes called the *news-making process* is the result of a daily bargaining process between various personnel in newspapers and broadcast stations. Editors look at the world they cover with particular standards and measures. They attempt to direct reporters to cover the most interesting, newsworthy material. There are some generally accepted definitions of news, and these provide the justification for what appears in the newspaper and on the newscasts. But many competing forces want space in the news columns and on newscasts. Some are self-serving, external persons who want their stories told sympathetically and well; others are reporters who want their work in the paper; still others are subtle influences ranging from values and habits to personal preferences.

A standard view is that, at the bottom line, news is determined by od itors and that editors' (or other gatekeepers') judgments should, in fact, decide what is news. There can be no mechanical standard, it is said, because the news of the day is dynamic and its results are uncertain. Therefore the well-trained editor or news director makes judgments reflecting prevailing journalistic practices and the specific needs of the audience as perceived by upper management. This, it is further stated, is the essence of journalistic (and other media) leadership. It is, after all, the job of editors to edit.

CHALLENGE

Dennis: Market forces, not editors' judgments, should decide what is news.

There is a long-standing debate among media professionals and media critics about what news is and who should make decisions about it. Editors and reporters say with much assurance that they and they alone should determine what will and will not appear in the news columns and on newscasts. Some critics of the press, for example people in business, say that the sources of news, those quoted in stories or covered in some fashion, should have a role in defining and shaping the news. In actuality, news decisions are made by journalistic professionals with little guidance from anyone, no matter how much their detractors may complain. This situation is changing, though, as intuitive judgments are being challenged more and more by market forces, which we learn about most effectively through market research. In my view, this change is good, and I hope that before long many of today's smug, all-knowing editors will replace their seat-of-the-pants (or skirt) decisions with more thoughtful, better-researched, systematic decision making. To such persons, this position is heresy, of course.

For as long as anyone can remember, editors (with the help of various minions) have decided what will grace the pages of newspapers and appear on newscasts. They have engaged in a hard selection process, elevating some items to importance and public exposure while relegating others to the wastebasket. Editors are hired to make these judgments, and for the most part they do so with the best of intentions. But how are these judgments made and are they the right ones? Against what set of criteria are news items and stories selected? On what basis are others deemed unworthy of coverage?

Most editors would tell you that they make their choices from among those news stories that they assign or that flow in from their regular channels (such as wire services), and they do so with proper regard for their audience. They would also tell you that they rely heavily on the "budgets" of the wire services (priority lists of stories deemed important or significant), as well as take cues from such major national media as the *New York Times, Washington Post,* and the three major television networks. What will interest the audience is of paramount importance, for, after all, if readers and viewers are not attentive, newspaper circulations may drop and broadcast ratings may falter. This situation would push revenues down and the editor might be fired or see the paper die.

It came as a surprise to many editors when in 1947 the Hutchins Commission on Freedom of the Press, a privately funded, blue-ribbon group that evaluated the news media, suggested that the media were failing to give readers a representative account of the day's news, let alone present a "representative picture" of the constituent groups of society. As with most media criticism, however just, editors rejected these ideas wholesale. The issue raised by the Commission, however, continues to raise its head at professional meetings and in scholarly critiques of the media. The definition of news is the subject of much wrangling—and for good reason. I believe that a new approach to news decision making is needed more than ever.

1. News is a highly complex formulation that requires the best intelligence and a thoughtful strategy for professionals to fashion it properly.

2. Editors and reporters are elitists, unrepresentative of their readers and viewers and unable to act effectively on their behalf.

3. A marketing approach to news is the most effective and efficient way to select and present news that is of interest to and pertinent for the audience. In such a system, market research findings, which indicate reader and viewer preferences, are used to decide news.

Ask journalism students if they know what news is and they will tell you, "Yes, of course." Ask them to define it and confusion sets in. News is difficult to define, a fact that explains why there is a lively continuing debate among many persons trying to sort it out. All kinds of people—journalists, sociologists, political scientists, news sources, and others—have engaged in this exercise. It is more than a theoretical discussion because knowing and understanding what news is can have real payoffs. Imagine the political candidate whose idea of news differs radically from that of the local editor. The candidate is likely to be a defeated candidate if that view persists. The same is true for others who want to place something in the news.

In a rather scornful view of news, Henry David Thoreau once wrote:

> I am sure that I have never read any memorable news in a newspaper. If we read of one man robbed, or murdered, or killed by accident, or one house burned, or one vessel wrecked, or one steamboat blown up, or one cow run over on the Western Railroad, or one mad dog killed, or one lot of grasshoppers in the winter—we never need read of another. If you are acquainted with the principle, what do you care for myriad instances and applications? To a philosopher all news, as it is called, is gossip, and they who read it or edit it are old women over their tea. (1854, 148–49)

Thoreau clearly identifies some of the negative characteristics of news. Some commentators have tried to explain the difference between facts, truth, and news with less than full success. Walter Lippmann once wrote that "news is not a mirror of social conditions, but the report of an aspect that has obtruded itself." One famous definition of news is attributed to John Bogart of the *New York Sun,* who allegedly said in 1880, "When a dog bites a man, that is not news, but if a man bites a dog, that is news!" Newscaster David Brinkley would seem to agree: "News," he said, "is the unusual, the unexpected. Placidity is not news. If an airplane departs on time, it isn't news. If it crashes, regrettably, it is."

Some of the standard criteria that are said to make up the news are the following:

1. Conflict (tension-surprise)
2. Progress (triumph-achievement)
3. Disaster (defeat-destruction)
4. Consequences (effect upon community)
5. Eminence (prominence)
6. Novelty (the unusual, even the extremely unusual)
7. Human interest (emotional background)
8. Timeliness (freshness and newness)
9. Proximity (local appeal)

Sociologist and distinguished analyst of the news Bernard Roshco says that all news has a dual origin. It is a *social* product that represents an effort to make sense out of what is happening in society, and it is an *organizational* product representing what the news organization decides to do with it.

After reading scores of articles and treatises on news, Melvin DeFleur and I came up with this definition that reflects some of the factors that go into news:

> News is a report that presents a contemporary view of reality with regard to a specific issue, event, or process. It usually monitors change that is important to individuals or society and puts that change in the context of what is common or characteristic. It is shaped by a consensus about what will interest the audience and by constraints from outside and inside the organization. It is the result of a daily bargaining game within the news organization that sorts out the observed human events of a particular time period to create a very perishable product. News is the imperfect result of hurried decisions made under pressure. (DeFleur and Dennis, 1996, 446)

This is not to suggest that a definition of news changes daily. There is considerable consistency over time as to what editors deem newsworthy; the similarity (some would say sameness) of our newspapers and newscasts suggests considerable agreement about what news is, under most conditions.

One aspect of what constitutes news is to be found, then, in the external events that await report. In addition, the consideration of what is news depends partly on the audience to whom it is directed. The journalist and the editor are supposedly acting as and on behalf of "everyperson" in deciding what is worth reporting. It is said that they have a built-in understanding of their readers and viewers if they are any good in their jobs; after all, readers and viewers are the journalists' next door neighbors, friends, companions at sports. While this vision of the journalist may be true in very small communities, however, for the most part it is far from the mark. Editors and reporters are part of an elite. They simply are not like most of the citizens of the community. They are better educated, more liberal politically, less religious, and more likely to be single, to live in an apartment (as opposed to a single-family dwelling), and to have both social and cultural values quite distant from those of others around them. National studies have documented this condition for a number of years, drawing a portrait of journalists as relatively isolated from and out of touch with their communities. As one reporter was quoted in a 1982 study:

> It is an inherent problem; inbred newspapers don't trust the people they are writing about. . . . Especially the younger reporters are getting removed from society. They come from different backgrounds than the average public. [Theirs is] a snobbish view of the world. (Burgoon, Burgoon, and Atkin, 1982, 5)

That study, based on a national survey conducted for the American Society of Newspaper Editors, went on to say that journalists underestimate reader intelligence, have a poor understanding of what people will actually read, and simply do not comprehend the role of television in delivering news to people who also read newspapers. The report was a stinging indictment of the press that was not out of line with a more impressionistic speech by Kurt Luedtke, mentioned earlier in this book. Luedtke charges that his former colleagues in the media suffer from the twin perils of "arrogance and irrelevance." Arrogance keeps them unpleasantly off the track with readers; irrelevance could spell doom in an era when other information sources (data banks provided by cable systems or the telephone company) can supply much of the factual information (sports scores, weather reports) that people now gain from newspaper and television news. There are a number of steps that editors and reporters can take to get and stay in touch with their communities, but nothing will change the inevitable. Journalists will continue to be elitists, continue to be unlike their readers and viewers.

A marketing approach to news makes news decisions less of a guessing game and more of a thoughtful, systematic process that takes into account the interests and needs of the audience. The marketing approach to news is nothing new. In fact in the 1970s, when newspaper circulations were sliding downward, a national Newspaper Readership Project—

which has been written about in many books on newspapers and news reports such as Leo Bogart's *The Press and the Public* (1989) and *Preserving the Press* (1991)—collected data about reader interests, preferences, and reading habits. As a result many American newspapers changed their formats radically, offering special sections on lifestyles, neighborhoods, and entertainment. News was packaged differently, with livelier design and more vivid writing. For example, a news story on a zoning ordinance would begin by suggesting the consequences of the news story for potential homeowners, rather than simply summarizing the action of the zoning board in a procedural manner. The story would likely be presented with striking photos or line drawings and readable, attractive headlines.

The marketing approach to news depends on a regular and accurate flow of statistical data about the audience. The data are then used as one factor, a central one, in determining what will be offered to the audience and in what manner. News is matched to the interests and potential interests of that audience. Some critics have called this approach "soft and sexy in the afternoon," suggesting that a marketing approach must always emphasize soft news rather than important news of public affairs. The best papers using the marketing approach, however, have an effective blend of editorial leadership, wherein professional journalists make news selections and prepare material with strategies for reaching the reader. Those strategies depend largely on marketing research data. This process is not a mindless one whereby journalists succumb to cold statistics while ignoring professional ethics and a desire to be complete in their coverage of a community issue or problem. Information is a calibrating tool that, when used by intelligent people, can result in a higher-quality product. Market information gives news organizations a continuous source of feedback from their readers and viewers, something that is lacking in many places today.

Any discussion of the marketing approach to news naturally revives the old debate of whether the press should give readers what they want or provide leadership that gives citizens what they need. I believe that the two are not incompatible, that the public is ultimately better served if market information plays a more important role in guiding editors' decisions. If today's newspapers and television stations guided mainly by intuition are so far out of touch, it is worth making our best effort to bridge the gap. Market information, intelligently used, will do it.

Argument summation: Market forces, not editors' judgments, should decide what is news.

Editors have too much control over selecting what news to present to the public. Selection emphasizes the editors' personal biases and fails to give a representative account of the day's news. Since news is difficult to define and numerous perspectives exist on what actually is news, it is preferable to have news selection determined by market forces, which give a broader account of events rather than relying on an editor's preferences alone. Research shows that editors tend to be part of an isolated elite and that this lack of interaction with and understanding of the public results in poor decisions about what is news. A marketing approach focuses instead upon a regular and accurate flow of statistical data about the audience. This systematic criterion based on market forces is preferable because it relies on the interests and needs of the audience in defining "news."

RESPONSE

Merrill: Editors' judgments, not market forces, should decide what is news.

Unfortunately perhaps, my coauthor has challenged a proposition that is not contradictory to what he is advocating. What Dennis seems to be saying, though he only gets to it in the last several paragraphs of his essay, is that news should be determined by a regular and accurate study of audience desires. In this view, the audience and not the editor determines what is news. The editor, in the Dennis perspective of news, is consigned to a mechanistic role in which he or she serves as a short-order cook preparing only what the customer orders. This is harsh pragmatism, crass capitalism carried too far, in my opinion.

The marketing approach to news relegates the press to a powerless dispenser of desired services. Editors take on a strange role; they do not make decisions but only grant requests. They do not determine what their audiences need or should have; rather they provide the news that the audiences—the real editors in the marketing approach—say they want. In effect, if Dennis's concept of editorial leadership were taken very far, journalism would become a passive and uninspiring vocation.

Now Dennis realizes this danger, and he tries to moderate his advocacy of the marketing approach to news by conceding that the "best papers using the marketing approach, however, have an effective blend of editorial leadership, wherein professional journalists make news selections and prepare material with strategies for reaching the reader." In other words, Dennis would have editorial leadership, while editors follow the dictates of audience research. He wants it both ways.

If this is the case, then I have very little to argue against. For I agree that market forces enter into the editor's decisions about news. Any American journalist who has ever dealt with determining what news is and how to play it has recognized the natural symbiosis between editorial decision making and audience desires. Only the most naive person would think that the editor's judgment and the audience's preferences are mutually exclusive.

I am arguing that the editor (or some journalistic decision maker) should decide what is news. He or she may do this while either taking audience desires into consideration or simply ignoring what he or she believes to be the will of the audience. In other words, market forces may or may not enter into the determination of news. I see news as an editorial matter, not a public matter. This is the main business of the editor: determining what news is and how it shall be played.

No editor has ever ignored the audience, so in that sense at least, editorial determination of news has always taken market forces into consideration. But editors have generally prided themselves on their own ability to recognize and determine news. They have seen themselves as independent decision makers in journalism and not simply reactors to their audiences. I feel that they have been justified in this image of themselves. Anybody who has worked for a news medium knows full well that the great majority of news decisions are made by journalists without evidence of what the audience wants. News is determined quickly, stories are selected from the many available without too much deliberation, and journalists make these determinations almost instinctively. They certainly do not have the luxury of holding various stories in abeyance until they can survey their readers to find out which of the stories might be desired. The pragmatics of journalism militates against the marketing approach to news.

This approach does not mean that the reasonable news executive does not have some general guidelines for news based on inferences drawn over time from the audience. My coauthor has already presented some of the standard criteria that help determine news—and, of course, these criteria did not suddenly leap full-grown from the editor's head. Over the years, journalists came to the conclusion that *generally* these were criteria that were agreeable to news consumers. So the editors did have some overall, long-range guidelines for news, but on a daily, decision-by-decision basis they made their own determinations as to what would be news in their media.

As Dennis says in his "challenge," all of this brings up the old debate of whether the press should give readers what they want or what they need. I believe that the press should give readers what the editors think they want and what they need. This is, really, what the press does. What the people want can also be what they need. What they need may not, however, be what they want—that is, unless they are made somehow to realize that there are some things they need that they have not thought about needing.

A good editor is one who recognizes that it is a journalistic responsibility to provide the reader with some significant, useful news which may or may not be of great immediate interest or appeal; at the same time, editors know that, in order to get the reader exposed to such news, they must also provide types of news of a shallower—perhaps even sensational—nature. The good editor is a pragmatist and a realist, not a one-dimensional person seeking either to entertain or to educate. The good editor wants to do both and other things as well. But in addition to being a realist, the editor is something of an idealist also, believing that readers should get certain information that they might not choose if given the chance. In this sense the editor is much like an educator.

Editors may very well use marketing information for some of their decisions. Certainly they have access today to a considerable amount of such information. They may, however, decide not to use marketing data for their news determinations; in fact, they generally do not. They use intuition, instinct, and perceptions of news value stemming from experience and common sense. They often project their own likes and dislikes about news to their readers. This may not be scientific, but it is useful and quick—and it works very well. An editor is a kind of one-person sample, projecting to the newspaper his or her own news values. As such, the editor can retain at least the illusion of independent editorial news determination while taking into consideration the assumed interests and desires of the audience.

Perhaps the philosophical rationale for audience-determined news is the same one that has resulted in a shift in several areas from an emphasis on the press to an emphasis on the public. Examples: increasing talk about "public access to the media" and the "public's right to know." Now we have people talking about the "public's right to determine what is news." Granted, the public (nonjournalists) can consider anything it desires to be news. As a member of the general public I have a right to determine what I want to call news, and I can press this information on to whomever I wish. But in the context of *journalism* such determination is up to journalists, not members of the public.

Said another way, as a private citizen I have the right to make home movies and to show them to anyone who will watch. But I do not have a right to determine for a cinema owner or a television director that my home movies will be shown in their facilities. In effect, I *can* indeed determine what I want to consider a "movie," but this does not and should not imply that I will determine what is to be shown as a movie through the mass media. Doing this is the prerogative of the media decision makers. Market forces, of course, must be taken into consideration, for no medium of mass communication is an island. But news determination, like movie determination, lies with the disseminating medium.

Only a stupid or unrealistic editor would continue providing readers with news that was not wanted or read by these readers. In fact, the newspaper would not exist very long if this were done. So it can be assumed that, in the case of viable newspapers, the editors are taking the news values of the readers seriously. However, they are not being dictated to by the readers; they can and often do go against the wishes of the readers. Admittedly, many journalistic news determiners do bow to the wishes of segments of their readership; this pandering often results in shallow, largely sensational material with negative overtones being the main news fare. Some editors do indeed stoop to the lowest common denominator.

But the question here is whether this *should* be the case. Should market forces determine the news? My answer is: No! An editor or any journalist responsible for news judgments should make news decisions. This is the nature of journalism. This is the job of journalists as long as they, not nonjournalists, are in the business of news collection, definition, and dissemination.

Argument summation: Editors' judgments, not market forces, should decide what is news.

In a free-press nation like the United States, market forces, advertisers, government, and other institutions naturally have their impact on news, but the media managers should determine what to publish or broadcast. That is the essence of press freedom in America. Obviously editors will take audience desires into consideration (when they know what they are), but these desires should not determine news decisions in a microscopic sense. The daily pragmatic nature of journalism militates against the marketing approach to news. News ebbs and flows rapidly, and only journalists can make decisions as to how it is to be handled.

TOPICS FOR DISCUSSION

1. How can market research be used in the everyday newsroom decisions about news?

2. The marketing approach depends on a regular flow of statistics about the audience. Editorial staffers on a daily newspaper, therefore, would have to get this data constantly. Is accomplishing this possible? If they are successful in doing so, how might a publication's basic editorial policy be affected?

3. If editors gave over their news determination right to the audience surveyors, would they lapse into being mere functionaries with no decision-making responsibilities? How would their jobs change?

4. Would a market research approach to news constitute a new people's right—the right to define news—and would such a right be consistent with traditional American journalism?

5. What might be a good compromise position in news determination? How would it work? It is different from what is presently done?

TOPICS FOR RESEARCH

1. Examine the proposition that editors should be quite conscious of their audience and target their work for the people who read, listen to, or view their reports. What role should the audience play in shaping the news?

2. Write a short paper on audience research in broadcasting or newspapers. What role does it play? How does it measure the relative health of a given medium?

3. What impact do ratings have on television news? Research this question by looking at the discussion in recent years involving people meters. Does the audience data yielded by people meters tell us anything about the demographics of the audience that will likely influence the news on television?

4. Discuss news decision making, consulting major books and studies on this subject. Can editors exercise professional standards and still please the audience?

5. Examine yourself as a consumer of news. If you could design your own paper tailored to your personal tastes and interests, what would it contain? What would it look like? Assume that you can create a new publication from scratch and select bits and pieces of several existing papers to create your personalized product. Discuss whether your paper would appeal to others. To whom would it appeal? Do you think there is enough of a market for it to create a niche?

FURTHER READING

Argyris, Chris. *Behind the Front Page: Organizational Self-Renewal in a Metropolitan Newspaper.* San Francisco: Jossey-Bass, 1974.

Bogart, Leo. *Preserving the Press.* New York: Columbia University Press, 1991.

———. *The Press and the Public: Who Reads What, When, Where and Why in American Newspapers.* Hillsdale, NJ: Lawrence Erlbaum, 1989.

Burgoon, Judee, Michael Burgoon, and Charles Atkin. *What Is News? Who*

Decides? And How? A report of the American Society of Newspaper Editors. East Lansing: Michigan State University, 1982.

Carey, James W. *Communication in Culture: Essays on Media and Society.* Winchester, MA: Unwin Hyman, 1988.

DeFleur, Melvin L., and Everette E. Dennis. *Understanding Mass Communication.* 5th ed. Boston: Houghton Mifflin, 1996.

Dennis, Everette E. *The Media Society: Evidence About Mass Communication in America.* Dubuque, IA: W. C. Brown, 1978. See especially Part II, "Looking Inside: The Media's Social Institutions."

Gans, Herbert. *Deciding What's News.* New York: Pantheon, 1979.

Gitlin, Todd. *The Whole World Is Watching: Mass Media in the Making and Unmaking of the New Left.* Berkeley: University of California Press, 1980.

Sigal, Leon V. *Officials and Reporters: The Organization and Politics of Newsmaking.* Lexington, MA: D. C. Heath, 1973.

Thoreau, Henry David. *Walden, Or Life in the Woods.* Boston: Houghton Mifflin, 1854.

Chapter **11**

NEWS-GATHERING TACTICS

Deeply rooted in American journalism is the notion of the journalistic reporter. Reporters are trained in the journalistic method, which gives them the tools and wherewithal to cover almost any situation they may confront. Essentially journalistic training means knowing how to gather the news—how to sift through documents, do background research, interview sources, and so on—and how to write a story using the usual news and feature forms employed by newspapers and broadcast outlets.

In the midst of this seemingly routine task, however, come all kinds of ethical issues (tactical decisions) including "checkbook journalism," fabrication of sources, false identification, and lying. Some of these issues, being topical, come and go. But many are recurrent.

As with news gathering methods and writing methods, competent reporters and editors are expected to handle tactical or ethical dilemmas. But do these problems require precise and differing tactics for different situations, or should responses be based on *consistent and universal* standards? While such questions are regarded as worthy of discussion, most reporters believe that they have somehow internalized professional values and competencies that will help them resolve any problems that may occur.

CHALLENGE

Merrill: News-gathering tactics should be situational and relative.

We come now to discuss a very real and important everyday concern of journalists: reportorial tactics, journalistic ways and means of gathering and writing stories. Should these tactics be situational and relative or should they be, as Everette Dennis will argue later, consistent and universal? I maintain that they are situational and relative; even more, I insist that they *should* be situational and relative. This position, of course, gets us into the realm of ethics.

Opposing my view is a considerable theoretical tradition in this country, even if it fails to manifest itself in common practice. It is safe to say that an accepted truth in American journalism is that journalists should be consistent in their methods and their actions: They should all subscribe to universal standards and should, if they are responsible and "professional," have a profound respect for predictable and consistent practice. Consistency and predictability, we are led to believe, are foundation stones of professionalism.

Unpredictability, on the other hand, is associated with amateurism, inconsistency, and relativity, which are seen by many as deleterious to journalism, harmful to the journalist, and frustrating to the audience. I would maintain just the opposite: that consistency in journalism—the journalist always using the same tactics and dealing with the elements of the story in the same way—makes for a deadly dull journalism, keeps the individual journalist from full self-realization, and prevents the audience from being exposed to the multifaceted, rich, and diversified aspects of similar (but different) stories.

Perhaps it is more comfortable and satisfying for journalists to have hard-and-fast rules as to tactics of reporting. This proposition seems reasonable, but I cannot believe that it is in the best interest of the newsperson or the public to have the press tied to an absolute tactical system. Most printed codes of ethics fail because they present absolute rules or standards (or because they are so fuzzily written that they in essence say nothing meaningful). But perhaps their failure is, paradoxically, a good thing—for such failure ensures that tactical situationalism and relativism will thrive in the absence of absolute ethical codes.

Ethics, of course, is very closely related to the subject of journalistic tactics. One cannot really separate them. Should I lie, either while getting a story or while telling the story to my readers or listeners? Should I reveal the source of certain statements or quotes that I use in my story? Should I give my readers or listeners all of the information that I have collected and verified?

CHAPTER 11. NEWS-GATHERING TACTICS

Here are just a sampling of questions that are both ethical and tactical:

Should I *ever* lie as a reporter in order to get a story?

Should I *always* reveal my sources? (Or *never* reveal them?)

Shall I try to ascertain the *whole truth* (as much of it as I can) for my audience?

Here we have introduced the possibility of tactical consistency or absoluteness. Such consistency has a notable appeal. If I am going to reveal the source in one case, why should I not reveal all sources? If I am going to lie in one case, why not in all? If I am going to withhold part of a story in one case, what would be wrong with withholding parts from any story?

Let me give an example of each of the two tactical positions:

1. Absolute: *Always* ascertain the names of victims of all crimes.

2. Relativistic: Ascertain the names of victims in *some* crimes but not in others.

The first tactic (the absolute) does indeed simplify the journalist's decision making. If this tactic is accepted, all that has to be done is to identify all victims—juveniles, the mentally ill, rape victims, and so on. The second tactic (the situational) is more difficult because it forces the reporter to discriminate, to think. The reporter must see distinctions and think about consequences; in short, the reporter must decide that it is not only all right but good journalism to make exceptions—to have double standards, if you will.

The reporter who is situational recognizes that there is a very important difference between a rape victim, for example, and a murder victim. Naming a rape victim can bring mental and emotional harm to the victim; naming a murder victim cannot harm the victim at all. The thinking reporter understands that the naming of a nine-year-old boy for shooting his father is quite different (in psychological if not in legal terms) from the naming of a thirty-nine-year-old adult for shooting his father. The reporter believes that it is his or her duty to make certain editorial decisions impinging on what is and is not published. After all, the reporter reasons, editorial decision is the nature of journalism: selection among facts is made to some degree in *every* story written.

I contend that a reporter must play this tactical game rather loosely—that he or she must not strive for consistency in tactics but must consider the specific circumstance. In short, the reporter (to be effective and in many cases to be ethical too) must determine not to be absolute and consistent, but rather to be situational and relative.

A reporter cannot subscribe to a tactic of always revealing a source, even if the reporter does maintain that the people have a right to know. In some cases, to reveal sources would be counterproductive as well as unethical. For example, the journalist may get information from a source who would be in great physical danger if his or her identity were known. The reporter not only wants to keep the source operative for another day, but also wants to avoid endangering the individual's life. In similar cases, the reporter might want to keep the source from losing his or her job.

Suppose a reporter writing a rape story has the name of the person arrested on suspicion of committing the rape and also has ascertained the name of the rape victim. The reporter decides not to use the victim's name but does not hesitate to use the suspected rapist's name. Inconsistent? Yes. This is, in effect, withholding information from the reader while at the same time providing the name of another person connected with the case—even though this person may not have committed the rape. The reporter feels no qualms about this inconsistent procedure, reasoning that in this case it is tactically prudent. The reporter justifies withholding verified information from the reader on ethical grounds, on a consideration of possible consequences to the victim.

The reporter in the hypothetical rape case certainly does not subscribe to a *universal* tactic. In a universal tactic, the reporter is obligated to report all the facts that he or she has, that are verified, that are pertinent to the story. Period. In this rape story, certainly the name of the rape victim is *pertinent to the story,* as we will be told by our absolutist reporter. After all, the reporter has found out who the woman is; therefore, should not the name be given, especially since the name of the rape suspect has been used?

Let me reply to this question with another question: Why *should* the reporter name all the names? The reporter is wise to subscribe to relativistic tactics, to play the story the way he or she wants to play it after consideration of possible consequences. Why should the reporter subscribe to the same tactics in every story? Straitjacketing oneself does not ensure better reportage. In fact, a relativistic tactical program is what is called for. Consider each story. Consider the ramifications of each story. Consider the importance of the story. Consider consequences or implications for certain persons in the story.

It may well be that when a reporter considers the importance to the public of a particular story, he or she will realize that normal tactics must be modified. A reporter may decide that the story is important enough, for example, to steal files (or at least to make copies of papers and return the files). A reporter may even feel that in a particular case there is justification to pose as someone else. The reporter might decide to eavesdrop on certain conversations and report on them, using or perhaps not using the names of those who spoke. A reporter might decide to bug a room or wiretap a telephone in order to get important information that the public should know. A reporter might tell a potential source that the reporter has heard certain things from someone else (which he or she really has not heard) in order to get a response. A reporter might decide to make up quotes and drop them into a story so as to prompt someone connected

CHAPTER 11. NEWS-GATHERING TACTICS

with the story to come forward to refute or to enlarge on the speculated or fabricated quotes.

We can justify these tactics by resorting to the "ends justifies the means" argument. We can say that we are thinking of the public's right to know. How can the public know unless we break through the barriers of secrecy with our situational tactics? Journalists thus must resort to these tactics *from time to time* in order to do their job, to live up to their responsibilities.

We can justify relativistic or situation tactics by contending that they are more ethical; we can also justify them pragmatically by saying that they are needed to accomplish our ends. In any case, in a country with a free press it is the right of a newspaper reporter to be inconsistent. If the reporter wants to reveal the source of a quote in one story and not in another, that is his or her right. In fact, if the reporter wants to reveal the source of a quotation in one part of a story and make all the other quotes in the same story anonymous, that is his or her right. Depending on the situation, there might be good reasons for:

Using the 5W lead in one story but not in another.

Using only indirect quotations in one story and using direct quotations or a mixture of indirect and direct quotes in another.

Giving the addresses of persons in one story and omitting addresses in another.

Going directly to persons for information in one story but going to someone for second-hand information in another or using old information from the files.

Giving certain personal data (such as age, race, occupation) about some persons in some stories but not about other persons.

What is the alternative to these inconsistent tactics? Consistent and universal tactics, we are told. The intelligent and dedicated reporter can only scoff at such an alternative, seeing it as a voluntary placement of the reporter in a straitjacket with little chance to achieve a primary goal of journalism: obtaining the story.

Why, asks the dedicated reporter, should I *never* deviate from a kind of traditional tactical program? If the normal tactics will not work, why not use others that will work? I may *usually* want to give sources of information in my story, but why must I always give them? I may *usually* want to avoid deceiving a person to get information, but why not deceive when I feel the issue is important enough to warrant deception? I may *usually* want to identify myself as a reporter, but there will be times when I need either to hide my identity or to pass myself off as someone else. I may *usually* want to get my interviews free as part of a news story, but why should I not pay someone for an interview if I feel my news medium wants it or that it is important to the public?

In short, I am not wise or very sophisticated if I always use the same tactics. Consistent and universal tactics are simply not instrumentally (or ethically, in many cases) conducive to effective journalism, nor are they in line with a journalist's dedication to getting the story and keeping the public informed.

As I have written elsewhere, relativistic ethics appears to be the only rational and situation-concerned ethical position for the journalist to take (Merrill, 1989). I suggested there what I called *deontelic* ethics (synthesis of deontological and teleogical ethics), combining a deep respect for moral principles with a willingness to deviate on occasion from such principles after much hard moral reasoning:

> Deontelic ethics is for the journalist who is both morally concerned and rational, who respects generalized ethical principles but who is willing to depart from them. . . . Deontelic ethics is a broad moral grounding, not a set of specific rules for right action. As such, it emphasizes the journalist's own reason, not his or her ability to conform or follow orders. It is truly a socially concerned, individualist ethics that respects the journalist's own freedom and reason but is built on a respect for others, too, and for the continued moral progress of journalism. (Merrill, 1989, 214)

Argument summation: News-gathering tactics should be situational and relative.

The tactics of news gathering should fit the particular case. In one case a reporter may have to promise a source anonymity, whereas in another there is no need. Closely related to ethics, such tactics must be flexible, and the reporter must think of *success* and *consequences.* Should a reporter *ever* lie to get a story? Yes. Should a reporter *ever* promise a source that he or she can see the story before publication? Yes. Tactics must vary to reflect the importance of a particular story. Important ends do indeed justify extreme means. Good journalists know that.

RESPONSE

Dennis: News-gathering tactics should be consistent and universal.

The preceding discussion of news-gathering tactics defends the status quo in American journalism. Reporters do use relative and situational methods when gathering the news. However, there are many agreed-upon general standards. These practical tactics for getting information are undergirded by ethical judgments that are self-contained, based mainly on the immediate situation rather than considered against the backdrop of long experience with similar cases. There is more than a slight temptation to reinvent the wheel with each ethical dilemma that arises.

That, in my opinion, summarizes one of the most serious problems in journalistic practice today—a thoughtless, seat-of-the-pants approach to reporting that eschews planning and thinking. It is the journalism of intuition. "Do what intuition tells you, and apply common sense to the situation" are accepted axioms. On the face of it this philosophy doesn't sound so bad, but consider the following:

A reporter for NBC News is asked how he knows when he has enough information to "go" with a story. "How," he was asked, "can you be sure that your information is complete, that you are not missing major sources that would turn a story completely around, maybe with a different interpretation altogether?" The reporter replied, "You just know. There is," he added, "no answer; things just click into place and it seems right."

An editor for a metropolitan daily newspaper is asked by a Harvard Law professor how far he would go to get a story. "Would you lie? Would you steal? Would you disguise your identity?" The editor thought for a moment, then responded, "Yes, under some conditions, I'd probably do all of those things, even though I might personally find some of them reprehensible." The professor wanted to know, "How do you make your decision; on what theory do you base your actions?" And the editor answered, "I have no theory, I just do what I think is right."

We would not accept this kind of thinking from doctors, lawyers, architects, or other professional persons, whom we expect to have standards, codes, and systematic bases for their decisions. We do accept it from journalists, perhaps because we have no choice, or because they convince us that news is unpredictable, a matter of timing that requires on-the-spot decisions governed solely by the facts of a particular situation. "You simply can't quantify these things," goes the incantation.

There is a prevailing myth in American journalism that planning news coverage runs counter to freedom of the press. Planning is thought to be dull and routine, not spontaneous and timely. It is further said that writers are creative persons who, if left to their own devices, will produce a better kind of journalism. And God forbid that journalists should have hypotheses. A hypothesis, which is an assumption that becomes an organizing principle, is thought to encourage bias and run counter to journalistic objectivity. There is also a prevailing view among many journalists that news really defies precise definition.

This "every-day-a-new-beginning" theme in many newsrooms, the operational rule of the status quo, needs rethinking. While it certainly is not always possible to predict with scientific certainty what will happen on a given day, journalism is much more routine than most of its practitioners know or will admit. They may not know it because American journalism is insulated and parochial. Many journalists have little work experience outside of their present assignments; few belong to national organizations where they come into contact with other journalists; few subscribe to professional publications or make any effort to keep up with the literature of their own field. Most sneer at the thought of reading "media sociology," systematic research that gives us data about patterns and practices across many journalistic organizations. Individual journalists may know their own organization intimately, but they often have little knowledge about the field generally. This situation is not unusual, because many professionals are so busy doing their jobs that they have little time to think about them or to make comparisons with their colleagues in other places. For a field that is supposed to demand so much creative calibration, journalism is remarkably predictable, routine, even stodgy. Send any five reporters to cover a city council story and you can predict with considerable certainty what they will write. Why? Because the coverage of public affairs, in particular, has been standardized. Journalists agree about the form and format of stories, about what essential facts should be included, and about what most editors will accept. Reporters know what is expected of them and generally they do it.

Of course, there are stories that are more complex, but even with these the traditional methods of news gathering pretty much dictate what will appear. And if this were not enough, we have "rewards and punishments" built into the journalistic system to guarantee conformity. At a positive level there are prizes (such as the Pulitzers) that honor imaginative work within the framework of traditional journalism. Journalism schools help out by promoting conventional approaches to news gathering through courses and books.

Journalists believe that their work is unpredictable, situational, and relative. Communications researchers say this is not true, that reporting is not nearly as uncertain as practitioners think. Journalists say that with regard to ethics, they live in a conceptual thicket that requires instant decisions of convenience, if not conviction. They tend to justify what they do without worrying whether revealing a source or lying is consistent with something they did before. Scholars, on the other hand, because they are trained to look for patterns of activity, can see a method, whether haphazard or well thought out, in journalistic work, just as they do in the work of firefighters and farmers. The way the newspaper or broadcast station is organized, the selection of personnel, their training and socialization, all have a hand in shaping news practices.

The once-similar (and now quite different) practices of journalists and social scientists explain some of this discrepancy. As Philip Meyer, well known for his work in precision journalism and a professor at the University of North Carolina, has written:

Social scientists used to be more like journalists. They relied on observation and interpretation, collecting the observations from public records, from interviews, from direct participation, and then spinning out the interpretations. Like many journalists they cheerfully accepted the American folk wisdom . . . that anyone with "a little common sense and a few facts can come up at once with the correct answer on any subject." (1979, 216)

But something changed. First with the development of inferential statistics and later with the advent of computers, social scientists no longer worked like journalists. Instead, they used powerful quantitative tools to deal with unwieldy and massive data. Now, says Meyer, social scientists are doing "what we journalists like to think we are best at: finding fact, inferring causes, pointing to ways to correct social problems, and evaluating the effects of such correction" (216–17). He charges that journalism is being left behind because it lacks a systematic approach to news gathering.

Systematic news-gathering tactics can bring a far richer yield than old-fashioned, impressionistic reporting. It is now possible to determine how much information, and from what sources, will be adequate. This does not mean that journalists should be exactly like social scientists. Press people have greater time pressures and are more concerned about immediacy.

The change toward more systematic reporting is under way. In addition to the "precision journalism" advanced by Meyer and others, there was also greater use of computer-assisted reporting during the late 1980s. At first, giant mainframe computers were used by reporters to access and sift through public records to get information on public officials and others. Then with new software developments, introduced mainly by Elliott Jaspin, a former reporter at the *Providence Journal* and now at the University of Missouri, it also became possible to do some computer-assisted reporting by plugging into massive government documents with a personal computer and a software package.

It is one thing to develop a strategy for news coverage that lists the tactics to be employed, another to actually use these tactics as specified. No situation is ever perfect and no prearranged rules ever work in all situations. For this reason some journalists throw out the rules altogether and make expedient decisions. It is threatening to ask: Is the information complete? Have I mined all possible (and reasonable) sources? Is the evidence strong enough to warrant the conclusion, actual or implied? Are various interpretations and leaps in logic justified? If such questions could have been avoided in the past, this is no longer the case.

Systematic news-gathering tactics are not simply a theory for journalism schools to trumpet, but something being demanded by the rest of society. One of the most compelling calls comes in the courts. Frequently in libel suits news organizations must offer evidence that their story has "an absence of malice." This requirement means that the story is not marred by "knowing falsehood" or "reckless disregard" of the truth. How is this honesty of intent determined? By showing that reasonable efforts, consistent with national news-gathering standards, were employed. If the paper admits they were not, there is the possibility for a whopping libel judgment. Sloppy reporting is expensive. Of equal or greater importance is the fear that journalists will not have the credibility they need and deserve unless their methods are respected by the audience.

People who argue against ethical standards or moral imperatives in news-gathering tactics usually suggest that each case is so distinct that rules will straitjacket the reporter. They add that general guidelines are so vague that they are meaningless. I disagree. We need a theory of journalistic ethics, a fundamental framework on which reporters base their decisions. This framework requires general understanding about ethical behavior, whether in reporting or in everyday life. It entails having a clear notion about how specific journalistic dilemmas ought to be handled. This general ethical understanding, however, does not mean that rules cannot be modified or tempered to meet particular situations. We need a thoughtful policy that serves as a conscience for individual journalists and their organizations. Such a policy should spell out standards of conduct for information gathering. One minimal standard is that journalists should obey the law. In most instances this principle means they should not lie, steal, or cheat. They should not wiretap or break into places not otherwise open to them. In rare instances a right-thinking reporter may want to be civilly disobedient, to break the law deliberately as a matter of principle because doing so will lead to a greater social good. In all instances where ethical questions arise, if there is not a clear answer, reporters should consider alternatives, not simply rush to judgment with the easiest solution. If a decision runs counter to conventional wisdom and standard ethical codes, there ought to be a clear and compelling rationale for making it.

For example, in most instances it is regarded as ethical to reveal one's sources in a news story. Doing so strengthens the credibility of the story and ties information to attributed sources. But if revealing names will put sources in great danger or make them reluctant to talk, a different decision may be appropriate. If it is determined that a source should not be named, the information should meet a test of public benefit, clearly agreed upon and understood by the reporter's supervising editors so that they can defend the action later. And the reporter, if subpoenaed by the courts, must be ready to go to jail if it comes to that.

The problem today is that many reporters do not have solid ethical training and do not have the foundation necessary for ethical decision making.

Journalists have gotten into trouble for being inconsistent in recent years with regard to fair-trial-free-press codes. The press was a signatory to such codes, which list tactical guidelines for covering criminal proceedings from initial investigations of crimes to court judgments. Reporters generally agree to withhold some information (such as prior arrest records) in the interest of not prejudicing a jury and of assuring the defendant of a fair trial. This understanding is a social compact between the press and the legal system. When the press violates this agreement or decides not to abide by a particular provision of the code, there ought to be a good reason (beyond curiosity seeking or pandering) to justify its action. If not, reporters and editors may have to answer in court. This happened in 1981 in a notable case in the state of Washington, where a newspaper was held accountable for violation of the fair-trial-free-press code. Naturally, it is always possible to substitute a "greater social good" argument or a "humanitarian" argument to explain why an individual journalist or publication may deviate from an accepted rule. I believe such exceptions should be justified on the basis of devotion to the public interest rather than petty or self-serving reasons.

Similarly, it is appropriate to reconsider rules that are regarded as journalistic conventions or articles of faith. Printing the names of persons involved in litigation is one example. Withholding the rape victim's name while printing that of the person accused of rape has been mentioned. This practice would seem potentially unfair to the accused. The press usually prints the name of the accused, but is it really necessary to do so? The reasons for printing names has to do with keeping the courts open so that they do not become secret tribunals. Thus we know who is being tried, for what, and why. But as long as the courts are open to the press and to spectators, why not defer printing this material until the trial is over? No great social good is done by heralding names of victims or accused persons in advance of trial, with some obscure exceptions.

Consistent and universal standards of reporting—with necessary escape clauses for unusual situations—will do much to enhance journalistic practice in America. Such standards, if widely known (and the press can virtually guarantee that they are, with adequate coverage), will do much to strengthen public confidence in the fairness and completeness of reporting. They will also have real advantages for individual newspapers and broadcast stations in an increasingly litigious society. Haphazard, thoughtless conduct that meets no standard but blunders along willy-nilly is neither appreciated nor rewarded by the courts. One of the most effective ways to put the journalistic house in order is to establish coherent policies and consistent practices. These are the essence of professional performance and distinguish competent performance from rank amateurism.

Argument summation: News-gathering tactics should be consistent and universal.

News reporting resorts too often to situational ethics instead of a planned approach to appropriate news-gathering tactics. Critics who argue that advanced planning or standards interfere with press freedom fail to recognize that journalism is already routine, as media sociology has revealed. There is much agreement about the form, format, and content of public affairs coverage, and the reward and punishment systems of journalism reinforce these norms. The problem is that these norms are haphazardly developed, relying on impressionistic reporting rather than on finding of fact and inferring of causes in a systematic manner. Guidelines, based on underlying ethical and moral objectives, should be developed to give journalists a clear framework on which to base their decisions in news gathering. At a minimum, these guidelines would require the journalist to consider the alternatives carefully and to develop compelling rationales when breaking the guidelines. The public interest is served best by a press that gathers news systematically, deviating from planned procedures only when doing so can be justified to serve that public interest.

TOPICS FOR DISCUSSION

1. Discuss how news-gathering tactics are related to a journalist's or to a medium's editorial policy and to a sense of ethics.

2. Explain why you feel news-gathering tactics should be determined a priori instead of as the situation arises. If you do not feel this way, explain why.

3. Do you think having definite ways of practicing journalism (tactics) that are considered "proper" or "sacred" is compatible with the American idea of press pluralism, individualism, and freedom?

4. Do you think tactics in American journalism are consistent or inconsistent? What are the advantages of each?

5. Why would a synthesis approach to tactics and ethics—called *deontelic ethics* by Merrill—be a solution to the absolute versus the situational tactical problem faced by the news reporter? If you don't believe it would be a solution, give your reasons.

TOPICS FOR RESEARCH

1. Prepare a report for your fellow students on the advantages and disadvantages of situational versus consistent news-gathering tactics. Take a position. To which approach do you subscribe, or do you advocate some other formulation?

2. Do a study of computer-assisted investigative reporting. Where has it been done? To what effect? Does it have advantages over more qualitative approaches?

3. How does professionalism affect news-gathering tactics? Does a professionally trained reporter work differently than someone with no such training?

4. To what extent does the law of communication, especially libel and privacy law, mandate more consistent news-gathering methods? When a court is asked to decide whether a particular story under scrutiny met professional standards, what would you want the attorneys for each side to argue?

5. Write a brief for the public that is an essay explaining what responsible citizens might want in their news coverage. What information should be offered? How should it be gathered, with what technical means, and with what ethical standards? How much evidence should be offered before a politician is accused of wrongdoing?

FURTHER READING

Bok, Sissela. *Lying: Moral Choice in Public and Private Life.* New York: Pantheon, 1978.

———. *Secrets: On the Ethics of Concealment and Revelation.* New York: Pantheon, 1982.

Diamond, Edwin. *The Tin Kazoo.* Cambridge, MA: MIT Press, 1975.

Hage, George S., Everette E. Dennis, Arnold H. Ismach, and Stephen Hartgen. *New Strategies for Public Affairs Reporting.* 2d ed. Englewood Cliffs, NJ: Prentice Hall, 1976.

Hulteng, John L. *The Messenger's Motives: Ethical Problems of the News Media.* Englewood Cliffs, NJ: Prentice Hall, 1976.

Jaspin, Elliott, "Out with the Paper Chase, In with the Data Base." New York: Gannett Center for Media Studies speech, 1989.

Klaidman, S., and T. L. Beauchamp. *The Virtuous Journalist.* New York: Oxford University Press, 1987.

Lambeth, E. B. *Committed Journalism: An Ethic for the Profession.* Bloomington: Indiana University Press, 1986.

Lowenstein, R. L., and J. C. Merrill. *Macromedia: Mission, Message, and Morality.* White Plains, NY: Longman, 1990.

MacDougall, A. Kent, ed. *The Press: A Critical Look from the Inside.* Princeton, NJ: Dow Jones Books, 1972.

Merrill, John C. *The Dialectic in Journalism: Toward a Responsible Use of Press Freedom.* Baton Rouge: Louisiana State University Press, 1989.

Meyer, Philip. *Precision Journalism.* Bloomington: Indiana University Press, 1979.

Rubin, Bernard. *Questioning Media Ethics.* New York: Praeger, 1978.

Chapter 12

JOURNALISTIC ETHICS

Ethics is a branch of philosophy concerned with the general nature of morals and specific moral choices that people make in relationships with others. *Journalistic ethics* is usually taken to mean the study and application of journalistic standards of conduct and moral choices. Journalistic ethics usually links a system of values and principles with choices that must be made in day-to-day media work and assignments. These value choices most often deal with "right" and "wrong," or degrees of rightness and wrongness, since many journalistic choices are difficult calls. *Values* refers to an ideal or highly desirable situation. For example, fairness is a value that most journalists and other media people would hail. But fairness to whom? To the person being interviewed? To the public? To one's employer? To oneself? When examined closely, fairness, which seems so obvious and easy from a distance, may be difficult in a given situation. Journalistic ethics most often relates to news decision making, and ethics in journalism has for the most part been a code of conduct expected of newspeople, especially editorial employees of news organizations.

Until recently the same ethical guidelines were not thought to apply to media owners, advertising and business personnel, and some special assignments personnel, for whom greater license has been accepted. That attitude is changing, however, as support for general business ethics has been advanced by educators, critics, and the public. Journalistic ethics are always seen in the context of the functions and purposes of the media, which include the delivery of information, opinion, entertainment, and advertising. In order to fulfill its information and news functions, media quite naturally confront conflicting rights and duties. When there is a conflict between the media's desire to publish a story that is important to the public but that violates someone's right of privacy, an ethical dilemma arises. The dilemma will be solved by one's determining what the responsible course of action is in this case. Sometimes doing this means balancing freedom and responsibility, in which case the freest choice to do what one pleases is not always the most responsible choice.

Journalistic ethics involves making choices in specific situations that are related to general rules and principles. For journalists and other communicators this means making choices that conform with the rules and conventions of the profession, which are guided by written codes of ethics. In a practical sense ethical choices suggest freedom in decision making when there might be degrees of rightness and wrongness to consider; there might not be a single "right" ethical choice in all situations. Some ethical values and standards become codified into law, the state requiring that a person follow a particular rule or convention in making choices. Journalistic ethics is thought to be a more voluntary endeavor, however, and the American system of freedom of the press allows considerable latitude not present in other professions, where ethical rules have the force of law.

Thus in a field where there are many standard practices but few absolute rules, the journalist has many independent choices to make in sorting out ethical from unethical conduct. In such murky water it is not surprising that there is little agreement about what, under all conditions, constitutes ethical conduct for a journalist. While seeking the truth is an ethical imperative for most civilized people, there are conditions where highly ethical journalists have lied for what they claimed was a greater public good. Media ethics proponents usually distinguish between general principles of ethics and the daily application of situational ethics, when ethical choices are made on the spot with little time for analysis or introspection.

CHALLENGE

Merrill: Journalists are essentially unethical.

Until the early 1960s little thought was given to the ethics of journalists. Of course the history of American journalism had instances of famous media hoaxes, instances of periodic wheelings and dealings by media publishers, sensational news and propaganda dissemination by men such as William Randolph Hearst and Joseph Pulitzer, and forays into yellow journalism, muckraking, and questionable publishing practices. But generally it was assumed that journalists were trustworthy, honest, dependable, just, unbiased, and concerned with uncovering and delivering the truth.

Now we are overwhelmed with publications, television round table discussions, Socratic dialogues, speeches, conferences, and workshops, all on the subject of journalistic or press ethics. Everybody has discovered that journalists have a big ethical problem. Journalists, who enjoy bashing everything and everybody in sight for ethical lapses, are beginning to get huge doses of their own medicine.

And it's about time. For too long journalists have been pushing their own ethical problems aside and enthroning their freedom, expediency, and self-interest. Pick up almost any copy of a magazine or journal, especially one dealing with the press, and you will encounter articles detailing some journalistic ethical lapse. The situation is so pervasive in the media that many critics—from Ben Bagdikian to William Rusher—have come to believe that "ethical journalism" is an oxymoron.

Some critics, admittedly, seem too extreme in their press condemnation. Janet Malcolm, for instance, lambastes journalists with these strong words:

> Every journalist who is not too stupid or too full of himself to notice what is going on knows that what he does is morally indefensible. He is a kind of confidence man, preying on people's vanity, ignorance, or loneliness, gaining their trust and betraying them without remorse. (1989, p. 38)

Malcolm proceeds to say that journalists "justify their treachery in various ways according to their temperaments." The "more pompous," she notes, talk about their freedom and the "public's right to know"; the "least talented" talk about art; the "seemliest" refer to earning a living.

Many journalists took Malcolm to task for her critical words, but not all. Jonathan Yardley, in a *Washington Post* column (March 27, 1989, C2), regrets the fact that Malcolm does not distinguish between the separate crafts of nonfiction and journalism, but he contends that journalists should take her criticism seriously. He concludes: "People who write nonfiction, whether books or journalism, are not responsible solely to themselves, which is a lesson all of us can learn to our profit."

John L. Hess, however, in *The Quill* (1989, 29), rebuts Malcolm's charges by saying that "the sins of journalists are more imagined than real." He dismisses Malcolm as an "apostate Freudian" who is "full of herself" as she relies on a "single case history" to make her point that journalists have little respect for the truth.

Hess represents the typical defensive reaction of journalists to criticism of their ethics. But in spite of their efforts, they are viewed (in public surveys) as arrogant, self-righteous, and power-hungry—never willing to accept responsibility for mistakes, always anxious (and able) to get the last word.

Some journalistic ethical codes (such as that of the Society of

Professional Journalists) insist that journalists "take nothing of value," that they refrain from political involvement, that they serve the truth, and that they show respect "for the dignity, privacy, rights, and well-being of people encountered in the course of gathering and presenting the news." Compare this rhetoric with the actual daily practices of journalists and you will quickly see that ethical *practice* has a long way to go.

And what is more interesting, journalists seem to have a difficult time accepting a major code admonition: that they "be free of obligation to any interest other than the public's right to know the truth." *Truth.* The gentlemen and ladies of the press enshrine the word but go about their daily business as if they were not bound by the truth. Half-truths, distortions, and outright censorship is the main game played by journalists. In fact, they even *purposely omit* or *distort* the truth when they feel it is necessary to do so.

Many journalists will tell you that, in spite of what their ethical codes say, there are some things more important than reporting the truth. So they fill their days with bits and snippets of the truth; they hide certain truths—often, strangely, because they feel it would be *unethical* to tell them. At least these journalists have an ethical motivation. Others, however, because of *personal biases,* withhold information and names, selectively quote sources, distort their stories, and tamper with the truth.

Press people, by and large, conceive of ethics as prudential actions which will achieve some preconceived plan, whether this is to get information from a source or to keep certain bits of knowledge from the public. Journalists often obtain their ends and then rationalize the means they used. If most journalists today have any ethics, it is a kind of Machiavellian ethics—the ethics of power and expediency.

Reporters have posed as mental patients in order to write exposés of mental hospitals, have slanted a story in favor of a preferred candidate, have fictionalized to make "lifelike" points (as in the Janet Cooke case), and have surreptitiously recorded a conversation or interview. In Cooke's case, she fabricated interviews for a story about a drug-using child. The story won a Pulitzer Prize, which was rescinded when the falsity of the account was revealed. Another celebrated instance of misleading journalism involved NBC's *Dateline* coverage of General Motors trucks in 1994. The program showed the trucks crashing and burning, but failed to mention that this was caused by a test firm hired by the network. In a discussion of "Machiavellian Ethics in Journalism," Ralph Lowenstein and I raise the question of American journalistic expediency-ethics and note manifestations of Machiavellianism (1990, Chapter 17).

Machiavellianism appeals to American pragmatic journalists. It appeals to the desire for power, for success. It appeals to individualism, dedication, and pride. Machiavelli (1469–1527) said all there is to say about a sizable slice of hard-nosed American journalists and their desire to "get the story at any price." Machiavelli might well be called the father of

American journalism, setting its tradition for competitive, bottom-line, winner-take-all, success-oriented media practice. The name of the game in this pragmatic media world is "using other people to achieve desired ends," as I elaborated in the British journal *Encounter* (April 1987, 80).

Certainly I am not maintaining that *all* journalists are unethical, but that *generally* the press and its practitioners indulge in unethical practices. Even the journalists themselves must recognize their general unethical status (at least *image*) in American society, for they are extremely defensive about the subject. If all is well in the ethics arena, as many of them insist, then why don't they just get on with their work and stop all their ethics dialogue, conventions, workshops, and speeches?

Argument summation: Journalists are essentially unethical.

Journalists are generally not concerned with acting rightly, doing the proper thing, informing and enlightening the people, telling the truth, and having standards that guide them. Self-interest and a kind of Machiavellianism guide their basic actions. Pragmatism, power, and success are their key motivations. Ethical journalism is oxymoronic. Ethical codes are useless and are mainly for public relations purposes. Journalists enthrone truth but deviate from it for a multitude of reasons. They talk of the people's right to know but impinge on it regularly. They invade privacy, tamper with quotes, select only certain stories and information that conform with their biases, and are basically arrogant, defensive, and self-righteous.

RESPONSE

Dennis: Journalists are essentially ethical.

Because journalists deal in the currency of information and news, their work is closely watched and often disputed. The reason, of course, is that they are (or ought to be) writing for their audience. While the best of them represent their sources fairly with accurate descriptions of events, situations, and quotations, there is often conflict because the source wants to be seen in the best possible light, even when his or her actions are reprehensible. The journalist is therefore put in an uncomfortable situation. One can serve the interests of the source, avoid conflict, and mislead the public, or one can pursue the truth, cover the news, and accept the consequences.

This is essentially the dilemma described, though somewhat unkindly, by Janet Malcolm. She was not, incidentally, the first person to suggest that writers always sell out their sources. An eloquent statement to that effect is found in Joan Didion's *Slouching Towards Bethelehem*. When it comes to dealing with the views of news sources, there are many complicated factors to consider in determining what is right. In *The Social Responsibility of the Press* (1963), J. Edward Gerald identified several factors in the ground rules that ought to govern reporters' conduct. First, he asks, "What are the conventions journalists are taught to respect?" Second, "What are the rules of their trade?" To this he adds, "What skills in communication entitle a journalist to the acclaim (of colleagues)?" And, "What errors bring loss of face?" Scores of books have been written exploring the points Professor Gerald introduced in these four questions, which travel over uncharted ground but also over much settled territory. While recognizing the foibles of individual journalists and other communicators such as public relations personnel, I believe that there is a great body of evidence, including books describing how journalists uncovered corruption from Teapot Dome to Watergate and Iran-Contra, that suggests journalists are essentially ethical.

Journalism both suffers and benefits from its enormous freedom. Freedom of the press allows enormous latitude in communication: No law can command a journalist to be responsible or fair or just. A journalist can be a highly ethical, moral individual who makes fair-minded choices, or he or she can be a mean-spirited polemicist who is out to get people. That is what freedom of the press guarantees, and through history there have been plenty of journalists who have not been nice people. But we are not talking here about eccentric exceptions, but rather about the norm, the typical journalist who is increasingly driven toward responsibility and fair play, in other words, ethical conduct. Why do I say this is so?

The majority of American journalists today are the products of journalism schools or have at least had some courses that indoctrinate them to their profession. That indoctrination includes values such as freedom of the press, responsible practices in news gathering, and rigorous fair-minded writing where accuracy, accuracy, accuracy is the clarion call. Journalists who do not go to journalism school have to possess writing skills and the ability to work within a media organization. Those organizations have written and unwritten rules about what is acceptable conduct for their employees. People learn these rules quickly and are governed by them; otherwise they are fired. There are also many professional organizations to which one can belong, ranging from editors' and reporters' groups to others for specialized journalists. Virtually all of them have codes of ethics that are widely distributed to their members. Nearly a score of new books on journalistic ethics have been published, even if they are not the fastest-moving best sellers.

In other words, information about journalistic ethics is readily available. There is an increasing amount of press criticism published in newspapers and magazines and also discussed on radio and television news programs. Mention almost any topic, and media coverage of it has been discussed somewhere recently. And what does that coverage and criticism typically address? You guessed it: journalistic ethics. In fact, I would guess that the typical citizen probably knows more about journalistic ethics than about medical or legal ethics. Why? Because the topic is front-row-center much of the time in our major media.

Studies of American journalists and journalism educators by David Weaver and G. Cleveland Wilhoit suggest that ethics is a serious concern among both groups. Similarly, the several studies of media credibility done in recent years (and stretching back for a half century) report that the public is very concerned about the ethics of journalists. While most people support the media and give journalists and others good grades, a vocal minority are dissatisfied. Media people pay attention to these report cards and often act upon them, especially if they feel the criticism is just.

Since the 1920s, every twenty years or so has seen a burgeoning literature of media ethics. There is discussion and debate for a few years, then the topic recedes into the background only to reappear later. That was true until the 1970s, but so visible are media issues and problems these days that the rush of articles and books has not abated. Excellent studies of situational ethics have been rendered by such educators as John L. Hulteng (1985), whose *The Messenger's Motives* is in its second edition. In *Groping for Media Ethics* Eugene Goodwin (1983) similarly looks inside newsrooms and observes problems. Philip Meyer (1987) in a study called *Ethical Journalism* even suggests that editorial ethics should extend to the business side of the press. Edmund Lambeth's (1986) *Committed Journalism* offers a coherent philosophy based, in part, on ethical imperatives as well as practical conditions. These books and others that are notable join several volumes on my shelf by John Merrill, who has been writing on media ethics for at least two decades. The literature is the tip of a very large iceberg, which includes increased instruction in media ethics in journalism schools, a trend that has been traced by Clifford Christians of the University of Illinois. There are centers for media ethics at the Poynter Institute, the University of Minnesota, and Emerson College. There are training programs in ethics for journalism teachers at the University of Missouri and scores of conferences that have been well attended for at least a decade.

Thus it seems to me that journalistic ethics is alive and well in the United States. But are journalists ethical? Yes they are, I believe, on the basis of studies, personal experience, and the various incentives that encourage ethical conduct. These include the reward and punishment system of American journalism, which rarely rewards reprehensible or unethical journalism; pressure from an increasingly sophisticated public, which is critical of the news it gets; and finally, the legal system, which in court takes an exceedingly unkind view of journalists who are regarded by their peers as irresponsible, reckless, or unethical. Mostly, though, journalists, like most people, are ethical because they want to do what is right. In one of the most celebrated cases of journalistic ethics in recent years, CBS News executive Burton Benjamin criticized a "60 Minutes" story about General Westmoreland in an internal report for the network; Benjamin's report was widely applauded for its ethical stance. The CBS story, the subject of a scathing cover article in *TV Guide,* led to an unresolved court case and to Benjamin's book called *Fair Play.* When television journalists are asked whom they admire most, who would most likely be their role model, the people who did the deeply flawed *60 Minutes* documentary or Mr. Benjamin, a man of principle, honor, and integrity, Benjamin won without dispute. That says something about the present climate for media ethics.

Argument summation: Journalists are essentially ethical.

While there are notable exceptions, as in any profession, ethical behavior is the norm in American journalism. The socialization of journalists, both through school and professional exposure, indoctrinates professional values which emphasize responsible news gathering, freedom of the press, and accuracy in reporting. Journalists who do not follow these unwritten rules of their organization do not have jobs for long. Studies confirm that journalists respond to criticism of media ethics and that there is a healthy debate regarding ethics; thus the profession is kept aware of a necessity for ethical behavior.

TOPICS FOR DISCUSSION

1. What do you think "being ethical" means to a journalist? Is it possible to justify or rationalize any journalistic action?

2. Where are the main ethical allegiances in journalism—to the general public, to the employer, to the media audience? How would you rank such allegiances in terms of importance?

3. Where do you think journalists derive their ethical standards? If they get them from various sources, how do they know, if they do, which sources are valid and reliable?

4. Do you think that codes of ethics are useful in a free-press society? How so? Do you think that a monolithic sense of ethics in the U.S. press would be good or bad for American journalism?

5. Give some evidence to substantiate the claim that "journalistic ethics is alive and well in the United States." How would we know if American ethics were sick or dead?

TOPICS FOR RESEARCH

1. Study the codes of ethics used by media organizations and professional societies. Compare and contrast them. How general are they? How specific? To what extent are they useful?
2. Interview one or more journalists from any medium. Ask them to articulate their "theory" of media ethics; that is, how do they define ethics in their work? How do they make ethical decisions? Ask for an example of a particularly difficult (or easy) ethical decision they recently had to make. Where does their knowledge of media ethics come from? How do they stay up-to-date?
3. Examine a major controversy in journalism in terms of ethics. Pick a case or controversy where the performance or behavior of a television or print journalist was under fire. What was the main issue? How was it resolved? Did this case serve the public well or not?
4. Write a review essay drawing on at least two recent books on media ethics. On the basis of these studies, how would you develop your own code of ethics? What advice would you give to a news organization about how they might write a code?
5. Read and analyze a recent biography by a media person. Examine the person's career and decisions on the basis of ethics. Is the person a good, mediocre, or poor model for others? What of his or her ethics?

FURTHER READING

Benjamin, Burton. *Fair Play.* New York: Harper & Row, 1988.

Christians, C. G., K. B. Rotzoll, and Mark Fackler. *Media Ethics: Cases and Moral Reasoning.* 2d ed. White Plains, NY: Longman, 1987.

Dennis, Everette E. *Reshaping the Media.* Beverly Hills, CA: Sage, 1989.

Dennis, Everette E., Donald M. Gillmor, and Theodore Glasser, eds. *Media Freedom and Accountability.* Westport, CT: Greenwood Press, 1989.

Fink, Conrad C. *Media Ethics in the Newsroom and Beyond.* New York: McGraw-Hill, 1988.

Gerald, J. Edward. *The Social Responsibility of the Press.* Minneapolis: University of Minnesota Press, 1963.

Goodwin, Eugene. *Groping for Media Ethics.* Ames: Iowa State University Press, 1983.

Hess, John L. "Who's Conning Whom?" *The Quill* 77, no. 5 (May 1989):29.

Hulteng, John L. *The Messenger's Motives: Ethical Problems of the News Media.* 2d ed. Englewood Cliffs, NJ: Prentice Hall, 1985.

Johannesen, Richard L. *Ethics in Human Communication.* 3d ed. Prospect Heights, IL: Waveland Press, 1990.

Klaidman, Stephen, and Tom Beauchamp. *The Virtuous Journalist.* New York: Oxford University Press, 1987.

Lambeth, Edmund B. *Committed Journalism: An Ethic for the Profession.* Bloomington: Indiana University Press, 1986.

Lowenstein, R. L., and J. C. Merrill. *Macromedia: Mission, Message and Morality.* White Plains, NY: Longman, 1990.

Malcolm, Janet. "The Journalist and the Murder." *The New Yorker,* March 13, 1989.

Merrill, John C. *The Dialectic in Journalism: Toward a Responsible Use of Press Freedom.* Baton Rouge: Louisiana State University Press, 1989.

———. *The Imperative of Freedom.* 2d ed. New York: Freedom House, 1990.

Meyer, Philip. *Ethical Journalism.* White Plains, NY: Longman, 1987.

Swain, Bruce M. *Reporters' Ethics.* Ames: Iowa State University Press, 1978.

Chapter 13

THE NEW COMMUNITARIANISM AND PUBLIC JOURNALISM

Onto the journalistic scene in the last few years has come a rather potent philosophical and sociological emphasis. It is called *communitarianism,* and in one or another of its sub-genres (e.g., public journalism or civic journalism) it is making inroads into the media and into academic discourse. The new communitarians are waging a rhetorical war against Enlightenment liberalism—against individualism and libertarianism. They proclaim the necessity for civic co-option of the editorial prerogative. In short, they would like to see the people as the journalistic agenda setters rather than the journalists.

Communitarianism's founder is the American sociologist Amitai Etzioni of George Washington University, whose book *The Spirit of Community* (1993) largely set the stage for the movement's recent popularity. Many other prominent thinkers, such as Joseph de Maistre, Alasdair MacIntyre, Michael Sandel, and Leo Strauss, have added their voices in praise of communitarianism. Perhaps the best book that is critical of the movement is Stephen Holmes's *The Anatomy of Antiliberalism* (1993).

In the academic world two journalism professors have been early supporters and advocates of media communitarianism. They are Clifford Christians (University of Illinois) and Jay Rosen (New York University). And in the newspaper world the *Wichita Eagle*'s editor Davis "Buzz" Merritt, Jr., has teamed up with Rosen in lectures, seminars, and workshops around the country to spread the word of what they call *public* or *civic journalism* (genres of, or synonyms for, communitarian journalism). Professor Edmund Lambeth of the University of Missouri's School of Journalism is also an active proponent of civic journalism. One editor who opposes this new movement is Howard Schneider of *Newsday.* He sees nothing new in this "public" journalism. "It's the most traditional thing that any newspaper worth anything has always done," he says (quoted in Shepard, 1994, 33). "Good newspapers go out to the community.... This is not a radical new notion that you also report on what the public cares about."

The communitarians (and their civic/public journalism cohorts) see traditional American press libertarianism as counterproductive, even harmful, to social stability and harmony. In short, they are pushing for what they refer to as "universal solidarity." This would mean, as Cliff Christians, says, having a "rich notion of accountability" that will "resonate in an organization's consciousness" and will have a "normative language for nurturing moral integrity in an age of fragmented lives" (1993, 16).

The Communitarian Network in Washington, D.C., has issued a platform statement indicating rights and responsibilities, which rightly and boldly states:

> Neither human existence nor individual liberty can be sustained for long outside the interdependent and overlapping communities to which all of us belong. Nor can any community long survive unless its members dedicate some of their attention, energy, and resources to shared projects.
>
> That's where the press comes in and, of course, it makes sense to join with like minded citizens in the community to improve all of our lives and lots. What better function for the press to perform? Enough of this irresponsible, disinterested standing back from the action. Let's get on with community improvement by becoming part of the action not just a curious bystander. We need more committed and more passionate journalism, and clearly communitarian journalism or as some call it public journalism is the answer. (The Responsive Communitarian Platform: Rights and Responsibilities, Washington, D.C.: Communitarian Network, 1994, p. 1)

For the communitarians the old ideas of Milton, Locke, Mill, Constant, Voltaire, and Madison may have been good in their day—but no longer. Instead of stressing individualism, rights, and freedom, the communitarians are emphasizing a more responsible media system in which journalists are willing to sacrifice their own freedom to the good of society or the community. Their ideas are somewhat similar to the basic tenets of the Hutchins commissioners of the late 1940s in their enthronement of social responsibility. They claim they are democratizing American journalism, giving the people the say-so in editorial matters.

This shift to a more communitarian journalism has been going on since the 1950s. Whereas previously the assumption was that the press and journalists were rational and capable of making their own editorial decisions, the emphasis has now shifted (or is shifting) away from such self-determination to become focused on the press's social *obligations* or *responsibilities.* These days the rationality and self-reliance of journalists have been called into question. The ability of the press to make its own decisions is now doubted. What is needed, the communitarians are suggesting, is a more monolithic and positive media system that refrains from polluting the intellectual environment and upsetting community stability.

CHALLENGE

Merrill: Communitarianism in journalism is a healthy trend.

The communitarians have a worthy goal. They want a better journalism—one that fosters greater public concern and a higher moral level. Almost anyone viewing the press today will be disappointed in its performance. The old eighteenth-century Enlightenment philosophy of the press simply does not work. It has led to all kinds of journalistic excesses, it is socially disruptive to the harmony of a community, it leads to cases of pompous and selfish individualism, and it fosters an egocentrism in journalism that leads to self-serving actions and a haughty demeanor.

It is refreshing that citizens *and* media persons are beginning to question the old atomistic, individual, rights-centered liberalism of the eighteenth century. And it is good that the emphasis is shifting away from egoistic and institutional media excesses. We should all be able to find congenial ideas in the emerging anti-liberal (elitist) social philosophy of communication and to applaud the more democratic or populist communitarianism on the horizon. Fortunately, people today are pulled toward a philosophy that offers social stability and freedom from the chaos and anarchy that rear their ugly heads everywhere. It would seem obvious that the community and its needs come before the individual and his or her rights.

And there is a need for uniform normative ethical standards. Journalists must understand their responsibility and recognize that they need to act in similar and predictable ways. A kind of discipline and commonality of values would ensure a far more smooth-running journalistic enterprise. A *people-based* journalism is more sensible than a *journalist-based* journalism—and this is what the new communitarians or anti-liberals are advocating. No doubt exists but that public faith in the mass media is slipping fast, and we can see media filled with cheap, superficial, and vulgar material. Tabloidism is taking over journalism. We see shoddy journalism and deceptive media practices all around us. Communitarians want something better; they say that libertarianism has had its chance—and it has failed.

What are some of the characteristics of this new communitarian journalism? Let me mention just a few, taken from Cliff Christians et al., *Good News* (1993). It is difficult to see how anyone could take issue with them, but I'm sure Ev Dennis will in his "response." Here are some of the "oughts" and "shoulds" proposed by the communitarians:

1. Journalists should publish those things that would bring people together, not fractionalize them.

2. Journalists should give the people of the community what they desire, not what the journalists want them to have.

3. Journalists should deal with positive news, with items that would not tear down community spirit but would solidify and promote it.

4. Journalists themselves—within the community of journalism—ought to agree on a common ethics and should not fall into the trap of embracing situational or relativistic ethics (pp. 54–55).

5. Journalists should discard the liberal politics of rights—which according to Christians et al. "rests on unsupportable foundations"; such rights should be "given up for a politics of the common good" (p. 45).

6. Journalists should throw out the old concepts of journalistic autonomy and editorial self-determination, along with individualism and what the communitarians call "negative freedom" (pp. 42–44).

7. Journalists should make news reports accurate, balanced, relevant, and complete (p. 55).

8. Journalists ought to hold fast to the underlying normative principles of truth telling and the public's right to know—"nonnegotiable principles" (p. 55).

9. Journalists should recognize that "morality always makes universal and categorical claims" (p. 61).

10. Journalists should realize that "universal solidarity is the normative core of the social and moral order" (p. 14).

11. Journalists should recognize the falsity of the concept of the "fourth estate" or the "watchdog" role of the press (pp. 70–71).

12. Journalists ought to realize that the Enlightenment philosophy of the press "currently generates confusion about the news media's rationale and mission, and excludes the substantive issues from our media-ethics agenda" (p. 44).

13. Journalists should reject "the Enlightenment's individualistic rationalism" (p. 185).

These, of course, are only a few of the suggestions made by the communitarians, but they are probably the main ones. Runaway individualism and irrational use of freedom simply cannot be sustained by thoughtful, moral people. So the communitarian proposals are most welcome. It is time to be concerned about the limits of individualism and freedom.

In conclusion, the day has come for a new concept of journalism such as the communitarians are proposing. Anything that makes our press more responsible, more civic minded, more democratic, and more concerned with the public interest is indeed welcome.

Argument summation: Communitarianism in journalism is a healthy trend.

The new concept or theory of communitarianism has made inroads into journalism during the last decade. It is a good and healthy trend because it takes the emphasis off the atomistic, individualistic, and libertarian outdated philosophy of the eighteenth-century Enlightenment and places it on the good of society, on the harmony, stability, and progress of the community.

Communitarianism places the group or the community ahead of the individual. It places obligations ahead of rights. It (and its close relatives—public and civic journalism) comprises a theory that enthrones a common normative ethics of journalism, that promotes positive and helpful news, that scorns negative and divisive journalism, that makes the public and not the media the agenda setter, that calls for accuracy and thoroughness in reporting, that seeks universal solidarity, and that denies the concept of the press as a "fourth estate" or government "watchdog."

RESPONSE

Dennis: Communitarianism in journalism is an unhealthy trend.

My colleague John Merrill challenges me to rain on a parade that is much discussed in American journalism today, one that arguably tries diligently to improve the quality of public affairs news that people get. Having sat in sessions of the communitarianism movement led by the eminent sociologist Amitai Etzioni, I know this movement to be a genuine effort to create more civic awareness and to improve the lives of all people. That's a worthy endeavor for community leaders, whether elected politicians or those who want to promote worthy causes that will improve the lives of citizens. But whether this is a function of journalism is another question altogether.

Professor Merrill endorses communitarianism rather uncritically and then goes on to mask his arguments for a new journalistic ethic behind the term *communitarianism,* which is used mostly by pretentious folks in the academy and a few community activists, but he avoids much discussion of the so-called journalistic "movement" more often represented in public or civic journalism. This somewhat evangelical effort to change the way newspapers and television stations report on local communities is strongly supported in the work of the Project on Public Life and the Press at New York University, which is headed by journalism professor Jay Rosen (see *The New News vs. The Old News,* 1992), and articulated in a book by *Wichita Eagle* editor Davis "Buzz" Merritt (1995). This project is closely connected to concerns regarding election coverage in 1992; newspapers in Charlotte (North Carolina) and Wichita (Kansas) agreed to take part in a project that resulted in more issue-oriented election coverage. While some public journalism proponents stoutly refuse to define it, arguing that you can't define a movement, which is a work in progress, this is a glib and unsatisfactory approach. Public journalism is generally understood to be journalistic practice at the community level that engages the reader and viewer more in defining what will be covered and why. Knight-Ridder's James Batten called it "customer service," while the Gannett Company's News 2000 Project uses former Gannett chairman Al Neuharth's term, "reader-driven journalism." The term probably dates to 1960s research on connecting the news and what the public thinks is salient. While advocates refuse to offer a simple definition—and believe me, this is not brain surgery—foundations that fund the practice, media firms that use it, and editors who oppose it all think they understand what they are talking about. Studies of the experiment by researcher Philip Meyer demonstrated that people would read stories that pushed candidates toward taking positions on issues that the newspaper thought were important and in need of action.

Three major foundations—Kettering, Knight, and the Pew Memorial Trusts—have provided funding for the NYU project and another headed by long-time broadcaster Edward Fouhy. These organizations are marching lockstep toward a new journalistic ethic that urges the media to get more involved in their local communities, to "join the parade," as one critic put it, and help frame and solve community problems. The newspaper industry, terrified that its medium is dying, has gotten on the bandwagon too and has mostly uncritically embraced public journalism as just the right medicine for its troubled industry. This is rather like a patient with incurable cancer glomming onto any potential cure because there is little to lose anyway. Believing as I do that the death of the newspaper industry is grossly exaggerated and that the future of that medium depends on a mix of ink on paper and electronic delivery modes with greater interactivity between media people and the public, I doubt that content per se is the real problem behind declining newspaper circulation. People aren't rejecting what they get in newspapers; they are simply finding it more efficiently and often in better form on television (see McGill and

Szántó, 1995). I believe the fundamental flaw of the public journalism movement is its assumption that better content will save newspapers as we now know them. Of course I'm supportive of anything that purports to improve the press, no matter how remote its ultimate success might be.

But wait. There is yet another problem with the public journalism/civic journalism/communitarian movement: It changes the basic function of the journalist. For decades social workers have advocated "community organization" to organize the resources of a community around solving a particular social problem, whether health care delivery, drug prevention, or something else. Here public and private agencies join together to solve problems and develop public policy. That's fine for social workers and for government agencies and private sector interests. It is not fine for journalists, whose job (last time I checked) was to cover the news and to report as impartially as possible on the passing show. As *Newsday's* managing editor Howard Schneider puts it, "Our job is to cover the parade, not to be in the parade" ("The Cronkite Report," Discovery Channel, March 22, 1995). The public journalism "movement," which really is not a movement for reasons I will detail later, is a traveling roadshow that urges journalists to become activists and cast their lot with solutions to problems of public life, to become part of the formulation of public policy by identifying worthy topics of such policy and by covering them in four-part harmony fashion. This is making news decisions based, in fact, on what a newspaper's editorial page thinks should happen or, worse yet, on decisions from its promotion department. This view is supported by *Washington Post* executive editor Leonard Downie, who says, "Too much of what's called public journalism appears to be what our promotion department does, only with a different kind of name and a fancy evangelistic fervor" (*Editor & Publisher,* November 12, 1994, p. 14).

When all is said and done and when one cuts through the hype, relatively few news organizations embrace public journalism and, at this writing, none of true national significance. The Wichita, Akron, Charlotte, and Seattle papers are among the largest to endorse the idea, but editors at the *Philadelphia Inquirer* and *Washington Post* have denounced it. Jay Rosen writes, "The test for any serious philosophy of journalism today is what it proposes to do about the troubles that plague public life" (*Editor & Publisher,* November 12, 1994, p. 14). Certainly the media should cover, analyze, interpret, and editorialize on the important issues and problems of the day, but to "do" something about them makes the journalist a player, an activist, an advocate, and possibly even a propagandist.

No, let's leave this task for the elected leaders of the community and for those who represent large institutions and interests. Once the press buys into a given community solution, it takes on a conflict of interest and no longer has a legitimate franchise to criticize. And worse yet, public confidence in the press as its representative rather than as a partner in a public policy venture is lost. At stake here is credibility. There are many ways to improve journalism, a goal that is worthy and important, but this is a bad idea, and people ought to step up to the plate and say so.

Argument summation: Communitarianism in journalism is an unhealthy trend.

Communitarianism is an academic description of a proposed public philosophy that is seen in journalism more often under the banners *public* or *civic journalism*. It urges the press, through its coverage of the community, to become engaged in solving community problems. This notion confuses journalism with community organization, a social work concept. Flaws in the public journalism argument are assumptions that better and more engaged content will stave off circulation declines for newspapers, something for which there is no good evidence; and that journalists should be activists taking positions on community issues, an action that would lose them any claim to impartiality and would sacrifice credibility. The journalist should cover the parade, not march in it.

TOPICS FOR DISCUSSION

1. How would the concept of communitarianism change the role of the media, and what would be different in newspapers, in magazines, and on television if this were the case?

2. Is there really a difference between a people-based journalism and a journalist-based journalism?

3. Why has the public journalism debate stirred such controversy in American media circles?

4. How do the principles articulated in the Hutchins Commission Report relate to the communitarian movement and its applications to the press?

5. What are the motives behind those who promote civic and public journalism? And what are the motives of their detractors?

6. Under the ideas of public journalism, how does a journalist differ from a community organizer?

7. Is there a difference between civic journalism and civic boosterism?

TOPICS FOR RESEARCH

1. Trace the development of the communitarian movement from the Enlightenment philosophers to the present. What are the main ideas expounded and how have they changed or matured?
2. Compare examples of "public journalism" with more traditional public affairs reporting.
3. Do a survey of local media in your community or state to determine how they feel about public/civic journalism and whether they practice it.
4. Compare and contrast the approaches of two newspaper groups—the Knight-Ridder group's interest in public journalism and the Gannett group's "News 2000" project. Do they differ? Are they similar? Do they represent major changes in journalism or not?
5. Try to determine the extent to which public journalism has been embraced by media in the United States—print and broadcast—and how it is practiced on a day-to-day basis.

FURTHER READING

Christians, Clifford, John Ferre, and P. Mark Fackler. *Good News: Social Ethics and the Press.* New York: Oxford University Press, 1993.

"Civic Catalyst," Pew Center for Civic Journalism, Washington, D.C. The newsletter of the Pew Center for Civic Journalism.

Dennis, Everette E., "Questions About Public Journalism," *Communiqué,* Freedom Forum Media Studies Center, June 1995, p. 2. Reprinted in *Editor & Publisher,* July 29, 1995, p. 48.

Etzioni, Amitai. *The Spirit of Community: Rights, Responsibilities, and the Communitarian Agenda.* New York: Crown, 1993.

Holmes, Stephen. *The Anatomy of Antiliberalism.* Cambridge, MA: Harvard University Press, 1993.

Lambeth, Edmund B. *Committed Journalism.* 2d ed. Bloomington: Indiana University Press, 1992.

McGill, Lawrence, and András Szántó. *Headlines and Sound Bites, Is That the Way It Is?* New York: Freedom Forum Media Studies Center, 1995.

MacIntyre, Alasdair. *After Virtue.* Notre Dame, IN: University of Notre Dame Press, 1981.

"Media and Democracy," *Media Studies Journal,* Summer 1995. Includes material on and related to civic journalism. Freedom Forum Media Studies Center, New York.

Merrill, John C. *The Dialectic in Journalism.* Baton Rouge: Louisiana State University Press, 1989.

Merritt, Davis. *Public Journalism and Public Life: Why Telling the News Is Not Enough.* Hilldale, NJ: Lawrence Erlbaum, 1995.

Rosen, Jay, and Paul Taylor. *The New News vs. the Old News.* New York: Twentieth Century Fund, 1992.

The Responsive Communitarian Platform: Rights and Responsibilities. Washington, DC: The Communitarian Network, 1994.

The Responsive Community (the journal of the communitarian movement, edited by Amitai Etzioni and published by the Center for Policy Research, Washington, DC). The Spring 1994 issue, "Rights and Responsibilities," includes articles on the communitarian movement and the media.

Shepard, Alicia C. "The Gospel of Public Journalism." *American Journalism Review,* September 1994.

Chapter 14

PROPAGANDA AND THE MEDIA

In its most basic formulation, *propaganda* is a neutral term for the spread of ideas. In *A Dictionary of the Social Sciences* propaganda denotes: "The techniques and methods of influencing or controlling the attitudes, and behavior . . . by the use of words and other symbols" as well as by "the statements and impressions issuing from the use of such techniques or methods." Propaganda is a communication process that makes use of certain techniques and methods to accomplish its ends. Although the term originated with the Roman Catholic Church and had to do with the "propagation of the faith," it made its way into political communication by the early twentieth century. World War I was said to have involved a propaganda battle between the British and Germans, and the U.S. public was the target of messages delivered in pamphlets, tracts, posters, cartoons, and other forms of communication. During World War II the Nazis developed an elaborate system of propaganda to build support for the regime, both within Germany and outside.

During that period the Institute of Propaganda Analysis promoted a serious study of propaganda, defining the term as "an expression of opinion or action by individuals or groups deliberately designed to influence opinions or actions of other individuals to predetermined ends." Propaganda usually involves the state's (or government's) promoting a point of view to gain influence or even control. George Orwell's novel *1984* is the story of a state where propaganda is used to control thought and action. Social scientists studying propaganda and the press have identified various propaganda techniques, ranging from name-calling to glittering generalities, testimonials, and bandwagon devices.

The interest in propaganda presupposed powerful media effects, but as this view of media lost ground in the 1940s, so did propaganda analysis. In time, the term was all but shelved among media scholars and used only occasionally in media and communication studies. Except for references to Chinese or North Korea propaganda, where the government and press were commingled, the term had an antiquated ring in America. This view changed by the 1990s as students of the media abandoned the minimal-effects model. While media in the United States are not official instruments of state propaganda as they once were in Russia, they are sometimes accused of being instruments of propaganda for various interests.

The term *propaganda* now has a clearly pejorative connotation to the general public. Among media scholars the prevailing view is that the press is independent and acts as a shield against propaganda. But some critics argue that media are manipulated by propaganda, whether that of our own government or that of other nations. They charge that the U.S. press is subject to influence from various interests, often through propaganda and public relations. Conservative critics accuse the media of having a liberal bias.

CHALLENGE

Dennis: Media are defenses against propaganda.

Those who readily use the once-discarded term *propaganda* to examine and assess the U.S. media have to accept one of two views: Either the media are being manipulated by external influences and are thus unreliable, or they are staffed by people who willingly participate in the deception. In such a system the media are either willing or unwitting soldiers in the propaganda war.

In North Korea and a few other countries the media are, in effect, part of the government and have a propaganda function. They follow a line like that practiced in Russia before the fall of Communism, but not practiced now. Another example of a media system under strict government control is that of the People's Republic of China. Although Chinese newspapers, wire services, and television were liberalized to the point of engaging in something closer to Western-style reporting, this quickly ceased after the student revolt of 1989, when key editors were replaced by government functionaries. In both the North Korean and Chinese examples the media are typically, though not always, instruments of propaganda.

Is there any fundamental difference between what the media do and what propaganda agencies do? I would argue in the affirmative. Propaganda agencies typically are government agencies, and their main function is to support and nurture their backers. They do this by persuading, sometimes overtly with great passion and sometimes through a complex web of subtle messages. They are simply a channel between government and people, and they almost always promote the status quo or change that will give the government greater authority and power.

Media typically exist to communicate with audiences, either on their own behalf or on behalf of their owners and managers. They are guided by international standards of journalism or media entertainment fare. If they are an uncritical mouthpiece for a government, business, church, or other entity, they are still instruments of mass communication, but they are hardly independent media operating in concert with media elsewhere in the world. During the Cold war, a newspaper funded by the CIA or the KGB was regarded by journalists the world over not as an independent newspaper, but as a suspect and captive voice.

Of course governments can publish newspapers or magazines or engage in state broadcasting, but the products they produce will be perceived for what they are. The BBC, for example, is one of the most respected broadcasting systems in the world. It has always had great independence and operates with high professional standards. Its main product is unbiased information and news, as well as first-rate entertainment and cultural programming. Its relative independence of the partisanship of particular British governments is well known, and when Mrs. Thatcher complained during the Falklands War that the BBC was not enthusiastically pro-government, there was a firestorm of criticism mainly defending the BBC. Some media outlets in other countries are known to be sympathetic to the government, but few that survive long are slavishly so. Of course, some government-run news organizations in Third World countries are more propaganda organs than news organs. That is the reality of the situation, but for the most part, the world over, one can distinguish between the broad purposes of public media and the narrower concerns of government propaganda.

This brings us to the media of the United States and many other Western countries. They are hardly mouthpieces for propaganda, government or otherwise. True, for most of their history they generally followed the government lead on foreign policy, but even that tradition seemed to end during the Vietnam War.

Are the component parts of the U.S. media system either willing or unwitting instruments of propaganda? Of course not. Whatever its faults—and they are many—the U.S. press is independent and vigorous. Ask any recent American president whether the press was a cheerleader for his administration and the answer will come back a resounding "No." The Congress too is often under fire in the press, with charges of gridlock. Such coverage probably played a role in the Republican takeover of the House of Representatives in 1992 and the rise of Speaker Newt Gingrich.

Similarly, the Supreme Court hardly gets a free ride. Its decisions are watched and are dissected and analyzed. Even the private sector gets fairly tough and independent reporting. Ask business leaders whether they like the way they are portrayed in the press generally or even in such publications as the *Wall Street Journal, Forbes,* and *Business Week.* Conservative critics claim that the media are too liberal and that journalists are biased. Some scholars who call themselves critical theorists and who generally oppose many of the capitalist values of the media say that the U.S. media do have an ideology and that this ideology generally supports business and the status quo. I agree with one commentator, who said, "Yes, the media are ideological, and for American media the ideology is objectivity." Objectivity, for all of its faults, is a defense against propaganda. The tendency of the American media is to ignore the commonplace and to highlight differences. Hundreds of honest politicians are virtually ignored while a corrupt one is pilloried.

The American press and public are particularly sensitive to the blandishments of propaganda. The South African government, for example, has tried to propagandize the U.S. press with little success. Other foreign governments and interests have had active campaigns to change their image in America. Typically the American press views such efforts with caution and even with criticism. The *New York Times* has, for example, carried paid advertising supplements from the Japanese government while vigorously investigating influence peddling by the Japanese in Washington. On occasion media critics have feared that the press has been getting too cozy with a particular government official. No doubt this happens, but so does criticism of the kind that uncovers it.

No, the American media may have many faults, but being fall guys for propaganda is the exception. Perhaps this is why the term *propaganda,* which only recently came back into use by scholars who had for years abandoned it as meaningless and pejorative, still seems a bit passé.

Argument summation: Media are defenses against propaganda.

Media cease to be news organs and become tools of propaganda when they are captive voices. For example, the press in China and North Korea could be characterized as propaganda organs because of their institutional ties to the government. In the United States the press is independent and vigorous—hardly a mouthpiece for propaganda, government or otherwise. The media's criticism of the President, Congress, and the courts bears out its adversarial relationship to government, and the private sector too is covered critically, a fact disproving any claim that the U.S. press is a propaganda organ. By encouraging detached commentary on events and even criticism of fellow media members when they become too supportive of a single viewpoint, the objective style of American journalism ensures that it is a defense against propaganda.

RESPONSE

Merrill: Media are instruments of propaganda.

We have just been treated to the case of media as protectors of the public against propagandistic assault. It is somewhat surprising to hear that media are basically innocent of propagandizing and seldom turn themselves into vehicles of the propaganda of others.

Of course, one big initial problem in such a controversial issue as "propaganda in the media" is how we define the term *propaganda*. If we limit it to overt and large-scale lying or purposeful misleading, then perhaps we can say that the media are not major participants. But if we take a more realistic view of propaganda as intentional persuasion toward some belief or action, then the media are filled with propaganda.

In a basic media-and-society textbook my coauthors and I suggested a *PASID* formula, identifying propaganda as Persuasive, Action-oriented, Selfish, Intentional, and Devious or Deceptive (Merrill, Lee, and Friedlander, 1990). Such a formula is necessarily superficial, but it is handy in summarizing propaganda's key characteristics.

Many persons will insist, as Dennis does earlier, that media seldom try to practice deception in order to persuade. My study of and familiarity with a wide assortment of journalists convinces me, however, that purposeful persuasion—along with techniques of bias and deception—is far more common than Dennis and others believe.

Biases exist in journalism. And they manifest themselves in stories and filmed reports through purposeful selection of acts, sources to be interviewed, the types of questions asked, emphases and deemphases. These and other techniques are used by skilled journalists to distort, bias, and persuade in subtle ways.

One reporter will use direct quotes (to depict a person either positively or negatively), while another will use indirect quotes. A journalist will quote one person in a story to provide a "typical" viewpoint. A faculty member at a university will be quoted to let the public know what the faculty is thinking. This "one-person cross-section" device of propaganda is commonly used in journalism. And reporters often quote out of context, giving one impression when another could be given if proper context were provided. And who has not seen the common sentence, often at the end of a controversial story, that "Mr. X was unavailable for comment"?

A journalist who is covering a debate between political candidates will be prone to "push" his or her favorite, playing up parts of what this candidate says that show the candidate in a good light and minimizing (or omitting) comments that are illogical, crude, ungrammatical, or otherwise easily open to criticism. It may be that what the journalist does choose to report is true, at least in the sense of being accurate in those parts reported. And of course the journalist will be sure that his or her favorite's opponent receives neutral or negative treatment. A journalist who is a photographer can do the same thing with a camera—looking for certain angles, awaiting the proper smile or frown or scowl or what have you. In one sense, a picture may not "lie," but there is no doubt but that a picture can propagandize by giving impressions that are false to reality.

A reporter might provide a source in Case A but not in Case B. News management, propaganda, forthright reporting? The reporter might use such generalizing devices as "Americans believe that the South African government is immoral and must change . . ." or "China experts are predicting that the hard-liners in Beijing will be toppled in the next few weeks." Which Americans? Which China experts? How did the reporter come to these conclusions?

Another reporter digs out of the library old quotes of a person currently in the news and weaves these quotes into the story to substantiate a dominant position being taken—often not even making it clear that they are old quotes. The reporter often gives "the other side" a chance to have a say (thereby feigning objectivity), thus telling the audience, in effect, that complex issues have only two sides.

Journalists, of course, never speak of themselves as propagandists. The term has a negative connotation and usually is applied to persuasive efforts during wartime—or perhaps to efforts made by politicians, evangelists, and advertisers. After all, are not *journalists* above such things? Are they not concerned solely with "truth" and even-handed presentation of information? Are they not persons with no axes to grind? Such questions as these only reveal the sophistication of the "antipropaganda" propaganda of institutionalized journalism.

What journalist can say that he or she is guiltless of intentionally persuasive techniques? Who in journalism does not indulge in reportorial half-truths, distortions, news "management," exaggeration, false analogies, ad hominem tactics, hidden evidence, emotional appeals, Machiavellian strategies, and other purposeful techniques to achieve special objectives?

Hiding propaganda in what purports to be impartial news is, of course, extremely effective because of the faith most people must have in such reports. In *The Information Machines* Ben Bagdikian wrote: "There are growing numbers of men who understand how news is generated, organized, and transmitted, and it would be unintelligent of them if they did not use it to their own advantage" (1971, 293).

I am maintaining that journalists are propagandists in the sense that they "propagate" or spread their own biases and opinions as they attempt intentionally to affect attitudes and actions of their audiences. Large numbers of journalists, among them the so-called straight news reporters, spread propaganda every day—if not their own, then somebody else's. Leading propaganda scholar Terence H. Qualter says:

> Any doubts that even the news columns have propaganda significance can be settled by comparing the way in which several papers react to the one story. Each paper will make its own decision on the importance of the story—a decision which will be reflected in the page on which the story appears, its position on that page, and the size and style of type used in the headlines. . . . At one time it was customary to distinguish the expression of opinion on the editorial pages of a paper from the straightforward presentation of facts on the news pages. With the growing appreciation of the extent to which opinion governs the selection and manner of presentation of news, it has been concluded that this division is unrealistic and it is now generally admitted that the news columns can also contain propaganda. (91)

Many people, especially journalists, disregard contentions like those made by Qualter, claiming that the readers already have a certain opinion or ideological position and are simply seeking newspapers that reflect them. Jacques Ellul, an acclaimed French writer on propaganda, considers such a reaction "simplistic, removed from reality, and based on liberal idealism." He also says:

> In reality, propaganda is at work here, for what is involved is a progression from vague, diffuse on the part of the reader to rigorous, exciting, active expression of that opinion. A feeling or an impression is transformed into a motive for action. . . . The reader is subject to propaganda, even though it be propaganda of his choice. Why always fall into the error of seeing in propaganda nothing but a device to *change* opinions? Propaganda is also a means of reinforcing opinions, of transforming them into action. The reader himself offers his throat to the knife of the propaganda he chooses. (1965, 104)

Some propagandistic journalism is rather overt and crude. Sophisticated and skilled journalists, of course, make every effort to avoid this kind. They propagandize in far more subtle, effective ways. Instead of injecting their own values and judgments into their journalism in readily recognizable ways, they resort to subterfuge, accomplishing their purposes through tactical selectivity and emphasis. And instead of expressing a point of view, a position, or an opinion *themselves,* they let others speak for them. They quote selectively using the device that *U.S. News and World Report* pioneered and best exemplified. It is a common practice among journalists, and most honest ones will admit that they are guilty of it.

Propagandistic inclinations of journalists make it difficult for the audience to know when they are getting the truth. Nobody, of course, receives the full truth in journalism. Truth put into the journalism grinder comes out in bits and pieces, incomplete and sifted through the subjective value system of the journalist, so the truth is something that is tarnished when journalists finish it. One should remember Jefferson's famous quote in his later years when he wrote to a friend that "truth itself becomes suspicious by being put into that polluted vehicle [the press]." Media play their parts in spreading the propaganda of others. In so doing they inadvertently (or purposely) propagandize.

I am not maintaining that journalists alone participate in propaganda. We all do. Even academic persons who, like journalists, uphold the ideal of neutrality and dispassionate search for truth. Scholars push their pet theories and emphasize their favorite political figures; they quote most often their ideological allies, and they make sure their students get nothing or very little of the ideas of their ideological foes. It has been said that you can tell the politics and values of teachers by noting whom they quote and by looking at the footnotes and bibliographic entries of their publications.

In the case of advertisers, public relations people, politicians, and evangelists, there is a normal expectation of propaganda; nobody contends that these people are not advocating something, trying to "sell" something. There is no hypocrisy here. Academics and journalists, however, claim that they are not grinding axes. Here are practitioners who pay allegiance to fairness, balance, an unbiased perspective, and a desire to get at the truth. Their audiences do not *expect* to get propaganda.

No hypocrisy adheres, of course, to some journalists—editorial writers and columnists, for example. Propaganda in their products does not surprise us. But with reporters it is different. Perhaps it should not be, however. Perhaps we should expect propaganda from *all* journalists. I certainly do.

Argument summation: Media are instruments of propaganda.

Practitioners both transmit the propaganda of others and initiate their own. Probably three-fourths of all media content (maybe more, considering advertising) contains propaganda for some cause, policy, idea, institution, party, or person. Journalists especially are people of strong beliefs, and their biases come through in their journalism. Innumerable ways exist for journalists to propagandize—selection of information for stories and use of quotes, for example—and the journalists make use of them. Advertising, of course, is almost all propagandistic, and without a doubt it accounts for the bulk of media content. Media are in the ax-grinding business as well as the information and entertainment business.

Fortunately, a pluralism of propagandas keeps the activity from doing great social damage. The people can select their favorite propaganda from the variety furnished by the media.

TOPICS FOR DISCUSSION

1. Discuss the value of the acronymic formula P-A-S-I-D as a useful definition of propaganda.
2. Explain how many persons would see the media as "shields against propaganda." Do you think this is a valid view?
3. Why is propaganda so often identified with *government* communication efforts rather than with other groups or with individuals, such as the press or the television anchor?
4. Discuss why propaganda in the U.S. media would not be as effective as it would be in the media of Iran or China.
5. Is there a natural inclination for people in control of mass messages to propagandize? Give some examples of journalism that you feel *do not* indulge in propaganda.

TOPICS FOR RESEARCH

1. Write an essay on how propaganda got a bad name. After all, it was once a neutral term.
2. Prepare a report on governments and propaganda. How do governments develop propaganda machines? How do they work? To what effect? Mention both democratic and authoritarian societies.
3. Read two or three books about propaganda and write a review essay, asking whether propaganda is still a useful modern concept.
4. Considering changes in the Soviet Union and Eastern Europe, examine the changing role of propaganda. Does a more pluralistic press challenge propaganda?
5. Examine the claim that public relations and propaganda are one and the same. True? False? How do you know?

FURTHER READING

Altschull, J. Herbert. *Agents of Power: The Role of News Media in Human Affairs.* White Plains, NY: Longman, 1984.

Bagdikian, Ben. *The Information Machines.* New York: Harper & Row, 1971.

Christians, Clifford G. "Jacques Ellul and Democracy's 'Vital Information' Premise." *Journalism Monographs,* August 1976.

Ellul, Jacques. *Propaganda: The Formation of Men's Attitudes.* New York: Alfred A. Knopf, 1965.

Ewen, Stuart. *All-Consuming Images: The Politics of Style in Contemporary Culture.* New York: Basic Books, 1988.

———. *Channels of Desire: Mass Images and the Shaping of the American Consciousness.* New York: McGraw-Hill, 1982.

Gabler, Neal. *Winchell: Gossip, Power and the Culture of Celebrity.* New York: Alfred A. Knopf, 1994.

Gitlin, Todd. *The Whole World Is Watching.* Berkeley: University of California Press, 1980.

Jowett, Garth S., and Victoria O'Donnell. *Propaganda and Persuasion.* Beverly Hills, CA: Sage, 1986.

Lemert, James B. *Criticizing the Media: Empirical Approaches.* Beverly Hills, CA: Sage, 1989.

Merrill, John C. *Existential Journalism.* Ames: Iowa State Univ. Press, 1995.

Merrill, John C., John Lee, and Jay Friedlander. *Modern Mass Media.* New York: Harper & Row, 1990.

Merrill, John C., and Jack Odell. *Philosophy and Journalism.* White Plains, NY: Longman, 1983.

Qualter, Terence H. *Propaganda and Psychological Warfare.* New York: Random House, 1965.

Schiller, Herbert I. *Mass Communications and American Empire.* Boston: Beacon Press, 1971.

———. *The Mind Managers.* Boston: Beacon Press, 1973.

Sproule, J. Michael. "Propaganda Studies in American Social Science: The Rise and Fall of the Critical Paradigm." *Quarterly Journal of Speech* 73 (1987):60–78.

Chapter 15

RACE AND ETHNICITY

Drop in at any convention of editors, publishers, broadcasters, or journalism/communication educators and almost immediately the word *diversity* is mentioned. Diversity is a euphemism for race, ethnicity, national origin, and sometimes gender, but in the 1990s diversity in media circles usually refers to race and ethnicity and traces its recent origins to the famed Kerner Commission Report of 1968 when the government-appointed group declared that the United States was not one, but two societies: "one black, one white, separate and unequal." The commission found the media of the day especially wanting—both in their failure to have diverse, representative staffs and in their failure to cover news of interest to minorities. For the next quarter of a century leaders of media organizations pledged to hire more minorities—usually defined as African-Americans or blacks, Hispanics or Latinos, Asian-Americans, and Native Americans. Other large ethnic groups such as German- or Irish- or Italian-Americans are not usually part of this discussion since they are regarded as white rather than "people of color" and are assumed to have equal opportunity, not suffering the kind and degree of discrimination that African-Americans have, for example.

Almost immediately there was an effort to increase minority hiring in news organizations and journalism schools. The American Society of Newspaper Editors stepped up to the plate in 1978 and pledged to make their newspapers truly representative, with the same ratio of minority staff members as is found in the general adult population, by the year 2000. Other organizations and groups followed suit, and the idea of having racial and ethnic minorities well represented on and integrated into news and other media staffs has become well accepted. At the same time, there has been a similar effort to make the content of the press more representative. Once there was little coverage of minority communities and no concern about this void, so again leaders of the media urged broader, fuller, and more representative coverage. Like some political leaders, they vowed to make the media "look more like America."

In 1994 a unique gathering took place in Atlanta, Georgia. Called "Unity '94," the event was the first national convention of the several ethnic-minority organizations of "journalists of color," as they referred to themselves. These organizations included the National Association of Black Journalists (NABJ), the National Association of Hispanic Journalists (NAHJ), the Asian-American Journalists Association (AAJA), and the Native American Press Association (NAPA). In moving accounts and lively conference sessions several thousand minority journalists inventoried their concerns and complaints about the staffing and coverage patterns of America's media. While acknowledging progress since the Kerner Report, they collectively expressed disappointment about progress toward full representation and the extent to which so-called mainstream (usually white-owned and -dominated) media seriously portray ethnic and racial minorities and minority communities.

In an era when the term *political correctness* has emerged to describe an ideological commitment to particular political positions and policy choices, diversity is said to be "politically correct." Often people who question various diversity objectives are dismissed as uncaring, insensitive, or outright racists. While virtually every formal organization in the U.S. media world endorses diversity of staffing and content, most also admit that goals set long ago have not been met and that true diversity remains a distant dream. The basis for supporting diversity has always been the democratic theory that all members of the society ought to participate fully and completely in the processes of democracy. In such a scheme, the press is an important instrument in the democratic process. It also follows that full and representative coverage of society requires coverage of ethnic and racial groups and communities.

Some of the arguments made in favor of diversity are moral and philosophical, positing that it should happen "because it is right," while others suggest that diversity is also "good business," because it engages more of society as readers, viewers, and workers in media industries. It is almost universally agreed that diversity is a good thing and that all people of good will who are not racists should support it. At the same time, there is a backlash against diversity—by white males, in particular, who argue that they are being disadvantaged by quotas and preferential hiring practices, which, they say, are inherently undemocratic. But clearly the accepted and prevailing sentiment today is that diversity is not only a good thing but a noble cause as well, one around which arguments and critiques are not usually welcomed.

CHALLENGE

Dennis: Diversity needs rethinking and reassessment.

Let's face it, nearly three decades after the Kerner Commission Report there has been considerable progress toward diversity goals, but not perfection. And while much good has been accomplished in terms of more representative staffs and broader coverage of all people, much of the diversity movement today adds up to a great complaint that it neither advances the cause of ethnic and racial groups nor builds bridges to others in American society who were once sympathetic but are now resentful.

Without disputing the rightful claims of African-Americans, Latinos, and others who were effectively barred from newsrooms and covered in the news only as problems for most of the media's history, it is discouraging to see the rise of a new divisiveness that can only hurt everyone in the end.

Diversity's quiet and often frightened critics, whom I have encountered in the newsroom of the *Philadelphia Inquirer* (where a quota policy for minorities caused white males to rebel), argue that quotas and preferential hiring are inherently undemocratic, even un-American. They argue that equality of opportunity is all that is required with regard to participating in the media workplace, not certainty of outcomes. To explain, the critics I have met say that they think everyone should have an equal chance at getting into journalism schools, for example, as well as into training programs and entry-level jobs. At that point they part company with minority critics who say that progress must be measured at all levels—when people are hired, at promotion time, in middle management ranks, and in the executive offices as well. The critics argue that the onus is thereby put on the employer to give preferential treatment to minorities, while no one stands up for the rights of the majority. Richard Bernstein, a *New York Times* reporter and critic, who wrote a controversial book about multiculturalism called *Dictatorship of Virtue* (1994), has described "race censors" and "intellectual intimidation" in America's newsrooms, which lead to thought control. He argues that "truth and fairness are falling victim to the demands of racial and ethnic self-esteem." In an interview Bernstein noted that while top editors at one leading U.S. daily praised staff members who joined minority media organizations with a strong political agenda, it denied others the right to join political organizations and even frowned on union membership. To Bernstein and a few other critics, diversity is a political movement aimed at benefiting a few people who rightly want their place in American life and society.

Of course Bernstein and a few other journalist-critics of multiculturalism and diversity are joined by conservative commentators such as Pat

Buchanan and Rush Limbaugh, who say that a new favoritism is sweeping the country and that it will lead to greater divisiveness whereby principles of fair play and equal opportunity are lost. Columnist Carl Rowan decries these views as a "civil rights backlash," which would undo what thirty years of progress in race relations has accomplished.

To many, however, the troubling question is to what extent the news media should openly become a political battleground for various groups and individuals arguing the rightness of their cause. Should there be color-blind journalism as the Supreme Court once urged, or color-sensitive journalism wherein the racial and ethnic agenda of the reporter is on display and poised for action. Author and journalist Ellis Cose, whose book *The Rage of a Privileged Class* (1993) captures the dilemma of successful minorities living uncomfortably in a still-white world, writes:

> Journalists, of course, are supposed to be different from ordinary citizens, at least when it comes to confronting difficult truths. But race, it seems, can make cowards of us all. It is not merely cowardice, however, that makes honest racial dialogue difficult. The difficulty also derives from the fact that perceptions vary radically as a function of race—or, more accurately, as a function of the very different experiences members of various racial groups have endured. (1994, 2)

The racial-ethnic debate gets more complex when one looks carefully at the different groups who are part of the equation, realizing that while they share some common goals about hiring and media coverage, they also have differences with other groups and within their own "group." For example, Hispanic journalists, who often prefer the designation "Latino," include in their ranks Mexican-Americans, Puerto Ricans, Cuban-Americans and others from the Caribbean, Central American, and South America. This is not one lockstep group but people who generally, though not always, share the Spanish language but little else. Still, as has been the case with European immigrants, groups gather together for political reasons to achieve their goals.

Beyond the broad goals of equitable hiring and adequate coverage of minority communities, questions have been raised regarding racial-ethnic identification among reporters. From the beginning, minority reporters, editors, and broadcasters have argued that they have sometimes been typecast and their assignments have been limited to covering their own communities, though this practice is changing. Some newsroom critics say that one cannot be an advocate for a cause—any cause—and also be an impartial reporter. One critic I know says that sometimes this problem can be overcome in the covering of a volatile issue or person. For example, in regard to Nation of Islam leader Louis Farrakhan, most whites and some blacks in one Chicago newsroom were clearly biased against the controversial leader, while two reporters, both black and with a more open-minded outlook, developed stories that pointed up beneficial aspects of the Nation of Islam movement, something that a white-only newsroom could not have done.

Prior to the post-Kerner concern over race in the media, it was rare for any ethnic group to push their cause openly in American journalism, although author Gay Talese, an Italian-American, once noted how few members of his nationality made it in American journalism. Now to some extent the danger in ethnic-specific demands and requirements is said to be lack of openness to the needs of other neglected groups. And occasionally there has been open hostility. Some Latino journalists, for example, have openly clashed with gay and lesbian journalists, and Hispanics often argue that minority hiring almost always means black or Asian. Another problem is the presumption that race is all-defining when, in fact, some minority journalists come from truly dispossessed backgrounds and others are people of privilege. One activist minority journalist told me that some media outlets in the United States take only upper-class minorities out of Ivy League schools or "fudge" their numbers by hiring international journalists of color instead of those born here. "There is a merging and blurring," he said, and therefore he found it "difficult to see any real gains."

Another justifiable complaint: The news media, notably newspapers and broadcasters, are light-years ahead of other media and communications organizations in hiring. For example, newspapers claim that 10.9 percent of their staffs nationwide are minorities, while broadcasters boast a heftier 18.2 percent. Yet newspapers have been out front pushing diversity while broadcasting has been largely influenced by government mandates and regulations, common in an era of regulation but no longer as stringently enforced. Magazines don't keep statistics about their racial and ethnic numbers, and neither, it seems, do advertising and public relations organizations, all of which are said to lag well behind the news media.

Thus I believe that lockstep assumptions about diversity are misguided, if not wrong. All hail the progress that has been made and the principles on which those achievements have been made, but we must be careful that there not be a litmus test for multiculturalism or diversity wherein all people in the media have to hold the same views. Let's recognize also that minorities too can be intolerant and engage in racial censorship that is not healthy in what ought to be a free and open society wherein the media are conduits for democracy, not the instruments of group think. The media may be guilty both in their professed (though not often achieved) hiring policies and their coverage patterns of shutting down debate, driving honest differences and what might have been open racism underground. Even racism in the open is preferable to censorship, as honest debate and persuasive arguments can improve the racial and cultural climate for all people everywhere.

Argument summation: Diversity needs rethinking and reassessment.

Diversity, which translates into equal opportunity and better coverage of minority Americans in the news media, may be undermining its own cause through various excesses. Diversity may turn into divisiveness instead of producing a more civil and humane society. While the media should be open and should foster diversity in staffing and in news coverage, doing so should not be mandated or prescribed in such rigid fashion that it becomes unfair behavior itself. Diversity efforts in the past have led to many achievements in the staffing of America's media organizations, and much more is still needed. The same is true for diverse, multicultural news coverage. The main effort now ought to be on careful assessment of major areas of needs and deficiencies, especially in and among media that have not been successful in diversity efforts. At the same time, all citizens and media people should guard against intolerance.

RESPONSE

Merrill: Diversity is still one of the media's greatest failures and needs constant attention.

Initially let me say that I don't really know just what *diversity* in the news media means. Dennis has limited the term mainly to racial categories, namely whites (European-Americans) and blacks (African-Americans). Of course, there are Hispanics, Asian-Americans, and Native (Aboriginal) Americans to be considered, along with a conglomeration of other diverse types. Just how diverse news media staffs should be is indeed an important question. What about handicapped persons (physically disadvantaged)? What about people with low IQs? What about former prison inmates? What about street people? What about Pentecostals, Quakers, Mormons, Baptists, Roman Catholics, Muslims, Hindus, or Buddhists? Should all these and many other groups be represented in the American newsrooms? And to what degree?

Although, as has been pointed out, since the Kerner Report in 1968 there has been considerable progress in diversification of news media staffs, many groups (actually no more than three) are still maintaining that American media are still too white-owned and -dominated. It is still widely believed that minority and ethnic communities are not adequately represented among media agenda setters and reporters. Underrepresentation in the media workforce results in less than adequate coverage of minority communities. This perhaps explains why the reader of newspapers and magazines finds basically a white world presented—and a male one at that. Ellis Cose gives a good example of this world:

> Today, though we live in a world (as we constantly remind ourselves) that is increasingly multicultural, much of conventional journalism remains fixated on the lives of the white and the wealthy. I was reminded of that earlier this year, when my issue of *New York* magazine arrived. It featured an article that purported to identify the best places to find any number of products and services one might search for in New York City. I was struck by the fact that in a city that is a virtual United Nations—it is said that more than 119 languages and dialects are spoken in New York—practically every face attached to the magazine's recommendations was white. Clearly, New York, as viewed by the magazine's editors, remains a very white place. (1994, 8)

A look into most newsrooms of the United States will reveal that European-American males dominate, especially in the higher administrative ranks. Let us admit that the *rational* basis for diversity in the newsrooms is suspect, as Dennis has said in his "Challenge." Admittedly there is no real evidence that an African-American can, because of his or her color, report—even on racial issues—any better than a white reporter. Nevertheless, greater diversity is a worthy goal in journalism and is one to which most American journalists have always paid lip service.

The journalist diversity in the media is improving but is still rather undernourished. For instance, the American Society of Newspaper Editors in 1993 reported (*Quill,* April 1993, p. 21) that minorities made up only 10 percent of the total newsroom work force and that African-Americans accounted for only 4.8 percent of all journalists, although they make up about 12.5 percent of the general population. As to gender, men comprised 65 percent (54 percent white men) in TV and 69 percent in radio, with women accounting for some 35 percent (27 percent white women) for TV and 31 percent for radio (*Communicator,* August 1994, p. 17). And according to a Scripps Howard Newspapers study (*Media Studies Journal,* Winter/Spring 1993, p. 179), men hold 85 percent of newsroom management positions.

Pluralism—or diversity—is one of the valued principles of American journalism. The greater the diversity of ideas and informational perspectives, the better the news package: This is a widely held belief. So why not apply this to racial, gender, and ethnic makeup of news staffs? A story written by a black American, for instance, may be no better written than one by a white American but at least it will provide a different angle, viewpoint, perspective, or emphasis. Or at least there is a good chance that it will. Reporters and editors reflect their various cultures—their upbringing, their religion, their values, and their experiences.

Most often the culture reflected in the media is a white culture—and a middle class white culture at that. By 1993 the Bureau of the Census

(*Quill,* April 1993, p. 22) showed that minorities accounted for 26.8 percent of the population, and the estimate was that by the year 2050 the U.S. population would be 47 percent minority. No doubt this shift will be seen in the makeup of media news staffs; certainly the newsrooms will evidence a much greater pluralism—if not out of philosophical considerations, at least out of economic considerations.

I doubt if any reasonable person wants to see what Dennis in his "Challenge" calls "lockstep assumptions about diversity"—quotas, for instance. But a natural, evolutionary assimilation of many cultural and racial groups into journalism should be a goal worth working toward. And as more and more diverse groups get larger representation in our journalism and communications schools, this natural assimilation into the media is indeed taking place.

Forced diversity may, as Dennis says, be leading to divisiveness in our media, but a white-dominated media system also results in divisiveness. This is really the nature of any institution—especially the press: Divisiveness is natural, to be expected. And a certain amount of it is perhaps good for journalism. Stuart Silverstein, a writer for the *Los Angeles Times,* notes (May 3, 1995, p. 2A) that because they have been targets of the "angry white male" backlash, some companies have scrapped diversity-training sessions. Other companies run diversity programs "out of economic self-interest, predicting that the initiatives will help attract talented workers, reduce turnover and unleash creativity." This is undoubtedly the case; we can see today a plethora of African-American journalists, in print and in broadcasting, who were invisible ten to twenty years ago.

Multiculturalism in *our society* must, it seems to me, be reflected (but to what degree, I don't know) in multiculturalism in *the media* that reflect and interpret our society. Therefore we need diversity—more than we have—in our news media. Preferably it will come naturally, and if it does, it will not do so equally; some races, sexes, groups will be larger than others in the makeup of the staff. If it is somehow forced, then we will have a tightly controlled, mathematically determined, highly regimented journalism, and few Americans would want that. For example, if 5 percent of a town's inhabitants were lesbians, few people in their right minds would insist that 5 percent of the town's newspaper staff should be lesbian. Yet it might be well if the newspaper had a lesbian or two on its staff; but then, again, it might not.

In conclusion, I would say that diversity in the news media is still a great failure. We have too little of it—but "too little" is of course quite subjective. At any rate I think we need more diversity of all kinds in our news media: conservatives, moderates, liberals, socialists, libertarians, radicals, communitarians, and individualists—as well as racial, gender, and cultural "rainbow" representations. In all of this, however, we must remember that freedom is also an important concept for the news media;

they should have diversity, but they should freely bring it about with no coercion from outside sources.

Some readers may think that I am weak willed in dedication to diversity. Not so. I am all in favor of justice (if we can find out what it is), but I don't want anyone to *force* me to be "just." Similarly, as a newspaper editor I may want "diversity" on my staff, but I don't want anyone to *force* me to have diversity. My newspaper may make great efforts to have diversity; your newspaper may not. This, in one sense, is adding to the equation another kind of diversity: some staffs with diversity and some staffs with little diversity. *C'est la vie!*

Argument summation: Diversity is still one of the media's greatest failures and needs constant attention.

Although diversity within the staffs of the news media—at least the kind of diversity that will please everyone—is perhaps impossible to achieve, there is still much that can be done in this area. Media practitioners are still mainly white, Anglo-Saxon males, and this is especially true in the higher echelons of media institutions.

One of the basic value-tenets of American journalism is *pluralism,* the idea of a great variety of news and ideas making their way into the media. *Person pluralism* should also be valued, and as large a diversity of "people-types" as possible should be found on news staffs. This process, however, should be a natural and voluntary one, one that is not forced upon a news medium by any outside force. One does not correct one problem in the media (lack of diversity) by instituting another problem (restriction of press freedom). Voluntary inclusion or self-determined diversity by the media themselves is the correct answer.

TOPICS FOR DISCUSSION

1. What do statistics about racial/ethnic representation in various media fields, such as newspapers, broadcasting, and others, tell us? How useful are these kind of data in keeping track of progress? Are there dangers in relying too heavily on statistics rather than looking carefully at different kinds of media organizations (big papers vs. small) and particular jobs (reporter, managing editor, station manager)?

2. What is the philosophical basis for diversity in the media and how does it comport with the theory of democracy?

3. What were the benefits of Unity '94 and how did the major news media react to that historic gathering?

4. Who are the most visible and important leaders in the media diversity movement? Are they known beyond the media fields to the general public?

5. When you think of visible minorities in the U.S. media, who comes to mind? How many of these persons are quite senior? How many younger? Are some media more likely places to find minority journalists and media executives than others?

TOPICS FOR RESEARCH

1. What did the Kerner Commission say about the news media of its day? To what extent are its conclusions still relevant or now outdated?

2. Some commentators argue that market segmentation in the media will benefit minority hiring and minority coverage because advertisers wanting to reach particular segments of the audience will have greater influence. What is the relevance of this idea to diversity, and what do you think of the argument?

3. Consider doing a sketch history in which you compare and contrast two minority media or journalism organizations at the state or national level. If possible, interview active minority journalism organization leaders in the process, in person, on the phone, or through e-mail.

4. Consider the following proposition: A journalist or other communicator who is an activist for his or her color, ethnicity, or community can/cannot be fair and impartial as a communications professional.

5. Do a brief content analysis of your local newspaper or the local evening newscast to determine the nature, amount, and quality of minority community coverage.

6. Read a week's run of a leading newspaper. Look for news of special interest to African-Americans, Latinos, Native Americans, and Asian-Americans. Pay attention to photographs and then write a comparative essay citing specific evidence from your study.

FURTHER READING

Bernstein, Richard. *Dictatorship of Virtue—Multiculturalism and the Battle for America's Future.* New York: Alfred A. Knopf, 1994.

Cose, Ellis. *The Quiet Crisis: Minority Journalists and Newsroom Opportunity.* Berkeley, CA: Institute for Journalism Education, 1985.

———. *The Rage of a Privileged Class.* New York: HarperCollins, 1993.

———. "Seething in Silence—The News in Black and White," *Media Studies Journal,* Summer 1994.

Dates, Jannette L., and William Barlow, eds. *Split Image: African Americans in the Mass Media.* 2d ed. Washington, DC: Howard University Press, 1994.

Dawkins, Wayne. *Black Journalists: The NABJ Story.* Sicklerville, NJ: August Press, 1993.

Fielder, Virginia Dodge. *Minorities and Newspapers: A Survey of Newspaper Research.* Reston, VA: American Society of Newspaper Editors, 1986.

Fisler, Paul L., and Ralph L. Lowenstein, eds. *Race and the News Media.* New York: Praeger, 1968.

Jackson, Anthony W., ed. *Black Families and the Medium of Television.* Ann Arbor, MI: Bush Program in Child Development and Social Policy, 1982.

Jhally, Sut, and Justin Lewis. *Enlightened Racism:* The Cosby Show, Audiences, and the Myth of the American Dream. Boulder, CO: Westview Press, 1992.

Lewels, Francisco J. *How the Chicano Movement Uses the Media.* New York: Praeger, 1974.

Martindale, Carolyn. *The White Press and Black America.* Westport, CT: Greenwood Press, 1986.

Martindale, Carolyn, ed. *Pluralizing Journalism Education: A Multicultural Perspective.* Westport, CT: Greenwood Press, 1993.

Muted Voices: Frustration and Fear in the Newsroom. Reston, VA: The National Association of Black Journalists, 1993.

"Race: America's Rawest Nerve." *Media Studies Journal,* Summer 1994. New York: Freedom Forum Media Studies Center.

The Report of the National Advisory Commission on Civil Disorders. Washington, DC: U.S. Government Printing Office, 1968.

Smith, Erna. *Transmitting Race: The Los Angeles Riot in Television News.* Cambridge, MA: The Joan Shorenstein Barone Center for Press, Politics and Public Policy, 1994.

Wilson, Clint C. II, and Felix Gutiérrez. *Minorities and Media: Diversity and the End of Mass Communication.* Beverly Hills, CA: Sage, 1985.

Chapter 16

ADVERTISING

Advertising is both a communication process and an industry that is inextricably linked to mass media in America and in some other societies. It is defined in dictionaries as the action that attracts public attention to a product or business, as well as the business of preparing and distributing advertisements. According to the American Marketing Association, advertising is "any paid form of nonpersonal presentation and promotion of ideas, goods, and services by an identified sponsor." Advertising has also been called controlled, identifiable information and persuasion. Advertising becomes a matter of controversy for several reasons. Its role in society and in the economy has often been debated.

Advertising has a well-established place in American life. The component parts of the advertising industry—ad agencies, media service organizations, media advertising departments—employ nearly 200,000 people and generate about $100 million in gross revenue annually. Advertising is generally accepted by most Americans, who recognize that it funds most of the media they enjoy, provides consumer advice, and promotes a capitalist economy. It has been said that American society is a commercial culture and advertising is an essential ingredient in that formulation.

While advertising is a historical reality and one that provides "fuel" for most commercial media in the United States, there are those who would prefer a communication system without advertising. Questions are frequently raised about whether advertising unnecessarily stimulates needs and wants of people, whether it encourages class consciousness, materialism, and other values that are not universally applauded. Such discussion is related to advertising's impact on society, an influence assessed by historians, philosophers, social scientists, and media researchers.

The social criticism of advertising often centers on whether advertising is truthful. While few critics today advocate the abolition of advertising, there is an active movement to control this form of controlled communication, presumably in order to serve the public interest. Special attention has been given to the impact of advertising on children, to the portrayal of women and minorities in advertising, and to other topics that have generated controversy.

CHALLENGE

Merrill: Advertising is a negative social force.

A principal deity of a capitalist society and of a competitive marketplace media system is the Great God Advertising. GGA is everywhere, raising its gaudy face across the land, beaming its insistent messages into our offices, cars, and homes. It fills billboards along our highways, drops in the form of coupons from our magazines and mailboxes, blares at us in all of its resplendent redundancy from our TV screens, and fills our newspapers.

The power and crassness of the advertiser is a negative social force. It contaminates our country from one end to the other. This advertiser power has been called by diplomat and scholar George F. Kennan "the greatest evil of our national life." How can we, asked Kennan, have a healthy intellectual climate, successful education, a sound press, or "a proper vitality of artistic and recreational life" until advertisements "are removed from every printed page containing material that has claim to intellectual or artistic integrity and from every television or radio program that has these same pretensions?" (1968, 201).

These are strong words from one of twentieth-century America's foremost diplomats. But that's not all Kennan had to say about advertising:

> Is it a revolution I am demanding? Yes—a revolution in the financing and control of the process of communication generally. And if this revolution brings in the government as a replacement for the advertiser in many of these processes, I still wish for it. The government's commitment and conscience as an educator—its commitment to truthfulness and integrity in communication—may not be all that we could want. But it has at least *some* responsibility here to the public weal, and *some* obligation to keep in mind the public needs. This is more than one can say about the advertiser. (1968, 201–2)

Another luminary of the twentieth century, Aldous Huxley, with his exceptionally keen eye for blemishes in social institutions, devoted all of Chapter 6 of his well-known *Brave New World Revisited* (1965) to the "arts of selling," with special emphasis on advertising. He speaks of propaganda in the West as having two faces—one (Dr. Jekyll) the democratic editorialist, the other (Dr. Hyde) the antidemocratic person in charge of advertising.

This propagandist—the advertising expert—is a Ph.D. in psychology and has a Master's degree in the social sciences. Here is part of Huxley's depiction of this advertising "Dr. Hyde":

> This Dr. Hyde would be very unhappy indeed if everybody lived up to John Dewey's faith in human nature. Truth and reason are Jekyll's affair, not his. Hyde is a motivational analyst, and his business is to study human weaknesses and failings, to investigate those unconscious desires and fears by which so much of man's conscious thinking and overt doing is determined. And he does this, not in the spirit of the moralist who would like to make people better, or of the physician who would like to improve their health, but simply in order to find out the best way to take advantage of their ignorance and to exploit their irrationality for the pecuniary benefit of his employers. (1965)

Irrational, exploitive, seeking pecuniary profit, manipulating the audience's desires and fears: This is the picture painted of advertisers. These two men have capsulized neatly the major characteristics and concerns of advertising in America. Obviously such advertising is not a positive force in our society.

Mention "Madison Avenue" and what comes to mind? The thoughtful, perceptive citizen does not have to read a book critical of the advertising business (like Samm S. Baker's classic *The Permissible Lie* [1968]) to feel antipathy toward the omnipresent commercialism that surrounds us all. Coke and Pepsi battle it out everywhere, each claiming superiority, with their slogans couched in abstract vagaries.

Brand X is best by taste test. Four out of five doctors recommend this mouthwash. Discerning people choose this brand. All one has to do is "squeeze" the toilet paper to know it's superior. My aspirin is stronger than yours. My automobile is like a bird; just watch it here on TV—it actually takes off and zooms into the night sky. Here come all the ads that hawk their products as "new" and "improved." And there is that advertising that insults one's intelligence; for instance, a commercial on television tells us that its product (a cereal) "might reduce the risk of certain types of cancer." It *might reduce* the *risk* of *certain* types. I am not reassured.

I sit before my TV set and, lo and behold, the alleged "positive force" of the commercials strikes me constantly. I learn useful and important things. I learn that "a double pleasure" is waiting for me if I buy a certain kind of chewing gum. I am urged to "come into Kirshmann's Furniture Store and feel the excitement." And, if "coffee tastes your way," it's X Brand. And if I drink this kind of beer, "the best comes shining through." And I'll get "taste free in every bite" if I eat a certain breakfast cereal.

Important stuff. A positive social force. Just knowing that there are double pleasures, the chance to feel the excitement, things tasting my way, having the best shine through, and getting a "free" taste with every bite. Now, that's a positive (useful, socially significant) social force!

But all is well, for the "Creative Code" of the American Association of Advertising Agencies (representing at least fifteen national communications groups) has determined to keep this "positive social force" intact and progressing. The public, we are told, has the right to expect advertising to be reliable in content and honest in presentation. And the code assures us that advertisers will "extend and broaden the application of high ethical standards."

Advertising, says the code, will not deal in misleading statements or exaggerations, present testimonials that do not reflect the real choice of the testimonial giver, make misleading price claims, makes insufficiently supported claims, or present statements or pictures offensive to public decency. I would say that advertising consistently does *all of these things*. If you don't believe it, just take a few moments and analyze the ads that flood from the media upon you.

Advertising a positive social force? I think not. Advertising causes people to buy what they don't need, causes people to discard perfectly good merchandise, causes poor people to want things they can't afford, spreads vulgar culture, and creates exorbitant and unfillable expectations, thus promoting a materialistic society.

Here is what Michael Schudson has to say about advertising:

> Whatever advertising's direct effect in stimulating and making people buy more goods, it fully merits its reputation as the emblem of fraudulence. . . . A great many [ads] are positively informational. But there is a persistent, underlying bad faith in nonprice advertising. I take as emblematic the old McDonald's slogan, "We do it all for you." That, of course, is a lie. (1984, 13)

As Samm S. Baker tells us, Madison Avenue condones and encourages half-truths and exaggeration. He adds:

> The overwhelming aim of advertising is to make a profit; to serve the public becomes a secondary consideration. A lie that helps build profits is considered a permissible lie. (1968)

Former magazine editor Richard L. Tobin quotes Samm Baker as saying, "In a single half hour of browsing through magazines I found more than a dozen ads claiming that their products were smoother; longer-lasting; cheaper; better; washed whiter; stayed fresh longer. . . . Are we really suckers that we swallow these pointless hooks?" Perhaps we are not so foolish as to swallow them, but even if they are relatively harmless from that perspective, it still seems rather obvious that such advertising does not serve as a positive social force.

Now my coauthor Dennis will surely maintain that much advertising is not of that type, that much of it is straightforward and factual and that it provides a much-needed public service. I must admit that this is true. There is *some* honest, informative advertising. But what about the generality? Advertising, *generally speaking,* is not a positive social force; it does more harm to the society than good, and certainly it should be deemphasized.

Advertising is to a newspaper as intercollegiate athletics is to a university. Both advertising and athletics deemphasize the real purpose of their carrier. Neither is perhaps bad per se, but, to quote two old clichés, each has gotten out of hand and we have a case of the tail wagging the dog. A newspaper (a misnomer these days when only about 10 percent of its total space contains *news*) reader must increasingly search diligently for tiny oases of editorial material, surrounded as they are by vast deserts of advertising.

In conclusion, I must contend that advertising is not a positive social force. It is simply the economic foundation for the money-making proclivities of media owners and the machine that stimulates exorbitant profits by manufacturers, wholesalers, and retailers. And what about *political advertising*? I won't even get into that—it's too sleazy—but I suppose that three out of four of the nation's politicians highly recommend it. Undoubtedly 100 percent of media owners give it the go sign. This, of course, must mean that it is a positive social force. But that's Dennis's position. I don't buy it.

Argument summation: Advertising is a negative social force.

Advertising clutters our media, overpowers serious news and discussion, encourages unnecessary buying, worsens class envy, and leads to wasteful consumption. Advertisements may largely finance American media, but that would be the only way it could be called a "positive force." Advertising exaggerates, misleads, appeals to sex and frivolity, gives irrational testimonials, creates exorbitant expectations, and generally promotes a materialistic society. At best, advertising in America is a necessary evil. It could hardly be called a positive social force.

RESPONSE

Dennis: Advertising is a positive social force.

If the reader were seated in front of a VCR, I would insert a selection of advertisements that urge safe sex practices to avoid AIDS, that promote literacy, and that encourage racial tolerance and environmental improvement. Then I would ask the reader to find equally powerful advertisements reaching mass audiences that promote the opposite of these causes and values or any other advertising that truly does damage to our way of life, fosters racism, or promotes pollution. I would guess that the reader would have difficulty with that assignment. I might then ask what in the world Merrill is talking about, but perhaps that would be too easy a response. So, I will respond to several of his protestations about the evils of advertising.

First a touch of reality. Advertising is a reality. It has been with us since ancient times and has played a particular role in American culture since before the Revolution. It is so well integrated into our commercial media—and that is most media sans public television and radio—that they probably could not survive without it. No one I know of, not even Merrill, is seriously suggesting that advertising be abolished or even curtailed by legislation. In fact, I doubt that doing so is possible, because it is well to remember that advertising is protected speech. It is commercial rather than political speech, but it is a form of free expression and it has some constitutional protection. With some irony, advertising executive John O'Toole writes:

> *The Pennsylvania Evening Post* of July 6, 1776 contained the text of the Declaration of Independence and ten advertisements, thereby exhibiting a certain insensitivity to a distinction between news and commercial speech that has taken on enormous importance over the ensuing centuries. (*Gannett Center Journal,* 1, no. 1 [Spring 1987]:97).

While once accorded less freedom than political speech, commercial speech has gained important ground over the last ten years, a trend that is likely to continue. So it seems that my colleague, who sees no problem with the free distribution of all kinds of political and social messages and generally abhors censorship, somehow is uncomfortable with the influence of what he calls "the great god advertising." I refuse to capitalize this rather hackneyed expression.

Of course, I am not so silly as to argue that all advertising is elevating and socially responsible, any more than I would make the case for all printed and electronic communication. Some advertising is misleading, unsavory, and generally reprehensible, but the vast majority of it is not, and if one really believes in freedom of expression, we take the good, the bad, and the ugly as part of the package, while hoping, of course, that positive social forces will reward responsible communicators and shun those who are not. In the case of advertising, ads that make fraudulent claims are subject to legal penalties, just as writers who libel others can be sued and thus punished. But that really isn't the point.

To argue that advertising has a positive social impact, I believe that its value is principally in providing consumer information to the public. Advertising is the means by which we learn about new products, services, and causes. Discerning people look at advertising with a somewhat skeptical eye because advertising is advocacy for a product and there are simply too many products for any of us to know, understand, use, or for that matter, afford. We know that there are many brands of cereal, all competing for our attention. Some will make nutritional claims, others emphasize taste. Probably no one—not even young children—accepts literally everything in an advertisement, even though it may be true, because there is something called "consumer choice," and we make our choices based on our own needs, interests, income, and other factors. Advertising thus provides an educational service.

Advertising stimulates the economy. One need only visit a socialist country to see how few products are available. And while it sometimes seems that our materialistic society has generated more products than we need or can possibly consume, if the choice is between the empty shelves of Moscow and the crowded displays in Los Angeles, I know where I would prefer to shop. Of course our economy does have a wasteful aspect—we have more firms and more products in the market than can possibly survive. Some do. Some do not. And advertising plays a role in showcasing both to the American public. On the positive side, advertising expands consumer choice and promotes diversity. If it were otherwise, someone would have to make arbitrary choices about which products would be manufactured and which ones would not be allowed to develop. In socialist economies this is done by the government. In our system, ultimately the consumers choose, and they are aided by advertising.

There is considerable controversy over whether advertising has any real impact on consumer behavior. Some economists and social scientists say it has little or none. Others argue that it is all powerful. Sociologist Michael Schudson, whom Merrill quotes, has some real doubts about the influence of advertising, arguing, "Advertising is much less powerful than advertisers and critics of advertising claim, and advertising agencies are stabbing in the dark much more than they are practicing precision microsurgery on the public consciousness." Still, in his book on advertising Schudson also concedes that "advertising serves a useful informational function that will not and should not be abandoned" (1984, 239).

Schudson is among those who doubt that advertising affects consumer choice all that much, but he does suggest that it may affect the goods available to consumers. Consumers are not the only factors to consider. The entrepreneurs want to create and sell products. They can do so efficiently and can try their wares on the public—sometimes successfully, sometimes not—because of advertising.

Modern advertising is not the carnival barker of old, nor is it indiscriminate shotgun messages sent out over mass media. It is carefully calibrated and controlled communication. It is aimed at a particular segment of the market or audience. A particular ad, for example, may target only black Americans or only persons in a particular income bracket or with a given educational background. This factor also encourages diversity and even stimulates the number and range of media organizations in the marketplace. The magazine industry, for example, exists mainly because of advertising aimed at specialized audiences. There are women's magazines, for example, mainly because there are products and services that are for women only. They advertise in *Ladies Home Journal* or *Ms.* to reach a selected, target audience. As some critics have said, this is not delicate brain surgery, but it is an efficient way to see that appropriate people know about certain products and issues that will influence them. Advertising ranges from national to local, from display to classified. It is hard to imagine that anyone, even Merrill, would argue against the utility and efficiency of classified advertising, unless, of course, it was the personals, which sometimes transgress good taste.

My colleague saves his final stab for political advertising, which he quite superficially denounces, and then with the dagger in his shawl he retreats from the stage. In light of the many attacks on political advertising in recent presidential campaigns, the subject is worth addressing here. Many will remember the Willie Horton ad run by the Bush-for-President campaign in 1988. It was said to be racist and misleading and I believe it was. At the same time, it was widely debated and I don't think, in the end, it unduly influenced anyone who wasn't already going to vote for George Bush for other reasons. Certainly there is no evidence to the contrary. True enough, there were misleading, low-grade political ads in the 1988 campaign, but they generally reflected an issueless campaign and the messages of the two candidates, both of whom were mean spirited. At the same time there were thousands of positive, elevating political ads used by candidates at the local, state, and national levels. And if past elections are any indicator, the general trend in political advertising has been quite positive, pointing up the virtues of a given candidate rather than tearing down that person's opponent.

The fact that there is so much discussion about the content of advertising suggests that people are paying attention to it. When ads have been sexist, there has often been an outcry against them. Fairly often these ads are dropped and new ones come on in their place. Is the net result here negative? No, not at all. The sexist ad, which probably was prepared to appeal to people's predispositions, was challenged and brought to public attention, thus unwittingly doing a service to the feminist cause. And it is through this kind of criticism and response that attitudes and public images do change over time. At one time minorities and women were portrayed in a denigrating fashion in the ads, or not at all. Now that practice is changing, reflecting changing social attitudes. That is for the better.

There will always be some offensive and potentially damaging advertisements, but in our system they can be challenged, criticized, and protested. That process is not a bad one and probably reflects the advance of civilization generally. After all, our culture wasn't created in a day, and it will continue to mature with the help of advertising, which is, of course, a positive social force.

Argument summation: Advertising is a positive social force.

There is no realistic justification for the restriction of advertising: It is a form of protected speech and is crucial to the financial survival of media industries. While some advertising is generally reprehensible, the vast majority is not, and there is virtually no advertising that promotes causes or values that truly do damage to American society. Instead, by providing consumer information to the public, advertising plays a positive social role. The public knows that advertisements are advocating specific views and accepts them with skepticism. Advertising also is a positive force for economic stimulation. Targeted advertising is valuable to increase the diversity and range of media organizations like specialized magazines in the marketplace. Political advertising, even when misleading, reflects the nature of the candidates and rarely goes unchallenged by the opposition or a critical news media.

TOPICS FOR DISCUSSION

1. What are some of the ways the American media system could be financially supported if we were to eliminate advertising?

2. Can advertising be considered a positive social force because it is "a reality" that has been with us from ancient times?

3. Does advertising in the United States keep the press free? If so, how? Could the press be just as free if there were no advertising? What does press financing have to do with First Amendment press provisions?

4. Make a case for political advertising. Do you know of anyone who voted for a certain candidate because of advertising? Have you or any of your family? Do you think political advertising is issue oriented?

5. Does most TV and newspaper display advertising appeal to one's reason or to one's prejudices and emotions? Explain and give examples.

TOPICS FOR RESEARCH

1. Look at public service advertisements that promote an important social cause or issue. Be specific and examine them in terms of their appeals and likely success (or failure).

2. After researching the topic of political advertising, write an essay on "Political Advertising: The Good, the Bad, and the Ugly." Give examples of positive and negative political advertising. Which kind works best? Why?

3. Is advertising a positive social force on the movement of goods and services? Compare and contrast the advertisements of two competitors. Do they distinguish their products? Do they make compelling cases? If this advertising were your only source of information about the products, which would you choose?

4. In recent years comparative advertising, wherein one product promotes itself by attacking a competitor either overtly or with subtlety, has been in vogue. Compare two advertisers who use this approach. Do you think it works?

5. Set up your own criteria and standards for advertising that is a positive social force. Then grade several ads or ad campaigns using your own criteria. Be a tough grader.

FURTHER READING

Baker, Edwin. *Advertising and the First Amendment.* Cambridge, MA: Harvard University Press, 1993.

Baker, Samm S. *The Permissible Lie: The Truth About Advertising.* Cleveland: World Publishing Co., 1968.

Huxley, Aldous. *Brave New World Revisited.* New York: Harper & Row, Perennial Library, 1965.

Jamieson, Kathleen Hall. *Packaging the Presidency.* New York: Oxford University Press, 1984.

Kennan, George. *Democracy and the Student Left.* New York: Bantam Books, 1968.

Packard, Vance. *The Hidden Persuaders.* Paperback ed. New York: Washington Square Press, 1980.

Pope, Daniel. *The Making of Modern Advertising.* New York: Basic Books, 1983.

Potter, David M. *People of Plenty.* 2d ed. Chicago: University of Chicago Press, 1969.

Rothenberg, Randall. *Where the Suckers Moon: An Advertising Story.* New York: Alfred A. Knopf, 1994.

Rotzoll, Kim B., James E. Haefner, and Charles H. Sandage. *Advertising in Contemporary Society.* Cincinnati: SouthWestern Publishing, 1986.

Sandage, C. H., Vernon Fryburger, and Kim Rotzoll. *Advertising Theory and Practice.* 11th ed. Homewood, IL: Richard D. Irwin, 1983.

Schudson, Michael. *Advertising: The Uneasy Persuasion.* New York: Basic Books, 1984.

Chapter 17

PUBLIC RELATIONS

Public relations (PR), like advertising, is variously a communication system, a subset of the media system, a series of practices, a profession, and the object of derision and scorn. The leading text by Scott Cutlip and colleagues says:

> The term public relations is used in at least three senses: the *relationships* with those who constitute an organization's public or constituents, the *ways and means used* to achieve favorable relationships, and the *quality or status* to the relationships. Thus the one term is used to label both *means and ends,* to name a *condition* and to express the *conduct or actions related to that condition.* (Cutlip, Center, and Broom, 1985, 120)

The field of public relations, like advertising, is part and parcel of the communication system in the United States. There are independent public relations firms, public relations offices in businesses and government, and communications consulting firms that do everything from training executives for television appearances to designing an information campaign and strategy for a political candidate or a foreign government. Hundreds of thousands of persons work in the public relations field and it would be hard to estimate the amount of money spent on this activity. While public relations certainly has its detractors, it also has a national professional association—the Public Relations Society of America—an accreditation procedure for professionals, a code of ethics, and a growing scholarly and professional literature. Some critics, especially some journalists, would abolish public relations altogether. That scenario, however, is an unlikely one, because public relations is nothing more than controlled and organized communication. And in a communication society, public relations has grown, since there is simply more demand for communication services. As information increasingly becomes a renewable resource through the recycling of messages, public relations strategies and services are needed to promote and market the product. Public relations differs in an essential way from advertising because it is not generally identified with a sponsor or product. When one sees a guest on the *Today Show*, chances are that person has been placed there by a highly paid public relations practitioner or firm, yet the viewer is never told of this aspect. Thus public relations can be more subtle and less visible than advertising.

CHALLENGE

Dennis: Public relations manipulates the news.

Pause for a moment and consider the general image that public relations has in American society. Public relations in the minds of many is equated with deception. A "public relations solution," for example, implies an emphasis on appearances and stage managing rather than a blunt recitation of facts. Remembering that public relations is an arm of top management, whether in the public or private sector, we can note that public relations is a process meant to benefit those creating PR messages. A company's public relations department is not charged with reporting bad news, should there be any in the firm. Instead their mandate is to put the best face on the situation, to explain and rationalize it. They can do this positively in a fashion beneficial to the public, but often they do not, since it is the client, not the public, paying the bill. Some argue that they are simply exercising the right to communicate and that all persons are entitled to put forth their views, with or without the help of a public relations firm. That concept is an important factor in the debate over the utility of public relations, since some critics argue that it not only tends to be deceptive, but also gives undue advantage to those who can afford to have their own public relations counsel. In general, even after years of high-quality professional attainment, the field of public relations still has a somewhat unsavory reputation in American society, and the term itself is much disputed. Whether this perception is fair and accurate or not is not the issue here. It is the prevailing image.

Even the origins of public relations in the United States are unsavory. Public relations historians are fond of recounting the history of this questionable enterprise, which they say was established by Ivy Lee, an ex-newspaperman who created a publicity agency. One of his clients was John D. Rockefeller, the oil tycoon, who had a deservedly bad reputation for his unfair business practices and his cruelty to his employees. The great muckraker Ida M. Tarbell documented Rockefeller's practices in her brilliant work "The History of the Standard Oil Company," which appeared in *McClure's Magazine* in 1902. Those articles and other social criticism brought pressure on Congress to clip Rockefeller's wings and those of other robber barons. The result was antitrust legislation and penalties for unfair and illegal competition. Rockefeller hired Ivy Lee to convince the public that he was a kind and loving family man (which he was) and generous as well (which he was not). Lee, for all his genius and his role in modern business communication, helped change Rockefeller's image and, in effect, manipulated the news media and public attitudes. Today Rockefeller is remembered more favorably than are those who campaigned against his excesses. Ivy Lee and public relations must share much of the blame.

Although there have been noble people associated with the public relations field, and some of them, like the pioneering Edward L. Bernays, campaigned for professionalism and ethical practice, it still must be said that public relations is a force that packages news and information on behalf of its clients. A vigilant press ought to be able to see through deceptive and dishonest communication—and it does—but still there is an advantage for those who are well represented by public relations counsel versus those who are not. Think of the homeless, for example, coming face to face with a giant developer who would remove them from a particular district of a large city. The developer will have a much greater capacity to argue his case in the press with the help of public relations people. There is nothing inherently wrong with this on a case by case basis, but, considered as a whole, there is no doubt that public relations strategies do influence press coverage and portrayals in the media. It isn't always a matter of money, but usually that is the case. Some social movements, from civil rights to the women's movement, have successfully marshaled public support with limited resources, while their opponents have sometimes failed to curry support even with superior budgets. These, however, are exceptions to the rule.

The excesses of public relations—and there are some—are less important than follies and foibles of a sometimes overworked, sometimes understaffed, often lazy and poorly trained corps of journalists in this country. There is simply too much information for most media organizations to cope effectively with it. Instead of hiring legions of specialists to help—they have hired a few—the media make heavy use of handouts (press releases) and other information provided free by public relations people. Clearly this practice is not fair and does not serve the American people well.

I know scores of talented public relations people and even more talented journalists. The PR people I know are, for the most part, responsible professionals. They have every right to do what they do, but they are paid promoters for vested interests, and those interests want publicity and public support. The PR people use many ploys to get their way with the news media and to influence the public through other means. To a large part they succeed and in the process are major information providers for the American people.

Argument summation: Public relations manipulates the news.

Public relations, by its very nature, is intended to benefit those creating the message, whether the source is public or private. In the information marketplace public relations manipulates the news by packaging information for the media with a specific client's interests in mind. While there have been laudable uses of public relations, on the whole the practice serves to flood the media with biased news. When the press is unable to verify the reports, because of the sheer quantity of information available or because of laziness, distorted public relations reports appear in the media as objective facts, and the news has been distorted to favor the public relations position.

RESPONSE

Merrill: Public relations provides an essential news service.

It has been said that public relations is a manipulative force in news presentation. Perhaps it is, to some extent. So what? There are many manipulative forces impinging on the news: editors' fears, reporters' biases, advertising pressures, government secrecy. Public relations, in spite of normal manipulative aspects, is a valuable—even essential—adjunct to the news dissemination activities of journalism.

It has been estimated, even by journalists, that nearly 50 percent of the news stories found in the media show some signs of PR influence. Journalists themselves must think PR sources are important to news gathering, for they certainly make use of PR releases and background material which is offered them by the PR establishment. It would be hard to deny that PR sources are helpful in supplying to news media background material and even some "hard" news.

Of course much PR material is ignored or discarded, but it is used more often than many journalists might like to admit. I myself have spent five years in college public relations and, on the basis of having kept careful clipping books and records, I can say that in this small PR sample *my public relations-generated news was used up to 80 percent on a weekly basis.* Use of releases by radio and TV was much less dramatic, but there is no doubt but that newspapers rely heavily on news releases coming to them.

Seymour Topping, curator of the Pulitzer Prizes and former managing editor of the *New York Times,* has said bluntly that PR people contribute to the news in a functional way: "Quite a lot of our business stories originate from press releases. Often the first hint of a newsworthy event is first heard of by us from a press release." Topping has gone so far as to say that PR is becoming a news network behind the legitimate news media, "a second network that feeds the real news media more and more of its news" (Blyskal and Blyskal, 1985, 46–47).

The Blyskals also quote Charles Staebler, assistant managing editor of the *Wall Street Journal,* who acknowledges the help provided by PR people. "We look at press releases positively as a source of tips. They can alert us to things that are going on." Staebler estimates that perhaps 50 percent of the average *Journal* stories are spurred by press releases, and he adds, "In every case we *try* [emphasis added] to go beyond the press release" (Blyskal and Blyskal, 1985, 47).

According to Scott Cutlip, long-time professor of PR, the 150,000 public relations practitioners play an important role in setting the public agenda and have a far more important role in opinion making "than the public perceives, or than journalists (who themselves are only about 130,000 strong) are usually willing to admit." And Cutlip estimates that 40 percent of all "news" content today comes from the desks of PR people. (*Gannett Center Journal,* Spring 1989, p. 105).

There is no doubt that PR does provide a news service. And in the common or loose sense of providing "essential" news, meaning a *very important* service, I would contend that public relations fills the bill. No one is saying that PR is journalistically relevant in all of its aspects, but in providing basic news, commentary on certain news events, tips on news stories, and access to news sources, the practitioner in public relations is extremely valuable to the news media.

In a strict sense of "essential" (meaning "absolutely necessary"), perhaps PR is not essential. True, a newspaper, for example, could provide news without any help from PR. But how thorough would it be? How many additional gaps would such news presentation have? One might as well say that the news media could "present news" without interviewing politicians. Certainly it could be done; there would simply be far less political news. So we might say that politicians are "essential" for *the best possible* political news and that public relations practitioners are "essential" for *the best possible news* related to the PR person's area of knowledge.

It may be true, as Dennis contends, that public relations manipulates the news. *All* factors impinging upon the collection and writing of news are manipulative to some degree. I could say just as well that reporters and editors manipulate the news. But since *manipulates* is a word with a negative connotation, it is not used to describe a journalistic function. With public relations, however, it is different: From the point of view of the journalist, any "news" function connected with PR seems to imply skulduggery and self-serving bias, with an intent to mislead the reader.

This may be true in some cases. But in others this is simply not the case. Truthful and conscientious reporting is not the sole province of the journalist. Such reporting can also be found among historians, sociologists, lawyers, and even farmers talking alongside a country road. Why not among PR people?

Because of its financial support by groups, organizations, and persons with vested interests, public relations is a field that is understandably suspect by news media people who pride themselves on being detached and unbiased in their news presentation. Perhaps PR people *are* prone to accentuate the positive when it comes to their special interests. But don't journalists generally accentuate the negative? Is negative bias any better than positive bias? Undoubtedly PR people do feel considerable loyalty to those who pay their salaries, but does employer loyalty necessarily imply dishonesty?

But let us assume PR people are biased. Are they more biased in their normal news-writing activities than are the general run of media reporters, who usually have their own strongly held values and biases, political and otherwise? This, of course, is a question that cannot really be answered. But it is worth asking.

In spite of biased news from PR sources which undoubtedly appears from time to time, there is no reason to believe that most PR people are not honest. Surely they *intend* to be honest, forthright, and truthful; for one thing, the Code of Professional Standards of the Public Relations Society of America (PRSA) says they must be. For instance, the Code stresses (in Standard Seven) that a member "shall not intentionally communicate false or misleading information and is obligated to use care to avoid communication of false or misleading information." That is strange wording, to be sure, but it points up PR people's concern for providing the truth. Earlier in the same code the PRSA members are urged to "adhere to truth and accuracy" and to refrain from engaging "in any practice which tends to corrupt the integrity of channels of communication" (quoted in Lovell, 1982, 41–42). Not much different from language in a journalist's code, is it?

William Ramsey, president of the PR firm of Bill Ramsey Associates, Inc., insists that public relations people "must communicate better . . . to the public" and that "we must tell the good news of our firm's accomplishments—and level with the public about our firm's or our institution's shortcomings." In fact, he says, "credibility is the key" (Haberman and Dolphin, 1988, viii).

In spite of PR people's attempt to professionalize, to write ethical codes, to use the status initials APR (Accredited in Public Relations) after their names, and to pay allegiance to truth and credibility, they still have a problem with the press. Journalists are suspicious of their forthrightness in news matters. Robert T. Reilly, APR member and professor at the University of Nebraska (Omaha), notes, "Even reporters who have never experienced a problem with a PR person harbor the concept of the practitioner as a self-serving person who will try to interfere with truthful encounter." He adds this backhanded slap at news reporters: "As reportorial success is measured more and more by exposé, and as media rely increasingly on the profession they criticize, you're apt to see this nagging hostility expand" (1987, 9).

But he's right. Journalists will undoubtedly continue to snipe at public relations people while using considerable portions of their news releases. In retaliation, PR people will take their verbal slaps at what they often see as the unrealistic and arrogant journalists who make no real attempt to understand and appreciate public relations.

All right. There's a kind of continuing cold war going on between the two "professions." Is that bad? I see it as a good thing, because this kind of mild adversarial relationship may help to keep both groups honest. Perhaps here we have another check mechanism in our society. But in spite of this unease that exists between the two groups, I still maintain that PR expands the public discourse, helps provide a wide assortment of news, and is essential in expanding the pluralism of our total communication system.

The image of PR is beside the point. The fact that ethical lapses occur in PR is beside the point. The fact that journalists are naturally suspicious of any other person or group in the "news" business is beside the point. The fact that PR people do have a loyalty to their clients is beside the point. What is not beside the point is that PR people do indeed provide news to various publics (including the general public through the mass media) and, in doing so, provide an essential public service.

Argument summation: Public relations provides an essential news service.

Public relations generates information for use by the media; it fills gaps in the news and provides services similar to those offered by advertising agencies. PR helps set the public agenda. It may not be "essential" in the ultimate sense, but neither is a newspaper or a TV station. Public relations may have an ax to grind, but so do advertising agencies. It is true that not all PR is ethical; is that not true of *any* institutionalized communications endeavor? Public relations serves as a supplement and aid to news media, a gap filler, and in general it does a valuable job of expanding message pluralism in society. A PR person may do many things other than news gathering and dissemination, but is this not also true of newspaper staff members?

TOPICS FOR DISCUSSION

1. Is truth related to a PR news release in the same way that truth is related to a news story on TV or in a newspaper?

2. Is it any safer to believe an advertiser than to believe a PR person? In what ways are the two types of practitioners similar? Different?

3. Why would a person who loves independence and truth want to be a part of a PR organization? How can there be so many PR people today who were news media reporters at one time?

4. The assumption is generally made that newspaper reporters are neutral, unbiased, and objective and that PR people are not. Is the assumption valid? Why or why not?

5. PR people work for and are paid by their clients. Media news people work for and are paid by their media. What is the difference? How does their employment status affect their loyalties? How do their loyalties affect their work?

TOPICS FOR RESEARCH

1. Study a local firm or nonprofit organization in terms of its public relations program, assuming it has one. What publics do they try to reach? With what methods or tools? How do they measure their effectiveness? How do you assess their efforts and success (or failure)?

2. Assume that you have been asked to document the public relations of your college or university. What is its prevailing public image? Does it differ with different publics, say students, faculty, and alumni? In your paper indicate how public relations is carried out at the institution, by whom, with what channels or tools, and to what effect. Does the effort work or not? Why?

3. Is there any "right" to public relations in what is increasingly an information or communication society? Argue the case that all people and organizations involved in public life need and deserve a public relations program. How can the public be protected in such a scheme?

4. Document the ethics movement in public relations. What does professional public relations do to ensure ethical practice? Interview a public relations practitioner on this issue. How would you assess that person's approach to ethical public relations? How are decisions made? With what help or sources?

5. Interview a newsperson about contacts between his or her news organization and public relations personnel. Is public relations a help or a hindrance? Be specific about the impact and influence of public relations, if any, on the basis of this interview.

6. What does the public need to know about public relations? Outline a speech you would give to a civic group about public relations and what citizens should know about it.

FURTHER READING

Bernays, Edward L. *Crystalizing Public Opinion.* New York: Boni and Liveright, 1923.

Blyskal, Jeff, and Mary Blyskal. *PR: How the Public Relations Industry Writes the News.* New York: William Morrow, 1985.

Bogart, Leo. *Commercial Culture.* New York: Oxford University Press, 1995.

Cutlip, Scott, Alan Center, and Glen M. Broom. *Effective Public Relations.* 6th ed. Englewood Cliffs, NJ: Prentice Hall, 1985.

Grossman, Lawrence. *The Electronic Republic.* New York: The Free Press, 1995.

Grunig, J. E., and Todd Hunt. *Managing Public Relations.* New York: Holt, Rinehart and Winston, 1984.

Haberman, David A., and H. A. Dolphin. *Public Relations: The Necessary Art.* Ames: Iowa State University Press, 1988.

Lovell, Ronald P. *Inside Public Relations.* Boston: Allyn & Bacon, 1982.

Pavlik, John V. *Public Relations: What Research Tells Us.* Beverly Hills, CA: Sage, 1987.

"Public Relations: The Manufacture of Opinion," *Gannett Center Journal,* Spring 1989.

Reilly, Robert T. *Public Relations in Action.* Englewood Cliffs, NJ: Prentice Hall, 1987.

Wilcox, Dennis L., Phillip H. Ault, and Warren K. Agee. *Public Relations Strategies and Tactics.* New York: Harper & Row, 1986.

Chapter **18**

JOURNALISM AS A PROFESSION

Although scholars and practitioners debate over what constitutes a profession, most journalists believe that journalism is a profession. There is a Society of Professional Journalists. Journalism is included in various standard listings of professions in America.

Even the most rigorous critics and scholars studying professional ethics include journalists in their discussions. Efforts to enhance the professionalization of journalists abound in seminars, workshops, codes of ethics, and other activities. Although it is said that freedom of the press, as guaranteed by the First Amendment, prohibits the control or licensing of journalists, newspapers still strive toward professionalism.

Clearly, journalists like to be associated with professionalism and they see no particular advantage in being members of a trade or a simple vocation. Professionalism is associated with competence, with training, with a body of knowledge, with standards of evaluation and improvement.

Is journalism a profession? If it is not, *should* it be? The debate goes on.

CHALLENGE

Merrill: Journalism is not a profession.

Contrary to conventional journalistic wisdom, journalism is not a profession. There really is not much tradition behind the idea of journalism being a profession. It is of recent vintage. For most of America's journalistic history, professionalism was no issue; if anybody thought of what journalism might be called at all, it was usually simply referred to as a trade, craft, or vocation.

Today the term and concept of *profession* has proliferated in journalistic rhetoric—in publications, speeches, and conversations. Journalists generally like to think of themselves as "professionals" and journalism as a "profession." I recently had a journalism student who was so emotionally tied to the idea that journalism is a profession that the very idea that it might not be distressed her greatly. "That's the reason I wanted to go into journalism—because it was a profession," she stated with apparent consternation.

Journalists seem to be impressed with the general esteem, respectability, and even awe that surrounds any organized activity carrying the name "profession." They have also observed that law and medicine, for instance, in being accepted as professions, have taken on an elite image and that their practitioners are generally paid better than are most nonprofessionals. It is understandable that journalists, often intellectuals or pseudo-intellectuals, find the lure of professionalism very strong. It would give them the aura of respectability, of public acceptance, of dignity, of exclusivity, and, at the least, the collective psychological comfort denied them if they functioned simply as "journalists."

The notion that journalism is a profession is undoubtedly growing in America, but individual journalists do not really know what journalistic professionalism entails, what being a "professional" really means. Even two journalists with similar backgrounds may act in ways that each would consider "unprofessional." Even members of the Society of Professional Journalists do not agree in many basic respects about journalism and its practices.

Professor Jay Black of the University of South Florida, editor of *The Journal of Mass Media Ethics,* writing on "Professionalism in Journalism," maintains that journalism is not a profession. Citing six characteristics of a *profession* (as provided by Abraham Flexner, writing on medical education in 1915) that have served through the years as a standard definition, Black shows that journalism does not have these characteristics: (1) an extensive and complex body of knowledge; (2) not only knowledge of the *what* and the *how* but also a theoretical grasp of the *why*; (3) a definite and practical goal; (4) agreement with other professionals about the ends to be served and about education necessary for practice; (5) common criteria or standards for practice—agreed-upon entrance requirements; and (6) a motivation that is altruistic, not self-enhancing or based on a profit motive. Dr. Black concludes that "clearly journalism falls short of being a full-fledged profession on several counts" (World Media Report, Spring 1987, pp. 13–15). Admittedly, some of Flexner's criteria for a profession are rather vague, but they are helpful.

Originally *profession* meant simply the act of professing; it has developed from that fundamental concept to mean, according to the *Oxford*

Shorter English Dictionary, the "occupation which one professes to be skilled in and to follow . . . a vocation in which professed knowledge of some branch of learning is used in its application to the affairs of others, or in the practice of an art based upon it."

Even now, professionals profess; they profess to know better than others the nature of certain matters and to know better than their non-professional clients what they need to know and in what proportion they need to know it. Professionals claim the exclusive right to practice, as a vocation, the arts that they profess to know.

William J. Goode, one of America's foremost sociologists, has insisted that professionals constitute a homogeneous community whose members share values, identity, and definition of role and interests. He has said that members of a profession "are bound by a sense of identity" and "share values in common." The observer looking at American journalism today can easily see that journalists really do not have a single identity, nor do they share the same values, nor do they have a common definition of their role.

The Bureau of Labor Statistics lists these requirements for a profession: (1) prescribed educational standards, (2) licensing, and (3) enforcement of performance standards by the profession itself.

Here are some other characteristics of a profession that are given in the influential *The Professions in America* (Lynn, 1965):

A member of a profession is expected to think objectively and inquiringly about matters that may be, for the outsider, subject to "orthodoxy and sentiment which limit intellectual exploration." (Is this true for the journalist?)

A member of a profession assumes that he or she can be trusted since he or she professes to have certain expertise that the layperson does not have. (Can a journalist say this with justification?)

A member of a profession believes in close solidarity with other members and thinks that it is a good thing to present a solid front to those outside the profession. (Is this true of a journalist?)

A member of a profession is able to meet various minimum entrance standards for the profession—such as a degree in the professional area, a special license identifying him or her as a professional member in good standing, and so on. (Is this true of a journalist?)

A member of a profession not only is certified or licensed but can expect to be put out of the profession if he or she does not live up to professional standards. (Is this true of a journalist?)

A member of a profession has a code of ethics governing his or her activities in concert with other professionals and submits to a high degree of group control. (Is this true of a journalist?)

A member of a profession participates in a system of rewards (monetary and honorary) for those who conduct themselves most notably within their code of ethics. (Is this true of the journalist?)

A member of a profession shares in a discrete and substantive body of knowledge available to those in the profession. (Is this true of a journalist?)

In light of this list of characteristics of a profession, is journalism a profession? Obviously it is not, although it has some of a profession's characteristics or it in some respects approaches a profession. (A donkey, we might say, has many of the characteristics of a horse—it "approaches" a horse—but we must say quite definitely that it is not a horse.)

There is no direct relationship between journalists and their clients. A journalist is not a self-employed person but rather works for an employer. In journalism there are no formal minimum entrance requirements; anyone can be a journalist who can get hired—experience or no experience, degree or no degree. No journalist is expected (or required) to abide by any code of ethics. No journalist is certified or licensed, at least in the United States. No professional standards are commonly agreed upon and followed by journalists. A person working for the *National Enquirer* is just as much a journalist as a person working for the *New York Times*. A person writing news for the *Podunk Weekly Bugle* is just as much a journalist as a newsperson working for the *Wall Street Journal.*

Journalists do not share in common a high degree of generalized and systematic knowledge. They do not claim the exclusive right to practice the arts (all borrowed from other disciplines) of their vocation. Finally, American journalists do not constitute a homogeneous community.

Here is what contemporary commentator Irving Kristol says: "Even to speak of the 'profession' of journalism today is to indulge in flattering exaggeration. Journalism has not, as yet, acquired the simplest external signs of a profession" (1975, 26).

Even though journalism is not a profession, it *can*—through increased stress on ethical codes, press councils, peer pressure, licensing of some kind, entrance requirements, and more rigorous standards for journalism education—grow into a true profession. I don't contend that it is impossible for journalism to become a profession, just that it has not yet happened. However, I think that it is *undesirable* that it evolve into a profession.

Philosopher William Barrett, writing about professions, states my feeling very well:

> The price one pays for having a profession is *deformation professionelle,* as the French put it—a professional deformation. Doctors and engineers tend to see things from the viewpoint of their own specialty, and usually show a very marked blind spot to whatever falls outside this particular province. The more specialized a vision the sharper its focus; but also the more nearly

total the blind spot toward all things that lie on the periphery of this focus. (1958, 4–5)

There appears to be a deep-rooted desire among press people to belong to a select group (a "hierarchical longing within the press," as Lewis Lapham called it in *Harper's*). It seems clear to me that this tendency, if carried very far, would stamp out unusual or eccentric concepts and, ultimately, also the journalists who embrace them. Lapham wrote that the more the press becomes a profession, the more it will "discourage the membership of rowdy amateurs" and, as it is with other professions, encourage the promotion of people who are "second-rate."

No doubt professionalism will certainly restrict the ranks of journalism, eliminate the "nonprofessional" from practice, and make the press appear more respectable, at least from the perspective of the elitists making up the profession.

In addition to a loss of diversity, another reason why journalism should not be a profession has been put forward on numerous occasions by James W. Carey of Columbia University: If journalism were a profession, its practitioners would increasingly turn inward on themselves, thinking more and more about their own vested interests and mechanisms for self-protection, and less about their responsibilities to their audiences. Professions, believes Carey, become ingrown and selfish, with a complacent and arrogant spirit contagious among their members.

I totally agree with Carey; it would be a pity if journalism, one of the most open, diversified institutions in the country—one that is dedicated largely to public service—were to change into a narrow, monolithic, self-centered professionalized fellowship devoid of an outward-looking service orientation.

So, I maintain that journalism is not a profession and that it should not be.

Argument summation: Journalism is not a profession.

Journalism is a vocation, an occupation, a craft, or something—but not a profession. It is a calling that is open to all, regardless of education. There are no entrance requirements, no discrete body of knowledge, no elite inner group to "de-press" wayward members, no code of ethics, and no licensing system for journalists. Naturally, journalism resembles a profession in some ways, but it is not yet there. *Harper's* editor Lewis Lapham was right to view the trend toward professionalization with alarm. He said that the more the press becomes a profession, the more it will discourage eccentricity and innovation, and the more it would encourage the promotion of second-rate people. Certainly journalism as a profession would shrink pluralism and cause journalists to think less of the public interest and more of their own interest.

RESPONSE

Dennis: Journalism is a profession.

Whether journalism is a profession is one of the oldest, continuing controversies in journalism. It used to be easier to take sides when the debate was simply whether journalism was a profession or a business. Liberals lined up on the side of professionalism, while conservatives liked to see journalism as a profit-making enterprise. But those were simpler times. Today we can look back on a half century of striving by journalists and journalistic organizations to achieve professional status.

Journalism is commonly regarded as a profession made up of professional communicators dedicated to professional standards. Journalists themselves believe this, and even some of the most elite of American institutions engaged in the study of the professions consider journalists—warts and all—to be professionals. The Harvard-Hastings Program on Ethics in the Professions, for example, has no problem calling journalism a profession. Neither do such distinguished sociologists as Morris Janowitz or Herbert Gans, who have contributed mightily to the literature of professionalism generally, as well as journalism specifically.

Admittedly some scholars quibble with this designation, preferring instead to call journalism a "subprofession." They would no doubt say that the terms *profession* and *professional* are too widely and indiscriminately used in America. The commonly understood definitions of *profession, professional,* and *professionalism* vary widely from those who say that a profession is simply a "principal calling, vocation, or employment" versus a more rigid view that insists a profession is "a calling requiring specialized knowledge and long, intensive preparation." (Both definitions are found in *Webster's Third New International Dictionary.*)

Most students of the sociology of work, concerned with professionalism, acknowledge that professions *evolve*. They are not created with all the finishing touches on Day One, with their standards and practices intact. Medicine, for example, had little in the way of universal standards or educational requirements in this country until after 1915. Some commentators say that the law did not truly become a profession until the establishment of law schools.

Journalism has most if not all of the distinctive marks of a profession and deserves to be so classified. This assertion reflects not a caving in to popular parlance (as with "professional" actors or "professional" athletes), but the fact that most of the major criteria that distinguish a profession from a trade or calling are integral to journalistic practice in America. What's more, dedication to professionalism is growing in journalism.

Like other professions, journalism shows most of the characteristics of professionalism, with different degrees of intensity. One of the primary marks of any profession (and not mentioned in the "Challenge") is the kind of work that has for its prime purpose the rendering of a public service. Journalism is in fact engaged in a public service—the free flow of information and ideas is at the core of First Amendment freedom in the United States. The press has special protection under the Constitution, not simply to allow newspaper and broadcast owners to make a profit, but because, as a matter of law and social policy, we believe that a free press is essential to a functioning democracy. Of course the press must make a profit if it is to survive, and reporters and editors have salaries and get various ego rewards for their work. Yet most of them would contend (and with justification) that they render a public service. Certainly law, medicine, architecture, education, and the other professions engage in public service activity and still provide a living for their practitioners. That fact does not exclude them from the august company of professionals. Under the most rigid definition probably only the clergy, and then only the highly trained clergy—could qualify as professionals.

For purposes of this discussion, I accept the standards set out in *The Professions in America,* even though they present a rather dated and stodgy view of professionalism. Does journalism qualify under this definition? I believe it does. Can a journalist "think objectively and inquiringly about matters" which by "sentiment and orthodoxy" limit outsiders? Certainly one of the purposes of journalism is to provide an impartial, disinterested synthesis of information. It identifies and explains conflicting viewpoints. This process helps the uninitiated understand what is happening in society without being subject to deliberate bias or distortion. Journalism tells us that a supply-side economist says one thing while a Keynesian says another.

Does a journalist have expertise that a layperson does not? Yes, of course. Journalists are experts at news gathering—searching out, assessing, and presenting information; standard definitions of mass communication specify that "professional communicators," not amateurs, are required.

Does a journalist have "close solidarity" and "a solid front"? Not in the sense that medicine might, but that is so because journalism is so diverse, involving many different kinds of media enterprises and professionals. Certainly journalists are organized through professional societies, guilds, unions, and other more specialized subgroups. I can think of few professions with more solidarity than journalism when a fellow journalist is jailed or when a lively First Amendment issue emerges. Powerful publishers join with lowly reporters to right a common battle. One of the clichés of the media when a story is attacked or seriously questioned is, "We stand behind our reporter."

What of minimum entrance requirements? While there is no formal licensing, most media organizations do have minimum standards of education or experience for hiring anyone. They can deviate from these requirements if they wish, but rarely do. Increasingly journalists are graduates of professional schools of journalism accredited by a national body that is sanctioned by the government through the U.S. Office of Education. This procedure is not the same as licensing, but there are many other types of "conformity" and "sanctioning" within journalism. There is considerable agreement among journalists on a whole range of values and craft attitudes, as studies by communications researchers have shown. It is by no means an "every man an island" profession.

Can someone be "put out" of the profession? Not by the government, but certainly by the informal hiring practices of media organizations. Someone who consistently violates professional norms and standards or who is regarded as sleazy by his or her colleagues may have difficulty getting a job at a reputable publication. There may always be an outlet for that person's work, say on TV's *Hard Copy* or in the *National Enquirer,* but not likely on the *Washington Post* or *New York Times.*

Journalism has codes of ethics, which help define professionalism and assist journalists with ethical dilemmas. On some newspapers a reporter who violates the code can be fired. In that instance, adherence to the code is a condition of employment.

The Editor & Publisher International Yearbook lists several pages of awards, both financial and honorary, available to journalists. Some of the most prestigious, such as the Pulitzer Prizes, Nieman Fellowships, National Magazine Awards, news Emmys, and Columbia-Dupont awards, can have a marked impact on their recipients' careers. These awards are given for exemplary performance.

The criterion of a "discrete and substantive body of knowledge" is more difficult. Because journalism is part of a system of freedom of expression, it is not possible or desirable to prescribe just what every journalist must know. However, there is a standard curriculum in the journalism schools that includes courses in communication theory, media history, law, and ethics, as well as other substantive topics. It is also generally agreed that journalists should be broadly educated in the liberal arts and sciences. In addition, professional schools have professional practice and skills courses in reporting, editing, photojournalism, and other topics. There is also a substantial literature of journalism, which includes both scholarly studies and such anecdotal materials as memoirs and media criticism. There are even subfields—journalism history, law, economics, theory and methodology, international communications, media sociology, and others—each of which has a corpus of scholarship worthy of considerable attention by scholars. Journalism studies are also part of a larger literature of mass communication that has strong links to psychology, sociology, anthropology, and political science. Students of journalism have a rich lode to consider if they wish to master the field. Of course there is no formal requirement that anyone do this.

More than half of the journalists in America are graduates of journalism schools, and virtually all have at least a liberal arts education. Increasingly, some journalists have specialized education or training in such areas as science, law, politics, or the arts. The diversity of journalism in America makes the implementation of one single model of education or training impossible. Some professional communicators in broadcasting must hold federally issued broadcast licenses attesting to certain technical competencies.

Fundamentally, journalists must know enough—gained either in formal education or on the job—to function in their work. If they do not, they are fired or otherwise excluded from the profession.

Just because all journalists do not march to the beat of a single drummer does not mean they are not professional. As Morris Janowitz has written:

> Practitioners in any particular profession hold differing conceptions of their tasks and priorities. The differences between the "public health" doctor and the clinician is a long-standing distinction that has had a strong impact on the practice of medicine. Since World War I, journalists have come more and more to consider themselves as professionals and to search for an appropriate professional model. The initial efforts were to fashion journalism into a field, similar to medicine, where the journalist would develop his technical expertise and also a sense of professional responsibility. (1975, 618)

That was the "gatekeeper" tradition, which emphasized the search for objectivity. Other journalists disagree with this view, saying that journalists instead should be advocates for causes and should participate in public affairs. This conflict, according to sociologists John Johnstone, Edward Slawski, and William Bowman, "would reappear to pit proponents of a professionalized objective, restrained, and technically efficient journalism against those advocating a socially responsible journalism inspired by some of the same journalistic norms which were the objects of earlier reforms" (1976a, 523).

Is journalism a profession? The evidence is resounding. Sociological quibblers can find flaws in all of the professions that might put them outside of purist definitions, but this approach is not realistic. Journalism is a profession not because its practitioners say they are professionals, but because it more than meets most of the criteria that, taken together, constitute a profession.

Argument summation: Journalism is a profession.

A profession is defined most narrowly as requiring "specialized knowledge and long, intensive preparation" and involving "rendering a public service." Whether journalism was a profession when it began, it has evolved (as medicine or law did) into one and deserves recognition as such. Journalism renders a public service by preserving the free flow of information. Even by the dated criteria suggested by Merrill, journalism possesses the objectivity, expertise, and organizational characteristics of a profession. A discrete substantive body of knowledge is required, in the sense that there is an expectation that journalists be broadly educated and there is a standard curriculum in the journalism schools. A uniform perspective of practitioners is not necessary for a field to be considered a profession; many doctors and lawyers possess differing conceptions of their tasks. Sociological quibblers might find distinctions that could put any profession outside a purist definition, but for all practical purposes journalism is a profession.

TOPICS FOR DISCUSSION

1. Why do you think many journalism students and journalists want journalism to be a profession?

2. Do you see any real dangers to journalism being a profession? If you do, what are they?

3. Can journalism be as diversified (pluralistic) as a profession as it can as a nonprofession?

4. More than half the journalists in the United States are journalism school graduates. What would the proportion be if journalism were a profession like medicine or law? Is common education really important for members of a profession?

5. Is a single code of ethics necessary for a profession? Why not have many codes, all similar, but differing somewhat? Should a professional code of ethics have teeth in it? Who should decide on such a code?

TOPICS FOR RESEARCH

1. Discuss the proposition that the public deserves professionalism in journalism. Indicate why and document your case carefully.

2. Study codes of ethics in terms of whether or not they promote professionalism. Be specific and give examples.

3. How do schools of journalism and communication promote professionalism? Does professionalism apply to all areas of communications?

Does professionalism apply to all media functions—information, opinion, and entertainment? Discuss and analyze.

4. Compare and contrast journalism as a profession with any other profession you choose. How do they differ? How are they similar? Be sure you consider the role of education, codes of ethics, licensing, and other issues.

5. Some critics say that professionalism is simply a control mechanism whereby owners of the media control their employees. Is this true or not? Is it a good or a bad thing? How do you know?

FURTHER READING

American Society of Newspaper Editors. *What Is News? Who Decides? And How?* Preliminary Report on the World of the Working Journalist, Washington, DC, 1982. Also cited in earlier chapters as Burgoon, Burgoon, and Atkin, 1982.

Barrett, William. *Irrational Man: A Study in Existential Philosophy.* Garden City, NY: Doubleday Anchor Books, 1958.

Gerald, J. Edward. *The Social Responsibility of the Press.* Minneapolis: University of Minnesota Press, 1963.

Janowitz, Morris. "Professional Models in Journalism: The Gatekeeper and the Advocate." *Journalism Quarterly* 52, no. 4 (Winter 1975):618–26, 662.

Johnstone, John W. C., Edward J. Slawski, and William Bowman. *The Newspeople: A Sociological Portrait of American Journalists and Their Work.* Urbana: University of Illinois Press, 1976a.

———. "The Professional Values of American Newsmen," *Public Opinion Quarterly* 36, no. 4 (1976b):522–40.

Kristol, Irving. "Is the Press Misusing Its Growing Power?" *More,* January 1975, pp. 26–28.

Lynn, Kenneth S., ed. *The Professions in America.* Boston: Houghton Mifflin, 1965.

Public Agenda Foundation. *The Speaker and the Listener.* New York: Public Agenda Foundation, 1980.

Southern Newspaper Publishers Association. *Education for Newspaper Journalists in the 1970s and Beyond.* Reston, VA: SNPA, 1973. See especially "Professionalism of the Press" by William E. Porter.

Stephens, Mitchell. *A History of News.* New York: Viking Press, 1988.

Chapter 19

GLOBALISM AND THE MEDIA

After nearly fifty years of East–West tensions that affected the whole world, the Cold War ended in the early 1990s. This event radically affected communication between and among peoples generally and the communication media specifically. The hostility between the United States and the former Soviet Union eased, and former Communist countries declared themselves democracies, throughout Eastern and Central Europe, across all of Russia and the former Soviet republics, in the Balkans, and elsewhere. At the same time, many authoritarian governments in Central and South America also initiated democratic reforms. It could also be reported that there was a new spirit of democracy in much of Asia, and even China began to loosen up its rigid system in spite of evident setbacks at Tiananmen Square in 1989, when the whole world saw a student-led democracy movement crushed. In most of the world the preferred form of government is now democracy (defined differently in different places depending on local cultural conditions) and also adopted market economies, again with different degrees of free market activity in different countries. In all this the press and news media played a key role, and the rise of independent media—media not controlled by the state—was seen in country after country.

Along with the sociopolitical changes sweeping the world and the embrace of market economies has come a trend toward globalism, wherein cultural products (especially media content of all kinds—information and news, entertainment and advertising) have an international audience as never before. The old barriers of borders and East–West restrictions have ended for the most part, and there is strong encouragement nearly everywhere for international and global communication, free trade and intercourse between and among nations.

At one level, globalism for the media seems to be a good thing, with more openness everywhere and the unembarrassed use of the word *freedom* to describe the condition in most countries. This means political and economic freedom and, of course, some measure of freedom of the media. For the news media it means that correspondents can travel freely nearly everywhere on the globe and generally report the news without restrictions and censorship. These trends have also accelerated the growth of large global media companies like Rupert Murdoch's News Corporation, Germany's Bertelsmann Company, and the U.S. giant, Time-Warner. Increasingly there is international ownership of local media in many countries. (Some, like the United States, still have rules that prohibit full foreign ownership of broadcasting, however.) Political changes that have gone hand in hand with economic changes have also been encouraged by a climate of deregulation; many rules affecting broadcasting and other media have been greatly relaxed in the United States, Europe, Russia, and other places.

Old arguments about the equitable distribution of all resources to all peoples, including access to communication—once a common feature of the East–West and North–South debate—were quite muted in the years after the Cold War. At one time, and for nearly twenty years, there was a fierce international debate—largely between developing countries and those fully industrialized—about the New World Information and Communication Order (NWICO), which expressed concern about the inequitable flow of news, which was going mostly from the big countries of the West to the developing world with little reciprocity. It was pointed out that cultural products like movies and news were dominated by the West because of its economic superiority. Connected to this issue was a UNESCO-sponsored policy (NWICO), which was interpreted by the West as an intrusion on freedom of expression, incompatible with an independent, nongovernmental media system. That debate, while still alive in some university circles, is all but dead in the media worldwide and is no longer a feature of the United Nations' UNESCO, which has rescinded the policy and urged a regime of international press freedom attended by market economies, a position quite popular in most countries of the world.

Instead of the New World Order arguments, we now have a great debate over the effects of globalism on media systems, individual media outlets, journalists and other media workers, especially the general public. The question most often raised is whether globalism in the media will be a liberating and beneficial influence or one that will constrain communication and deny access to those in poor countries where media markets at the moment are less than attractive. The dominant view in the world among governments, business, media companies, and most large institutions is that globalism is a positive influence, one that has its roots in utopian values promoting true international discourse among all the peoples of the earth, wherein communication solves problems great and small while at the same time the market benefits. On the other side are a few important critics and some scholars of communication. In recent visits to more than fifty countries and in extensive interviews there, the authors confirm the positive view of globalism as it affects the media, while at the same time recognizing that there are critical voices of those who worry about the effects of globalism, arguing that bigness is inherently bad and that diversity is nearly always good.

CHALLENGE

Dennis: Globalism greatly benefits people, the media, and freedom of expression.

The British commentator Anthony Smith has predicted that in the new communication age, national borders will be irrelevant. At one time the reach of most media was determined by the nation-state, with national newspapers and television systems being the best examples of such limitations, but now human beings have truly conquered time and space and the whole world is within reach. Smith argues that new technology has tremendous consequences for individuals and institutions and that, while big companies control much of the world's communication content, it has never been easier for new media products to enter the marketplace (Smith, 1991). Banking visionary Walter Wriston agrees, positing that borders are indeed "totally porous" and thus render "regulatory distinctions meaningless." In other words, governments can no longer control what comes into their countries nor can they stop the "inevitable global conversation" made possible by new media technologies and a global marketplace (Wriston, 1992).

This phenomenon is, of course, what the Canadian media guru Marshall McLuhan spoke of when he predicted a "global village" in the mid-1960s. And certainly one sees the global village idea—of messages reaching every corner of the world—in the presence of CNN almost everywhere. Be it in a great international hotel or a remote rural village, there is virtually no gathering of human beings in the world today that does not have access to CNN and other global satellite services including news, information, entertainment, and opinion fare. Similarly, I have watched the ever popular MTV and other music channels in Moscow, Santiago, Hong Kong, and elsewhere, something that would have seemed magical only a few years ago, when a visit to a Nigerian town meant cutting oneself off from the world altogether. What this new world means to individuals as well as whole societies is seen in the writings of Joshua Meyrowitz, who points out that it was once possible to "excommunicate" children from the family dinner conversation, sending them to their bedrooms as punishment. Now, says Meyrowitz, being banished from the family circle means going to a room filled with communications devices and services far more interesting and diverse than the family conversation.

The kind of global reach that media have today definitely benefits people, giving them access to a massive range of information and entertainment fare. In turn it helps the media organization that delivers the content, by building audiences, mass and targeted, and thus bringing revenues into the media's corporate coffers. Global media also benefit noncommercial public media, which beam their messages everywhere, garnering audiences.

Of course the critics worry that a few global companies will not only gobble up all of the media of the world but somehow enslave human beings through low-quality programming, cheap information, and entertainment junk food. Such warnings have been with us for a long time. The respected press critic Ben Bagdikian has been worried about big all-powerful newspaper companies for as long as I can remember. But in the mid-1990s, when big media deals were being made on Wall Street, these fearsome newspaper "giants" could rarely afford to be part of systems that involved telephone companies, cable firms, broadcasters, and movie companies, to name a few enterprises. Big media, which now operated with precious little governmental controls, live in the world of competition and to date can be credited with delivering the richest, most diverse storehouse of media content in the history of the world. These operations have benefited individual media companies and individuals themselves enormously. Instead of three or four channels coming into the home, there are scores and soon hundreds. True some of the material is junk, but much of it is not, and when people bother to open their eyes and look at the rich lode of media fare, they cannot doubt that big media companies have been a positive force.

Still the critics persist in saying that the big players limit the range of information and opinions, thus driving out alternative views. In fact, however, exactly the opposite is true. Even alternative journalism has benefited from the worldwide trends toward vigorous market economies. Former underground papers are now healthy alternative news weeklies, linked together by on-line services and connections. A magazine like *Utne Reader,* peddling alternative-media views, gets hundreds of thousands of readers/subscribers. Magazines of all kinds representing widely varying points of view are thriving today, just to name one media example.

The cry-baby critics have never had it so good, and instead of being dispossessed, they are communicating more vigorously than ever—electronically and by the wonders of desktop publishing, which now makes entry into the communication field easier than it has been in history.

All too often those who disparage the global media trends simply argue that bigness is bad, that all media power might be vested in a few hands, and that this situation is inherently bad. A closer look confirms that there are certainly large conglomerates, not only in the United States and Europe, where the biggest ones reside, but also in Latin America, where virtually every country has only a few well-heeled media companies that own media of all kinds. Yet at the same time, people create exquisite desktop newsletters and other new media that are highly professional. They also log onto an on-line service and create their own home pages on the Internet.

For a lucky few, a little enterprise, say a specialized newsletter or magazine, becomes so successful that a large company will buy it up from the individual who had started it with little or no capital. The individual could sell one enterprise and then start another, thus sharing in the bounty of big media.

What many of the critics of global media deny is the end of the Cold War, the end of public (color that "government") media. Some of them are bitter about the fall of former socialist states that practiced censorship as a matter of course. Only a few years ago there were "relatively uncontaminated" media systems that had little contact with the West, but as the historian Timothy Garton Ash has pointed out, many of these supposedly publicly supported media were nothing more than a colossal system of lies (Dennis and Vanden Heuvel, *Emerging Voices,1990*). The New World Information Order is dead; democracy and market economies are in, and that fact galls many critics who believe that commercially vigorous media are somehow inherently immoral.

Without our defending the dumbing down of American newspapers (a fragile technology desperately seeking a new future), the existence of tabloid television, and other less than elevating content, it is hard to imagine an intelligent person who cannot find a rich range of information on virtually every topic, whether at the public library, in a school database, or elsewhere. Much of the yield of new media is available free, not only in an institutional setting such as a school or library, but also on one's home PC. Globalism may have its flaws, but to date it has been far better for the world than were eight decades of Communism and its repressive influences. With interactive media, people can talk back to the media as well as communicate directly with friends and peers anywhere in the world. Of course there are some modest problems of access for all people to various video services and information, but I would counsel patience, because issues of access and the navigation of complex "files" are being extended and developed every day. I see new media as a tool for the citizenry and the large firms that produce these products—mostly beneficial in virtually every society they enter (normally by invitation from locals, by the way).

There will always be room for localism in the media industries, but at the same time person-to-person contact over many air miles also enhances the global conversation. Both greatly benefit freedom of expression and globalism, which follows the trends set by international business—a process that brings jobs and wealth to many. All this is just beginning, but the idea that big companies, which must court public favor, are malevolent has not yet been proven.

Argument summation: Globalism greatly benefits people, the media, and freedom of expression.

Globalism is a reality. The world now has a global economy wherein goods and services are marketed across borders by large firms that have a presence in several countries. Media, once creatures of the nation-state, are now increasingly global, what with global media companies and media that have worldwide reach such as CNN, the BBC, and MTV, to name only a few. The main benefit of global media, both mass media and cyberspace media such as the Internet, is that for the first time interactive communication among all people everywhere is within reach. It may not happen immediately, but it is possible. At the same time people are better informed and get a wider range of information and entertainment than ever before. People worry that a few companies will dominate world communication, but many small entrepreneurs are also flourishing, and entry into the communication market is easier than it has ever been in human history.

RESPONSE

Merrill: Globalism harms national and local media and can only impair freedom of expression and individual liberty.

We have just been told in the "Challenge" that the New World Information and Communication Order, pushed vigorously by UNESCO and the Third World during the 1970s and 1980s, is all but dead in the media worldwide. To some degree it may be ailing around the world, but in my view it is far from dead. In every Third World country I visit I find I have to try to defend Western journalism—and especially U.S. journalism—from the same old criticisms of the last twenty years. It may be that the partial demise of Communism has muted much of the criticism of

Western journalism—especially the debates surrounding press freedom. But this NWICO is not dead yet.

There are still the old complaints of Western information imperialism, inequity of worldwide news flow, Western stereotyping of developing countries, and the spreading of values and traditions harmful to indigenous cultures. And the danger of Western multinational media conglomerates is stressed probably more than ever before, with good reason. Western-style advertising, especially in the Muslim world, is seen as demeaning and harmful to religious values. Nonrational, emotionally charged advertising raises unrealistic expectations in the developing countries. All is not peace, light, and harmony on the world scene. Dennis sees no danger in the growth of big media companies increasingly controlling world communication, and he quotes Anthony Smith as saying that it has never been easier for people to get exposure to new media products. It's easier than ever for people to get exposure to AIDS also, but who would call that a good thing? In his "Challenge" Dennis also quotes visionary Walter Wriston as positing that borders are now "totally porous," thereby rendering governmental regulation of incoming messages meaningless. Perhaps. But the capacity to *receive* messages from abroad is not the same thing as having freedom of the press. What about the freedom from government control of domestic media? What about the availability of national leaders for reportorial interviews? What about national press laws? What about government control of newsprint? And on and on go the questions.

Dennis mentions that he has watched MTV and other music channels in places like Hong Kong and Moscow in recent years, something that was not available only a few years ago. All right; let us admit that more Western programming is reaching more of the world's people. But is the bulk of this material good for the world's people? Does it have a positive or negative impact on the various cultures? Does it do little more than perpetuate stereotypes and lower moral standards?

The new global reach of the media, according to Dennis, benefits people by giving them a massive range of information and entertainment. This is a statement of opinion, and certainly one that needs evidence. How do we know that a range of information, and especially entertainment, is of benefit to people? Common sense, you may say. I wonder. I have access to tremendous amounts of entertainment, but I doubt if it benefits me very much. In fact, it is probably true that the more messages we are exposed to from television and the print media, the less we live authentic, active, and productive lives. It might benefit me (especially if I live in a Third World country) far more to grow vegetables for my family than to sit and watch the *Oprah Winfrey Show*, or even the *CBS Evening News*.

Dennis mentions that the fear of entertainment "junk food" is unwarranted and that such a concern has been with us for a long time. True, we can live with junk in our media, and granted there is plenty of substantial material. But junk food, especially in the form of titillating, splashy, and mindless advertising, seems to be proliferating everywhere, and now flowing in large quantities into other countries and cultures.

If big media companies increase pluralism and alternative views, as Dennis contends, then we might assume that what we really need is *one* big multinational media company in the world so as to provide the greatest diversity in media messages. It would presumably spawn large numbers of short-lived mini-media, rising and falling as they constantly fertilize the Big Medium. And as to the desktop publishing and on-line services and connections being products of the big media conglomerates, this is quite dubious. Furthermore, computer networks and individuals talking to individuals via the Internet *are not journalism*; certainly they do not constitute the *news media*, any more than does one person talking to a neighbor over the backyard fence.

It seems to me that media's falling into fewer and fewer hands *is* bad. The fewer the companies, the less real diversity will be found in the total media picture. Bryce Rucker's *The First Freedom* (1968), as well as a number of works by recent media critics such as Ben Bagdikian in *The Media Monopoly* (1980) and Herbert Altschull in *Agents of Power* (1995), attests to this fact. Freedom of the press may not be impacted directly by the big conglomerates and media companies, but alternative perspectives reaching sizable audiences will tend to be squeezed out. Admittedly, research needs to be done on this hypothesis, but common sense says that it is true.

Dennis seems to feel that it is a healthy thing that some small specialized newsletters and magazines will be successful and will be bought up by big media companies. That is exactly what will probably happen. Big companies cannot stand seeing small individual publications succeed. They want to own them. This practice, then, further consolidates media in fewer hands and limits the individualistic flavor of the total media system.

People who see "bigness" and consolidation of media as harmful, contrary to Dennis's contention, are not those bitter about the fall of the former socialist states. We do not deny the end of the Cold War. But we do not think that the Cold War's end means that all is now good with the capitalist expansionism, cold bottom-line publishing, and dog-eat-dog competition. We still believe that variety is healthy in the media, that media values are not universal, that Western big media companies still dominate world news flow and flood alien values into the developing countries. Dennis triumphantly contends that "democracy and market economies are in" and all's well with the world. We critics of big media companies do not necessarily believe, as Dennis says, "that commercially vigorous media are somehow inherently immoral," but we do believe that it is considerably more difficult for a wealthy media company to enter the

Kingdom of Media Morality than it is for a small, public-service-oriented medium.

Globalism, says Dennis, "may have its flaws, but it has been far better for the world than were eight decades of Communism and its repressive influences." I wonder. Look at the countries of Africa, and many in Southeast Asia. Where are the healthy influences of the media? How is the Western-generated globalism helping these unstable countries? Where is the national harmony and stability?

Where are the reliable news and general quality in the media? Sure the Soviet Union is gone, but a kind of tribalism has taken its place all over the globe, and world stability and security are no better than before 1990. In fact, there are indications that nationalism, bloodshed, suffering, and hunger have grown throughout the world since that date. As the great globalized media companies spread their views of political disputes, revolutionaries and terrorists, nationalists, and tribal animosities, ideas are planted here and there in fertile soil. Is it any wonder that they grow rapidly?

As an institution grows, as a company expands, as a conglomerate globalizes, the individual shrinks in personal dignity and impact. This is a sociological truism. As a media company puts its tentacles into ever more projects, programs, and global enterprises, the *news* function of the company tends to get less attention. Entertainment and bottom-line considerations take over, and the news medium is transformed into a *business*.

Individual liberty suffers under such a system. Cooperation, stability, and lockstep thinking among the functionaries take over. Local media are minimized or subsumed by the big media, and the number of voices in the marketplace is restricted. The whole trend of international publishing—exemplified well by the giant Bertelsmann Company of Germany and several similar media behemoths of Britain and America—are little more than indications of capitalism gone wild. The health of the world's media system is anchored in local and national media, reinforcing indigenous values and providing home-grown entertainment and news. Localism, not globalism, of the media is the way to foster individualism and pluralism and to communicate with an increasingly tribalized international audience.

Argument summation: Globalism harms national and local media and can only impair freedom of expression and individual liberty.

The new trend toward globalism, toward big media companies expanding worldwide, is an unhealthy trend. There is no evidence of benefits to people, or to freedom of expression (within the countries receiving messages). Small local and national media are squeezed out of existence by the big companies (just as the mom-and-pop stores are killed by a Wal-Mart coming into the community). National values are endangered by the increased alien cultural material, especially advertising and entertainment of a sensational, vulgar nature.

TOPICS FOR DISCUSSION

1. What are the dimensions of globalism? How is it defined and to what extent are media the conduits for this process?

2. Discuss some of the most visible media barons and big media owners such as Ted Turner, Rupert Murdoch, and others. What impresses you about them? What does not? Do they have too much power?

3. One of the topics sparked by discussions about the New World Information and Communications a few years ago was the licensing of journalists. Is this justified? Does it impair free expression? Why or why not?

4. The world now has information societies such as the United States, Japan, Canada, Western Europe, and others. How have these areas advanced their cause in a global media economy? What about developing countries?

5. Debate the proposition that for media, bigness is bad and diversity is good.

TOPICS FOR RESEARCH

1. Compare the topics covered on a television network evening news show for a week and assess whether they are (1) diverse and (2) drawn from every continent.

2. Examine the basis for the annual "Censored Stories" survey done by Professor Carl Jensen of Sonoma State University in California and critique (1) why such material was left out and (2) what the media regarded as more important.

3. Write a paper indicating how the end of the Cold War affected news coverage. Possibly compare the contents of newspaper front pages in 1986 with those in 1996 or some other years. What are the differences and why do you think that is the case?

4. Compare and contrast arguments for and against public funding of public TV or some other policy issue that pits the public interest against private interests.

5. Document cases of successful small media such as desktop publishing ventures and other examples of individual initiative in your own community. Have some enterprises come and gone? Why?

FURTHER READING

Altschull, Herbert. *Agents of Power.* White Plains, NY: Longman, 1995.

Bagdikian, Ben. *The Media Monopoly.* Boston: Beacon Press, 1980.

Dennis, Everette E., and Jon Vanden Heuvel. *Emerging Voices–European Media in Transition.* New York: Gannett Foundation, 1990.

Gerbner, George, Hamid Mowlana, and Kaarle Nordenstreng. *The Global Media Debate: Its Rise, Fall and Renewal.* Norwood, NJ: Ablex, 1991.

Grunwald, Henry. "The Post–Cold War Press." *Foreign Affairs* 72, no. 3 (Summer 1993):12–16.

Hamelink, Cees J. *Cultural Autonomy in Global Communications.* White Plains, NY: Longman, 1982.

Horvát, János, with András Szántó. *The Travails of Objectivity—U.S. Media Coverage of Eastern Europe.* New York: The Freedom Forum Media Studies Center, Fall 1993.

Mattelart, Armand. *Multinational Corporation and the Control of Culture.* Atlantic Highlands, NJ: Humanities Press, 1979.

Meyrowitz, Joshua. *No Sense of Place: The Impact of Electronic Media on Social Behavior.* New York: Oxford University Press, 1985.

O'Neill, Michael. *The Roar of the Crowd: How Television and People Power Are Changing the World.* New York: Times Books, 1993.

Rosenblum, Mort. *Who Stole the News: Why We Can't Keep Up with What's Happening in the World and What We Can Do About It.* New York: Wiley, 1993.

Rucker, Bryce. *The First Freedom.* Carbondale: Southern Illinois University Press, 1968.

Smith, Anthony. *The Age of Behemoths: The Globalization of Mass Media Firms.* New York: Priority Press, 1991.

Wriston, Walter. *The Twilight of Sovereignty.* New York: Charles Scribner's Sons/Macmillan, 1992.

INDEX

Absence of Malice (film), 21
"absence of malice" standard, 141–142
access, right of public to the media.
    See public access to the media
access to information. *See* right to
    know
Accredited in Public Relations (APR),
    204
Accuracy in Media group, 70
advertising, 33, 36–37, 38, 55, 63, 80,
    96–97, 98, 173, 174, 187–197,
    199, 224
advocacy journalism, 114–115
Alien and Sedition Acts, 26
Altschull, J. Herbert, 36
    Agents of Power, 225
American Association of Advertising
    Agencies, 190
American Marketing Association, 187
American Press Institute, 37
American Society of Newspaper
    Editors, 37, 125, 176, 182
American Spectator, 70
analytic stories, 117
Annual Review of Psychology, 79
Ash, Timothy Garton, 222
Asian-American Journalists
    Association (AAJA), 177
Associated Press, 72
attribution, 108–109
audience, 35–36, 40, 93, 95–96, 97, 98,
    117, 122, 125–126, 127–130,
    150, 194
authoritarianism, 13, 14, 59, 60

Bachen, Christine, 79, 81, 82
Bagdikian, Ben, 34, 40, 148, 221
    The Information Machines, 171
    The Media Monopoly, 225
Baker, Edwin, 45
Baker, Ray Stannard, 95, 100
Baker, Samm S., 190
Ball-Rokeach, Sandra, *Theories of
    Mass Communication*, 81
Barrett, William, 210
Barron, Jerome, 56, 58–59, 62–63, 66
    Freedom of the Press for Whom?, 36
Barth, Alan, 113
Benjamin, Burton, *Fair Play*, 153
Bernays, Edward L., 200
Berns, Walter, *Freedom, Virtue and the
    First Amendment*, 14
Bernstein, Carl, 94–95, 100
Bernstein, Richard, *Dictatorship of
    Virtue*, 178
Bertelsmann Co. (Germany), 210, 226
Biagi, Shirley, 34
biases
    in journalism, 170–174. *See also*
        propaganda, and the media
    in media, 203
Bickel, Alexander, 11
Bill of Rights, 7, 10, 45, 46, 49, 58–59,
    62
Bill Ramsey Associates, Inc., 203
Black, Hugo Lafayette, 7–8, 11, 12, 46
Black, Jay, 208
Blasi, Vince, 28
Boccardi, Louis D., 72

229

Bogart, John, 124
Bogart, Leo
  Preserving the Press, 126
  The Press and the Public, 126
Bolten, James, 161
Boston Globe, 94, 102
Bowman, William, 215
Brandeis, Louis, 62
Branzburg v. Hayes, 46–47
Brinkley, David, 108, 124
Britain, 23, 25, 26
British Broadcasting Corporation (BBC), 23, 168, 223
Brucker, Herbert, 113
Buber, Martin, 110
Buchanan, Pat, 178–179
Buckley, William F., 69, 100
Buel, Ronald, 116
Bureau of Labor Statistics, 209
Bush, George, 194
business
  ethics in, 146–147
  press coverage of, 28
Business Week, 169

cable television, 39, 64–65
categorical imperative (Kant), 13–14
censorship, 5, 14, 26
Center for Media and Public Affairs, 70
Central Intelligence Agency, 25
Christians, Clifford, 152, 156, 157
  Good News, 159
civic journalism. *See* communitarianism
Clurman, Richard, *Beyond Malice*, 69
CNN, 39, 220, 223
code of ethics
  in advertising, 190
  in journalism, 134, 137, 139, 142–143, 144, 146, 147, 148–149, 150, 151, 158, 160, 210, 214. *See also* professionalism, in journalism
  in public relations, 203–204
Cohen, Jeff, 69
Cold War, 218, 222, 225
Columbia-Dupont award, 214
Columbia Journalism Review, 71
commentary, 71, 73
Commentary, 35
commercial speech, vs. political speech, 192

commercial television, 96, 98
Commission on Freedom of the Press (Hutchins Commission), 14, 23, 36, 63, 73, 122–123, 157
communitarianism, 114, 156–165
Communitarian Network, 157
competition, in the media, 23, 39, 72, 221
Confucius, 13–14
consequential stories, 117
Constant, Benjamin, 157
Constitution, U.S., 7
contract law, 9, 11
Cooke, Janet, 38, 149
Cooley, Thomas, 6–7
Cooper, Kent, *The Right to Know*, 50
copyright, 8, 9, 11
Corry, John, 70
Cose, Ellis, 182
  The Rage of a Privileged Class, 179
credibility
  of journalists, 142
  of the media, 32–33, 37–38, 40, 73, 74–75, 152. *See also* public trust, and the media
  of the press, 163
  in public relations, 204
Cross, Harold L., *The People's Right to Know—Legal Access to Public Records and Proceedings*, 46, 50
Cutlip, Scott, 198, 202

Daily Mirror (London), 99
Dateline (NBC), 149
defamation, 11
DeFleur, Melvin, 86, 124
  Theories of Mass Communication, 81
democracy, role of press in, 5–6, 10, 19, 29, 32, 44, 48, 50, 51, 52, 70, 177, 213
Democratic Party, 70
DeMott, John, 112
deontelic ethics, 138
deregulation, 219
descriptive stories, 117
desktop publishing, 40, 221–222, 225
Detroit Free Press, 21
Diamond, Edwin, 70
Didion, Joan, *Slouching Toward Bethlehem*, 151
diversity
  ethnic and racial, 176–186
  in media channels, 39–40, 194–195

Douglas, William O., 8, 46–47
Downie, Leonard, 162

Edelstein, Alex, 65
Editor & Publisher International Yearbook, The, 214
editorial autonomy (self-determination), 12–13, 14–15, 20, 24, 48–49, 51, 57–58, 59–61, 121, 127–130, 157–158, 159. *See also* news, definitions of
egalitarianism, vs. elitism, 93
electronic media, vs. print media, 55–56, 65–66
elitism
   vs. egalitarianism, 93
   in reporters, 63, 95–96, 98, 123–127
Ellul, Jacques, 172
Emerson College, 152
Emmy awards, 214
Encounter, 150
Enlightenment philosophy, 7, 9, 26, 156, 158, 159, 160
ethics, 9
   in advertising, 190
   in business, 146–147
   Confucian, 13–14
   in journalism, 24, 137, 139, 143–144, 146–155. *See also* code of ethics, in journalism
   in media vs. journalism, 146–147
   situational vs. absolute, 134–145, 147, 159
ethnicity, 176–186
Etzioni, Amitai, 160
   The Spirit of Community, 156
evil, 13

fairness, 146
Fairness and Accuracy in Media (FAIR), 69
fair trial, right to, 8
fair-trial-free-press codes, 142–143
Falklands War, 168
Farrakhan, Louis, 179–180
Faulkner, William, 94
Federal Bureau of Investigation, 25
fireside chats (FDR), 71
First Amendment, 5, 7, 8, 9, 11, 12, 14, 15, 34, 38, 45, 47–48, 50, 55, 56, 57–59, 62, 66, 207, 213
Flexner, Abraham, 208
Forbes, 169
Fortune, 21

Fouhy, Edward, 161
Fourteenth Amendment, 8
fourth estate, press as, 19, 20, 27, 159
Fox Network, 39
France, 26
Free and Responsible Press, A (Hutchins Commission), 36
freedom. *See also* freedom of the press
   absolute vs. conditional, 7–8, 11, 12
   essential nature of, 6
   globalization of, concept of, 219
   vs. liberty, 7
   meaning of, 13–15
   and responsibility. *See* responsibility
   utilitarian notions of, 14–15
Freedom Forum Media Studies Center, 37
freedom of expression, and globalism, 223, 226–227
Freedom of Information Act, 46
Freedom of Information (FOI) movement, 46, 49, 59
freedom of speech
   and advertising, 192–193
   Confucian notion of, 13–14
freedom-of-speech clause (First Amendment), 57–58
freedom of the press, 5–18, 20–21, 38, 50, 52, 55, 58–59, 61–63, 130, 213
   and ethical standards, 137, 139, 143–144, 147, 151
   international, 26, 58, 219, 224
   meaning of, 63–64
   preservation of, 26–27
free-press clause (First Amendment), 5, 47, 55, 57
Friendly, Fred W., 69

gag rules, 9
Gans, Herbert, 70, 71, 72, 212
Gerald, J. Edward, *The Social Responsibility of the Press*, 151
Gingrich, Newt, 69, 85, 168
Gitlin, Todd, 81–82, 84
Gitlow v. New York, 8
glasnost, 167
globalism, and the media, 218–228
"global village" (McLuhan), 220
Golden Rule, 13–14
Goode, William J., 209
goodness, 13–14
Goodwin, Eugene, *Groping for Media Ethics*, 152

Gorbachev, Mikhail, 167
government, relationship with media, 19–31, 167–169. *See also* national security; no prior restraint
Graham, Katharine, 39
Grenada crisis, 37

Hadwin, Arnold, 111
Haiman, Franklyn S., 48
Hall, Stuart, 84
Hard Copy, 214
Hartford Courant, 113
Harvard-Hastings Program on Ethics in the Professions, 212
Harvard Law Review, 56
Harwood, Richard, 83
Hayakawa, S. I., 107
Hearst, William Randolph, 147
Hemingway, Ernest, 94
Herbert v. Lando, 10
Hess, John L., 148
Hiebert, Ray, 34–35
Hocking, William Ernest, 63
Hoffman, Nicholas von, 100
Holmes, Stephen, *The Anatomy of Antiliberalism*, 156
Hook, Sidney, 8, 12
Horton, Willie, 194
Hulteng, John L., *The Messenger's Motives*, 152
Hutchins Commission. *See* Commission on Freedom of the Press
Huxley, Aldous, *Brave New World Revisited*, 189

Institute of Propaganda Analysis, 166
interactive media, 65, 222
Internet, 222, 223, 225
inverted pyramid news story, 106, 113
investigative reporting, 94–95, 98, 114
Irvine, Reed, 70

Janowitz, Morris, 212, 215
Japan, 169
Jaspin, Elliott, 141
Jefferson, Thomas, 173
Jesus Christ, 13–14
Johnstone, John, 215
journalism, as a profession, 207–217
Journalism Quarterly, 81
Journal of Mass Media Ethics, 208

Kant, Immanuel, 13
Kauffman, Irving, 47

Kennan, George F., 188
Kerner Commission Report, 176, 177, 178, 181
Kettering Trust, 161
King, Cecil, 99
Knight-Ridder, 161
Kristol, Irving, 210
Kuhn, Thomas, *The Structure of Scientific Revolutions*, 81

Ladies Home Journal, 194
Lambeth, Edmund, 156
  Committed Journalism, 152
Lapham, Lewis, 211
Lazarsfeld, Paul, 80, 81, 85
leaks, 23, 27
Lee, Ivy, 199–200
Lemert, James, 82–83
Lewis, Anthony, 46
libel, 7, 8, 10, 11, 46, 141–142
libertarianism, 20, 21, 25–26, 29, 50, 51, 52, 60, 156, 157, 158, 160
liberty
  vs. freedom, 7
  and globalism, 226
licensing, in journalism, 25, 207, 210, 214, 215
Lichter, Linda, *The Media Elite*, 71
Lichter, Robert, 70
  The Media Elite, 71
Limbaugh, Rush, 26, 69, 179
Lippmann, Walter, 13, 123–124
  The Public Philosophy, 14
literary magazines, 93
Locke, John, 157
Loeb, William, 26
Los Angeles Times, 37, 108, 183
Lowenstein, Ralph, 149
loyalty, 14
Luedtke, Kurt, 21, 48–49, 125
lying, as reporter's tactic, 135, 136–137, 138, 139, 142

Machiavellianism, 149–150
MacIntyre, Alasdair, 156
MacNeil, Robert, 38
MacNeil/Lehrer NewsHour, 69
Madison, James, 46, 157
Maistre, Joseph de, 156
Malcolm, Janet, 148, 151
Manchester Union Leader (New Hampshire), 26
marketplace theory, and the press, 36–37

market research, 40, 95–96, 114, 122, 123, 125–126, 127–130
Mattelart, Armand, 112, 117
Mattson, Floyd, 63
McClure's Magazine, 200
McCombs, Maxwell, 81, 86
McDonald, Donald, 110
McLuhan, Marshall, 220
media
  big conglomerates in global markets, 221–222, 224–227
  competition in, 23, 39, 72, 221
  diversification in, 39–40, 194–195
  electronic vs. print, 55–56, 65–66
  ethical standards in, 146–147. *See also* ethics, in journalism
  foreign vs. U.S., 99, 100–101, 106
  and globalism, 218–228
  interactive, 222
  international ownership of, 219
  ownership of, 11, 34, 39, 41
  political bias in, 69–77, 203
  power of, 78–91
  profit motives of, 33–37, 38, 40, 56
  and propaganda, 166–175
  public access to, 55–68
  and the public trust, 32–43
  quality in, 40, 92–105
  relationship with government, 19–31, 167–169
Mencken, H. L., 108, 112
Merritt, Davis "Buzz," Jr., 156, 161
Methvin, Eugene, 98
Meyer, Philip, 140–141, 161
  Ethical Journalism, 152
Meyrowitz, Joshua, 220–221
Miami Herald, The, 57
Mill, John Stuart, 14, 157
Milton, John, 157
Milwaukee Journal, 8
minorities, 36, 60–61, 63, 64–65, 176–186, 195
Ms, 194
MTV, 220, 223, 224
muckrakers, 95, 99–100, 147
Mungo, Raymond, 115
Murdoch, Rupert, 39, 219

Nation, The, 70
National Association of Black Journalists (NABJ), 177
National Association of Hispanic Journalists (NAHJ), 177
National Enquirer, 214

National Geographic, 35
National Magazine Award, 214
national security, 8, 9, 11, 12, 46, 48
Native American Press Association (NAPA), 177
Navasky, Victor, 70
Nazism, 166
Near v. Minnesota, 9
Neuharth, Al, 161
new journalism, 79, 106, 114
news, definitions of, 121–132. *See also* editorial autonomy (self-determination)
News Corporation, 219
Newsday, 156, 162
"news doctors," 96
news-gathering
  methods, 94–95, 133–145
  and objectivity, 116–117
  and public relations, 201–202, 204
  and right to know, 47–48
Newspaper Association of America, 37
Newspaper Readership Project, 125–126
newspapers, 34–35, 39, 93–94, 98, 100, 161–162, 163
News 2000 Project (Gannett Company), 161
News World Corporation, 39
New World Information and Communication Order (NWICO), 219, 222, 223–224
New York City, 64–65
New Yorker, 35
New York Sun, 124
New York Times, 9, 10, 35, 39, 72, 108, 122, 169, 202, 214
Nieman Fellowship, 214
Noelle-Neumann, Elisabeth, 81, 82, 86
no prior restraint, 5, 9, 11, 13, 58–59
North Korea, 26, 167
Novak, Michael, 109–110

objectivity, 71, 106–120, 169
opinion journalism, 71, 73
opinion magazines, 26, 93
Orwell, George, *1984*, 166
O'Toole, John, 192

paradigm change (Kuhn), 81, 83
Parker-Plummer, Bernadette, 108
people's press, 58, 66
People's Republic of China, 26, 66, 167, 169

Pew Memorial Trust, 161
Philadelphia Inquirer, 162, 178
Plato, 13, 14
pluralism, 20, 23, 36, 58, 182, 183–184, 204. *See also* diversity, ethnic and racial
Podhoretz, Norman, 100
political advertising, 191, 194
political bias. *See also* propaganda, and the media
   in the media, 69–77, 111
political correctness, 177
Powell, Lewis, 27–28
power, of the media, 78–91
Poynter Institute, 37, 152
precision journalism, 114, 115, 141
press
   definition of, 6
   and democracy. *See* democracy, role of press in
   as the fourth estate, 19, 20, 27, 159
   libertarian theory of, 20, 21, 25–26, 29, 50, 51, 52, 60, 156, 157, 158
   licensing of, 25, 207, 210, 214, 215
   and marketplace theory, 36–37
   meaning of, in First Amendment, 58
"press exceptionalism," 46
print media, vs. electronic media, 55–56, 65–66
privacy, right to, 7, 8, 11, 46, 62
process of reconciliation, 10
profession, definitions of, 208–210
professionalism
   and freedom of the press, 9–10
   in journalism, 72, 73, 74, 134, 207–217. *See also* code of ethics, in journalism
Professions in America, The, 209, 213
Progressive, The, 9
Project on Public Life and the Press (New York University), 161
propaganda, and the media, 166–175. *See also* political bias
property law, 9
Providence Journal, 141
public access to the media, 55–68, 129
Public Agenda Foundation, 97
Public Broadcasting System, 35, 69, 93
public interest, 27, 97, 143, 144, 188
Public Interest, The, 21
public journalism. *See* communitarianism

public opinion polls, 65
public relations, 11, 198–206
Public Relations Society of America (PRSA), 198
   Code of Professional Standards, 203–204
public service, 33, 34, 213
public trust, and the media, 32–43
Pulitzer, Joseph, 147
Pulitzer Prize, 140, 202, 214

Qualter, Terence H., 172
QUBE, 65
Quill, 98, 148
quotas, 177, 178, 183

race, 176–186
Radio and Television News Directors, 37
Ramsey, William, 203
Rand, Ayn, 57–58, 66
"reader-driven journalism," 161
Reagan administration, 37
Reilly, Robert T., 204
Republican Party, 70
Reshaping the Media, 38
responsibility
   vs. rights and freedom, 9, 10–11, 13–15, 147
   social, of the press, 52, 60
Reston, James, 100
The Artillery of the Press, 24
Reynolds, Frank, 108
Richstad, Jim, 63
right of reply, 55, 63
rights
   institutional (structural) vs. individual, 6, 25, 45, 46–47, 49, 62
   institutional vs. social, 52
   and responsibility. *See* responsibility
rights of man, 7
right to know, 44–54, 129, 148, 149, 150, 159
Rivers, William L.
   The Adversaries, 28
   The Other Government, 28
Roberts, Donald, 79, 81, 82
Robinson, John P., 81, 87
Rockefeller, John D., 199–200
Rogers, Will, 32
Roosevelt, Franklin Delano, 71

INDEX

Rosen, Jay, 156, 161, 162
Roshco, Bernard, 124
Rothman, Stanley, *The Media Elite*, 71
Rowan, Carl, 179
Rucker, Bryce, *The First Freedom*, 225
Rusher, William, 148

"salience information," 65
Sandel, Michael, 156
Sartre, Jean-Paul, 110
Saxbe v. Washington Post Co., 27–28
Schneider, Howard, 156–157, 162
schools of journalism, 140, 141, 151, 152, 214, 215, 216
Schramm, Wilbur, 81
Schudson, Michael, 109, 190, 193–194
  Discovering the News, 108
Scripps Howard Newspapers study, 182
secrecy, in government operations, 23, 25, 27, 44. *See also* national security
sedition laws, 25
service journalism, 114, 115
sexism
  in advertising, 194–195
  in media hiring and coverage, 182
Shaw, Donald, 81, 86
Silverstein, Stuart, 183
Sinclair, Upton, 40
Sixth Amendment, 8
60 Minutes, 10–11, 153
Slawski, Edward, 215
Smith, Anthony, 220, 224
Smith, Red, 94
social responsibility, of the press, 26, 52, 60, 157–158
Society of Professional Journalists, 148–149, 207, 208
sources, 47, 108–109, 135–136, 138, 142, 150–151
South Africa, 169
Soviet Union, 58, 66, 167, 169
sports, press coverage of, 28–29
spying, CIA, 25
Staebler, Charles, 202
stealing, as reporter's tactic, 136, 139
Steffens, Lincoln, 95, 100
Stevenson, Adlai, 71
Stewart, Potter, 25, 47
Stone, I. F., 29
Strauss, Leo, 156

Sulzberger, Arthur H., 39
sunshine laws, 27, 44, 45–46
Sweden, 13

Talese, Gay, 180
talk radio, 26, 71
Tarbell, Ida M., 95, 100
  "The History of the Standard Oil Company," 200
television news, 96
Thatcher, Margaret, 168
Third World, 168, 223
Thoreau, Henry David, 123
Tiananmen Square, 218
Tillich, Paul, 110
Time, 37, 69
Times Mirror, 37
Time-Warner, 219
Tobin, Richard L., 190
Topping, Seymour, 202
Tornillo, Pat, Jr., 56–57
Tornillo v. The Miami Herald, 56–57, 61–62
Tribe, Lawrence, 45
Tuchman, Gaye, 113–114
Turner, Ted, 39
TV Guide, 153

United Kingdom, 12–13
"Unity '94," 177
University of Minnesota, 152
University of Missouri, 152
U.S. News and World Report, 172
Utne Reader, 221

values, 146
Varey, James W., 211
verifiable journalism, 111
verification, 108
Vietnam War, 9, 168
Villard, Oswald Garrison, 40
Voltaire, 157
vox populi, 32

Wall Street Journal, 38, 72, 169, 202
Warren, Samuel D., 62
Washington Post, 9, 38, 39, 83, 113, 122, 148, 162, 214
Watergate scandal, 25, 94–95
Weaver, David, 71–72, 152
  The American Journalist, 70
Weaver, Paul H., 21
Westmoreland, William, 153

White, Byron, 47
Wichita Eagle, 156, 161
Wicker, Tom, 100
Wilhoit, G. Cleveland, 71–72, 152
   The American Journalist, 70
Will, George, 100
Winans, Foster, 38
Winship, Tom, 94, 102
wiretapping
   CIA, 25
   as reporter's tactic, 136, 142
Wiseman, Fred, 28
Wolfe, Tom, 94, 114

Woodward, Bob, 94–95, 99–100
World War I, 79, 166
World War II, 50, 52, 166
Wriston, Walter, 220, 224
writing, quality of journalistic, 94, 100, 102
Wylie, Philip, 15

Yankelovich, Daniel, 97
Yardley, Jonathan, 148
yellow journalism, 147

Zenger, John Peter, 25